A Life In Flying. Stories From A Pilot

Copyright © (

CW00763612

All r

ISBN: 978-178456-761-3

Paperback

First published 2021 by UPFRONT PUBLISHING
Peterborough, England.

An environmentally friendly book printed and bound in England
by www.printondemand-worldwide.com

A Life in Flying.
Stories From a Pilot.

A Life in Flying.
Stories From a Pilot.

JIM SNEE

publishers logo

About The Author.

Jim Snee was born in Taunton, Somerset in 1948. He spent his early years in both East and West Africa as well as spending time in Belize, Central America. Following completion of his education in England, he entered the world of civil aviation as a trainee pilot, gaining his professional flying qualifications in 1968 at the London School of Flying, Elstree.

In 1972 he joined British Midland Airways, later rebranded as BMI, where he spent the next thirty six years of his career until he retired in 2008. During his time with BMI, he flew various different aircraft types and at the same time enjoyed a variety of differing pilot management positions. He and his wife continue to live in the East Midlands. They have four children.

BMI continued as an airline until 2012 when it was bought by British Airways and absorbed into that company. Such was the camaraderie within the airline however, that several different groupings of former colleagues, inclusive of the author, continue to meet up socially on a regular basis.

Preface

My parents lived through interesting times and my sisters and I were party to many a fascinating and often amusing tale recounted by them about their experiences in the field. Most of these tales we've now forgotten and with both of my parents now long gone, there's no way of recapturing their anecdotes. I have always regretted that I did not encourage them to record their experiences and adventures so that they were not lost to those who followed. There are many questions that I would like to ask today but alas, their world is now a closed book. With that closed book a small part of the local detail, history and insight that spanned the last days of British Colonial rule, and the immediate years that followed, have been lost.

The purpose of my writing this book is not because I have any notion that anything I did in aviation was remarkable in any way. Far from it, the anecdotes I've written about all come from my tenure in the business, spanning forty or so years between 1967 and 2008. My guess is that they reflect a career common to many pilots and managers of that period of aviation. As the industry continues to evolve my time and experiences within its embrace is now also a closed book – hence the opening of this one.

The reason for recording these vignettes is that, as with my parents era, I now think that snapshots of 'the way it was' are worthy of preservation, even if hardly of earth shattering importance. I have bored innumerable friends over the years with a flying tale or two, when the occasion has prompted itself, and many of them have commented that I should write these stories down before they're lost in the mists of time.

As I've moved further into my years of retirement, so the aviation industry has also moved forward. So much so in fact, that I now sense a growing contrast between the way that we used to operate our aeroplanes and man our offices and the way that these activities are now undertaken. The world of the airline pilot [and the office] are now very different, carrying, as they both do, what I see to be as an ever growing burden of regulation, bureaucracy, political correctness, red tape, monitoring and an inevitable increase in the reliance of automation in the flight deck.

This contrast has now reached a point where I suspect that today's young pilots would hardly recognise the working world that I and my colleagues inhabited for much of our careers, certainly in my case, those earlier years. Indeed, I have a suspicion that many of today's crop wouldn't believe what went on and how it went on, were it not for the fact that a fair few of the players involved are still amongst us, many indeed remain flying as more senior captains in one airline or another.

And so I commit pen to paper. Partly, as I say, to hopefully give a flavour of the way it was but also as much to paint a picture of the people and the characters who populated my working life. Most of my anecdotes are more about the people, the humour and the vagaries of management style than they are about the technicalities of the flying and the aircraft. If you are looking for an illumination of pure aviation history and technical detail then this is not the book you need. If you want to read about the people in aviation, their foibles, their weaknesses, their strengths – and their humour – then turn a few pages and see how you get on.

As a footnote, especially to those of a nervous disposition about flying, I should make it clear that underlying any apparent notion of frivolousness reflected in my stories, the paramount goal of Flight Safety was always writ large. Safety was, and remains, at the very heart of everything a pilot [and indeed the whole industry] strives for.

Safety is one of the main reasons why there is now such a contrast between the way it was and the way it is. As the industry has evolved and become ever more mature, so practices and disciplines have changed and evolved. Airline flying was already safe when I started in the '60s, now it is even more safe. This is not a claim it is a categorical fact!

The thing is, looking back [doubters will say through rose coloured spectacles], my peer group and myself can safely say – to anyone who cares to listen – that we had the best years in aviation!

"I think it is a pity to lose the romantic side of flying and simply to accept it as a common means of transportation". Amy Johnson

Acknowledgements

As with most things that spring from human effort, this book did not suddenly and remarkably appear from entirely my own initiative or input. Much help and encouragement came from other quarters along the way.

Without the support of Carly, my wife, these stories would never have seen a page of print. Carly had to put up with some 40 years of marriage to a husband too often absent at work whilst she spent far too much time, effectively operating as a single Mum to our four sons, with me away and playing with my big boys toys. This sacrifice allowed me to indulge my passion for flying and to work on the management side of the business – as well as spending time accruing all the experiences and 'events' as described in the book. Whilst Carly doesn't entirely share my [perhaps misplaced] sense of humour, she nevertheless gave me enormous encouragement to write this biography and again put up with endless hours of solitude whilst I spent my time sitting in front of a laptop, laboriously typing away, instead of contributing to family life.

Likewise our four sons who all rather lost out in their younger days from enough quality time spent with their father, due to him being away so much. Even so, they were all wholly enthusiastic and encouraging in badgering me to finally put pen to paper.

It goes without saying that I also owe an enormous debt of gratitude to all those former colleagues who feature in the book. Without the antics, the foibles, the myriad talents, the mistakes and the friendships that so many of these indelible characters had to offer, there would be no story to tell. It would be unfair to name names here as many would be missed and the list would anyway be too long. Suffice to say that some appear in the book under their own names and there are others whose names have been changed to protect their modesty. I'm sure that they will know who they are – as will most of their former colleagues who also read these vignettes. Others will have to speculate as to the true identities of those featured!

On the issue of naming names, there are three who cannot be missed. Stuart Balmforth, [Sir] Michael Bishop and John Wolfe. These were the three partners who owned and ran British Midland for the majority of my career in the airline. Together, they provided me [and many others] with long and steady employment in a very volatile industry, in my case 36 years of it. Challenging times for all maybe but we had the best days available in aviation whilst they were at the helm. Their vision and hard work gave me the platform that led to the possibility of the book.

It would be remiss of me not to mention the many friends outside aviation who have also encouraged me to press ahead with this project. Not least amongst this group, those who frequent the Plough Inn in Diseworth and have been bored stiff, many a time and oft, as I have held court at the bar and repeated, yet again, one of my so called, more 'amusing' anecdotes. None more so than my good [but grumpy] friend Alan, whose discouragement has been a positive spur.

No budding author I'm sure, can sit in an empty room staring at a blank piece of paper [or computer screen] for hours on end whilst waiting for the right words, or inspiration to otherwise appear from somewhere, without a prop or two to help out. My grateful thanks are therefore due to Mr. Rington [from Yorkshire] who supplied the flavour for the endless cups of tea that I consumed whilst writing and also to Messieurs Courvoisier and Remy Martin who helped out when the going got particularly tough.

Finally, my ever grateful thanks go to my parents who spent a lifetime working hard to give my sisters and myself the kind of start in life that allowed me to transition from school to flying with relative ease. I also have to acknowledge that it was from my father, very much the gentleman and diplomat, from whom I inherited my inappropriate sense of humour. That, I hope, has been a significant theme in my writing. Alas, I know not where those other two characteristics went.

1. Customs and The Deluded Passenger

Every arrival back into the UK from abroad was a fraught affair for pilots and cabin crew alike.

Many years ago now – before the UK had been fully seduced into the EU – we still had 'Excise Duty' to pay whenever we returned from abroad and had with us more than the maximum 'Duty Free' allowance of imported booze and cigarettes, etc. This was set at 200 cigarettes and a single bottle of spirits per person and was policed by Customs Officers from H.M. Customs and Excise [long since merged with H.M. Tax Office to form our present H.M.R.C.]. These Customs Officers were a pretty fierce bunch of boys and girls, had immense powers, and were much feared by most of the travelling public. This, I suspect, was because people were all too often trying to smuggle in that extra bottle of illicit spirits or carton of fags and were terrified of getting caught.

On this particular day I had flown into Luton Airport from abroad as a passenger, I forget from where now. I'd taken a flight out to somewhere but was then next required back at base for some reason. Anyway, I had to clear Customs, just like everyone else, so had joined the queue in the 'Nothing To Declare' channel to await my turn of running the gauntlet of maybe being challenged and searched, or maybe not – all depended on the individual customs officer and his mood.

In front of me in the queue was a man with a young boy in tow, clearly a father and son pairing. The boy was maybe around eight or nine years old, no more than that [his father was somewhat older!]. We all moved slowly forward until father and son were at the front of the queue and facing judgement from the Customs official. Would he wave them through or would he question them? I was hoping for the former [the queue had been very slow and I had a taxi waiting outside for me] but the latter was to be the order of the day on this occasion.

Mr. Customs opened his conversation with the usual string of pleasantries: – "Good morning Sir. Have you been on holiday?, Where have you been?, Did you have an enjoyable time?" etc, etc, before cutting to the chase.

"Have you got anything to declare Sir?"

"No, only my duty free allowance Officer".

"And what would that be Sir?"

"Well, 400 cigarettes and two bottles of whiskey of course".

"I see, and where are they Sir?"

"In this carrier bag'.

Mr. Father produced the two bottles of whiskey and placed them on the low counter between the pair of them, two protagonists about to engage. Mr. Customs looked down at the whiskey, looked back up at Mr. Father, looked at Mr. Father's son, paused and then said: –

"I'm sorry Sir but you're only entitled to one bottle".

Yes, I know. That's one for me and one for my son".

"And just how old is your son, Sir?".

"He's nine but what's that got to do with it?" said Mr. Father.

"I see. Well, I'm afraid your son doesn't qualify for a duty free allowance. He's not entitled to duty free alcohol until he's aged eighteen. You'll have to pay duty on the second bottle you've got I'm afraid", countered Customs.

"Of course he's entitled, I bought him a ticket for the flight!", Father replied.

There then followed a long and circular argument during the course of which Mr. Customs remained resolutely calm and implacable whilst Mr. Father became increasingly heated and angry. Mr. Father turned from red to puce as his options were explained and were then repeated, several times, whilst his innocent son just stood there looking perplexed as he hopped from foot to foot whilst watching the unfolding verbal battle. I could sense that this was not going to finish well. Eventually Mr. Customs decided that the time had come to put an end to this rather sterile debate.

"I really must ask you to now make a final decision Sir. Do you want to pay the duty, put the bottle in the Bonded Store, or have it confiscated?"

"I'm not paying any duty, I'm not putting the bottle in the Bond and you're not confiscating it either!".

And with that Mr. Father picked up one of the bottles, held it aloft at arms length and, with great theatricality, he very deliberately let it drop from his grasp. It fell to the floor with a resounding crash and smashed into more pieces than Delboy's chandelier. Whiskey and broken glass fairly exploded all over the immediacy of the Customs Hall floor, leaving a fine mess.

Mr. Customs didn't blink, he didn't move, his expression remained completely unchanged. He stood there, statuesque and looking into the whites of Mr. Father's defiant eyes. There was a slight pause and then, with total calm and into the pregnant silence he said:-

"I'm very sorry Sir, but the bottle you dropped was yours, I still have to charge you duty on your son's whiskey – and then we can discuss the cigarettes!!".

What sangfroid, what a reaction, what an amazingly quick wit. I was singularly impressed with Mr. Customs [seldom a breed respected by pilots, we were always trying to beat the system and they were always trying to catch us out!]. How he managed to have the presence of mind to come up with that comeback line so fast – and without falling over with laughter – I'll never know.

Sadly, I never got to witness the end of this encounter. I think Mr. Customs now knew that he was in this for the long haul but, for whatever reason, he waved me through to my taxi before he resumed further battle. I somehow doubt that Mr. Father got home without having had to pay his dues. Customs, one – smugglers, nil.

My life in aviation was packed full with little vignettes like this, most with an amusing twist and without much consequence, some serious and some less happy.

To learn how it all started for me and to uncover more of my stories, read on.

2. Early Days and my Instructors

I went straight from school into aviation. I came from a background of boarding school having being bought up in East Africa. My father was teaching out there and, as was the way of things in those days for many 'ex pat.' children, I commuted by air to and from school in England throughout the course of my school career.

As a youngster I thought that this air travel was hugely exciting and I lapped it up, greatly looking forward to every trip I made. I also thought that it was perfectly normal too, after all, every other child I knew was, just like me, also flying to and from school. I was especially fascinated by the complexities of all the instruments in the flight decks that I visited and I wondered how anyone could master anything so difficult.

Flights then, to and from Nairobi in Kenya, were all by BOAC from a Heathrow airport that was very different from the vast and complex place that it was to become years later. I remember as a very small child flying from London [with my parents] when the terminal building was a marquee and the floor was made of duckboards simply laid over the grass and winter mud! Another early memory of aeroplanes that excited me was of RAF Vampire jets screaming overhead, at low level, as they came in to land and take off from the airport at a place called Tabora, in Tanzania, where we were living during the Mau Mau debacle in the early 1950s. I thought that these machines were wonderful.

It never crossed my mind that one day I would join the ranks of those people who were able to actually fly these amazing creations of might and mystery. I had no idea how anyone qualified as a pilot and I always assumed that I'd have a 'normal' job, just like everyone else.

Becoming a pilot was nowhere on the agenda. It wasn't until very late on in my school life that I even thought about flying as a career and that it might be possible.

The London School of Flying, based at Elstree Aerodrome [just north of London], was one of only three flying 'schools' then equipped and approved to train pilots up to professional UK licence standards in the 1960s. I had to pass an interview to be accepted onto one of its flying courses. I was young and very green behind the ears and I took it all very seriously. Learning to fly is an expensive business. Learning to fly to a professional standard is a very expensive process.

I actually knew precious little about flying and what it was all about but I'd gleaned all the information that I could get hold of in preparation [no internet back then and I didn't know anyone who was a pilot to quiz so I couldn't get much of an insight in advance]. I turned up for my interrogation in suit and tie, looking as smart as I was able and with some trepidation.

I was interviewed by the two owners of the flying school, a Mr. Kendall and his business partner, a Mr. Jaffe. If I'd been a bit more streetwise then than I was to become I wouldn't have needed to worry at all. These two were a pair of smooth operators who had little interest in any knowledge, skills or aptitude for flying that I might possess. They were interested only in taking my money – and a good deal of it to boot. Once it had been established that I had deep enough pockets for their purposes it was plain sailing all the way and I was duly enrolled.

The first two weeks of the course were spent entirely in the classroom learning basic theory. We didn't alas, get anywhere near an aeroplane, somewhat frustrating! We did however learn who our respective flying instructors were going to be. There were about a dozen people on any one course and there were three or four courses at various stages of the training process ahead of us.

As with students all over the world, those at Elstree were no different, they all had opinions on the relative merits [or otherwise] of their teaching staff. We learned from our peer groups who were the best flying instructors and who weren't. Apparently, top of the pile was a chap called Dave Rowley. He was reputed to be a hard taskmaster but if you were teamed up with him then you were quids in and you'd be OK.

Four of us would be teamed up with any one instructor and the distribution was decided by the teaching staff, not by us students. We all hoped we'd be teamed up with the mythical Dave Rowley but we had to await for the announcement which came close to the end of our fortnight's classroom prison sentence. Come the day and, as luck would have it, Dave Rowley had drawn the short straw and he found himself lumbered with me as one of his protégés.

Dave was a short, stocky chap. In a former life he'd been an engineer in the merchant navy and he still walked with that rolling gait that only sailors have. His reputation was well earned. He briefed us well, he had high standards and he expected us to strive for the same. He was indeed a hard taskmaster. He'd accept a mistake, debrief us, explain what was wrong, how to put it right and then make us do it again. Making the same mistake twice was not an option, he took no prisoners and he wouldn't accept second best. When it went well he would give credit, when it didn't you knew all about it! As a result of Dave's carrot and stick approach his students tried very hard to get it right first time. Mostly we did – because the alternative was never good – and thus we seemed to forge ahead of our fellow would be pilots with our flying progress.

To supplement my meagre bank balance and save myself from starvation I worked in the evenings as a barman at the Elstree Flying Club. This was a lively and well used watering hole peopled, as it was, by a clientele of wealthy North Londoners and acolytes from the nearby film studios. Dave Rowley was then a bachelor, a flying club member and he hailed from the school of Olympic standard beer drinkers. As time went on and we got to know each other we found that we got on well and many a wasted evening was spent in the bar in each others' company – along with fellow like minded travellers. Before I'd finished my training Dave decided that the time had come for him to move on to pastures new. However, in typical thoughtful fashion he took us through to the point of us successfully passing the flying exams for the basic Commercial Pilot's Licence before he left to join the British Antarctic Survey Team. I wasn't to bump into Dave again for another 10 years or more but he'd bequeathed an indelible mark on me and the quest for high professional flying standards.

I had two instructors for the second, and more advanced, part of the flying training on the course. The first was a chap called Keith Poynter. Keith had himself been a student at Elstree when I first enrolled so was very familiar with the whole process and he well understood the stresses and strains that us students felt. This enabled him to empathise well and teach at a pace that worked for each different student. I lost touch with Keith when I finished at Elstree but I think he went on to forge his flying career with British Airways.

My second 'Instrument Rating' instructor was a chap called Harry Langdon. Harry was another gentle character and a very accomplished aviator. He was older than most and had had a distinguished flying career in the war when he flew as a Mosquito pilot in one of the Pathfinder Squadrons. Not many were picked for this elite squad, which was indicative of the quality of the man. With these two teaching and mentoring me I went on to complete the course and emerge as a fully qualified 'professional' pilot without any great dramas.

I learned a couple of years later that Harry, having been through all that he had in the war – and survived – succumbed whilst reversing his car out of his own drive and into the path of an oncoming vehicle that he'd not spotted. I was much saddened by this news and have often wondered at the irony of the way Harry met his end. How is it that those to whom our generation owe so much can be so unlucky?

Above and right:
The Piper Cherokee basic trainer that
I flew with Dave Rowley

Below:
Twin Commanche. Advanced
trainer – in which Keith Poynter
and Harry Langdon taught me.

3. My Expensive Watch

Back in 1967 when I started my flying training the political world landscape was beginning to change with many former colonies achieving independence and starting to grow their own industries and their own airlines. To the fore in building their own National Flag Carrier airlines were some of the Middle East countries, now becoming wealthy through their oil production facilities. A consequence of this was that during my time at the London School of Flying at Elstree many of my fellow students hailed from that neck of the woods.

Pretty much all of these chaps either came from very wealthy families or were 'sponsored' by their national airlines at very generous levels, or both. This was all fine but it wasn't without its own problems. Partly this was because English was very much a second language for these guys and many of them struggled to grasp and learn what was necessary to both know and to pass the necessary written exams, particularly when it came to the technical stuff – of which there's quite a lot when it comes to aviation and aeroplanes. In fact very little doesn't have any technical content.

The other bit that was difficult for these people was that for the first time in their lives they were outside their own cultural norms and were exposed to the bright lights and seeming decadence of what was becoming an increasingly liberated western society. It was like all their Christmases had come at once. Here they were, immediately adjacent to all the excesses that London had to offer, especially to those who had deep pockets. And these boys certainly had those. And there was no one to hold them back – no parent, no family, no supervision and no censure from anywhere or anyone. Our Middle Eastern colleagues lived high on the hog and to the full.

In short, most of them spent more of their time driving to and from London's hotspots in their Ferraris and E-Types than they ever did studying in the evenings or attending their lectures. It was hardly surprising therefore, that a course that should have taken no more than a year was taking some of these students two or three years to finally finish and to qualify. The school itself was quite happy with this scenario. For them, the constant failures of these high living playboys merely meant that these same high rollers would simply chuck another load of money into the school coffers and pay to re-sit the course and the exams. All this activity driven by the hormone fuelled wants of unfettered youth, a win-win all round!

Another constant irritation for our high spending friends, ironically, was cash. Credit cards and cash machines hadn't yet been invented and we all, back then, relied on cash and/or cheque books. Also, the banks [the only source of cash] closed at 3.30 pm every day and didn't open at all over the weekends – how the world moves on!

These guys drank a lot, they gambled a lot, they drove lot and they spent a lot. They were always short of ready cash and if they hadn't managed to top up supplies on the Friday before going into London for the weekend they were pretty miserable because there was no money to be had until Monday. This eventuality would pretty much curtail their activities for the following two days – and probably impact on the profit margins of the Capital's more seedy, as well as high end, establishments.

One of these high rolling and long serving students encountered this precise problem on a particular Friday evening. He wanted to go into town but he was short of cash, could I lend him twenty quid?

Twenty quid? To his Red Rum sized war chest my pocket was a mere pit pony. Twenty quid was a mountain of money to me and I could no more raise that sort of cash than raise the Titanic itself [my weekly food budget then was ten shillings – fifty pence in today's language, [OK, money was worth more then but I still had to keep a tight hold on my purse strings]. I politely informed my friend that I didn't posses twenty quid, I only had ten pounds and I needed that myself. He went away to find someone else. Soon he was back again, there was no one else around to help him out, if I could lend him my ten quid he'd pay me back on Monday morning. I could actually probably have scraped by until Monday minus my ten pound note but again I declined.

He was back again a few minutes later with a new proposal. How would I like to buy his watch from him? The price he was asking was, by coincidence, ten pounds. Now this was a different proposition altogether! His watch was a Bretling Navitimer, the 'must have' chronometer for any aspiring airman. These things were in the same league as a Rolex or similar and any pilot who was anyone had one strapped to his wrist – large, black, it's face full of numbers and smaller dials within. A Breitling was way out of my league and cost more than a good second hand car. This man must have been desperate to get into town to make such a ridiculous offer! I couldn't quite believe that he was being serious. On the other hand who was I to look such a gift horse in the mouth?

Almost as fast as Paul Daniels could make a playing card vanish during one of his tricks on television my ten pound note was out of my pocket, in his hands and he had peeled off his watch and handed it over. He then shot off to London to make whatever assignation he had in mind and I spent my evening admiring my new toy and status symbol and wondering how I'd manage next week now that I was devoid of any real liquid assets. And that's the story of how I acquired my expensive time piece.

So what happened to my oversized but basement bargain priced piece of bling? Well, nothing is the answer, for several years. I wore it every day and very useful it was too, it not only told the time, it also incorporated a circular slide rule which was very useful [no calculators or mobile phones then] and a stop watch, another very handy flying aid.

Years later I was married and had managed to achieve my first command as an airline captain so some of our earlier financial constraints eased marginally. I'd always had a yen to own a sports car but had never really been able to afford one. Now was not really that much different but as we'd just had a new baby I realised if I didn't get one soon then it would never happen, a growing family would soon outpace any such aspiration. So I did the sensible thing and bought a Jensen Interceptor. These were high end cars at the time but mine was relatively cheap and somewhat second hand. It was also fitted with a 7.2 litre American V8 engine so it was a bit of a 'gas guzzler' to boot. I reasoned that if I did all the maintenance myself on this luxury item, then it's running costs would be reduced to affordable levels.

One sunny summers day I was working on the car, messing about with the exhaust system I think. Whatever it was for, the front end of the car was jacked up and on axle stands on our drive and I was lying on my back underneath and tinkering away. I'd carefully taken off my miniature version of Big Ben and put it on the front scuttle of the car, between the bonnet and the windscreen, to stop it getting scratched whilst I worked – a sensible precaution.

Our house was set back from the road, on the side of a hill and the drive was about 25 yards long up the slope of the hill. As I lay on my back under the car, parked at the top of the slope outside our garage, I watched this pair of legs walk up the drive, past the car, and on up to the kitchen door at the side of the house. No doubt it was either the postman or the milkman doing their daily chores. Thirty seconds or so later the legs came walking back down from the house and disappeared into the distance. I thought no more about this and carried on tinkering.

You're already ahead of me! When I emerged from my hiding place under the car, there was no longer any sign of my watch. It was gone, vanished, disappeared and never to be seen again. I never did find out who the offending tealeaf was but he was pretty deft in the way he'd lifted the item from my bonnet. Firstly, he did well to even spot it nestling there amongst the chrome of the car's windscreen, wipers, etc. and secondly he did well to take it without so much as a sound or even a pause in his gait. I suspected nothing until way after the event.

As it was he got an even better bargain than had I – he didn't even pay a tenner for his prize! Today those same watches are fetching circa £4 grand a pop – and I didn't even think to make a claim on my household insurance!

4. Rafik

Amongst the group of middle eastern students at Elstree whilst I was there was a chap called Rafik. Rafik stood apart from his fellow middle eastern cousins in that he seemed to be far less wealthy than the rest of them were. Indeed, he lived in a very restrained and frugal manner. He hardly ever went out anywhere save to buy his food and other necessities and he most certainly didn't flash his money about, unlike most of the rest of his peer group. Additionally, Rafik took his studies quite seriously and he spent many an evening burning the midnight oil in his efforts to keep pace with the syllabus and absorbing all the information and knowledge necessary to pass the exams.

Talking of Rafik and his frugal lifestyle, I remember inadvertently upsetting him greatly on one occasion. Rafik was a Muslim and unbeknown to me and he took his religion seriously enough not to eat the likes of bacon, etc. We shared the same digs and this meant that we also shared the same kitchen and cooking utensils [supplied by the landlord – i.e. the flying school]. One day I was cooking myself bacon and egg and was using a shiny new frying pan that I'd not seen before, simply assuming that the caretaker for the building had replaced the former, rather worn out, pan with this new item.

How wrong I was! Needless to say, it turned out that said new frying pan had been purchased by none other than Rafik, precisely so that he wouldn't have to use one sullied with bacon, or anything else, cooked by us heathen infidels. He wandered into the kitchen in my mid fry up and when he spotted what had happened to his very own private frying pan he went, not surprisingly, absolutely ballistic. It took me a long time and a great deal of diplomatic skill to finally calm him down but eventually he accepted that it was indeed a genuine error on my part. Even so, I had to I promise that I'd go and buy him a replacement frying pan p.d.q.. Even thoroughly washing out the one I'd just used wasn't going to cut the mustard with him!

The main trouble was that Rafik really did struggle with his English and despite his diligence and application this made it doubly difficult for him to stay abreast of everything that was thrown at him, from both the classroom and from the instructing that he received during his flying training. The consequence of these factors were that as our training progressed, the unfortunate Rafik fell further and further behind as he strove to keep pace and as he found himself constantly having to repeat great chunks of the course. This must have been very disheartening for the poor chap, as well as being expensive. He was having to pay again to re-sit those parts of the course that he'd already covered once. However, Rafik was absolutely determined to make the grade and he manfully shrugged aside all these various difficulties and setbacks as he stoically pushed on to achieve his end goal.

When I finally finished at Elstree, having taken just over twelve months to complete the course, happily with no delays or setbacks [save a few weeks lost when no flying could be carried out due to bad weather] poor Rafik was still not yet half way through his course, having been knocked back so many times. I was never to see Rafik again but I was to learn more about him a year or two later.

Now a qualified professional pilot I was looking for work but this was hard to come by and I wasn't getting anywhere, like most of my fellow graduates at the time. One day a fellow graduate and friend, Tristram, telephoned me. He'd heard that there was a chap in Bromley [South London] looking for a couple of pilots to do some intermittent ad hoc charter work. Tristram was going to see this chap that afternoon, did I want to go along too, to see if I could also get some flying and some much needed cash? Needless to say I jumped at the chance so we met up in Bromley and together made our way to the address Tristam had been given. Our rendezvous turned out to be in a backstreet garage, supposedly selling second hand cars and the chap we met indeed had a proposition. He was quite cagey to start with but little by little, as he worked out that we really were pilots who could fly light aircraft and that we were interested only in making money and nothing else, he opened up.

Now we could understand what all his earlier hesitancy and hedgehopping had been about. The deal was that we'd fly over to Holland, at night, to some unspecified flying strip, in a single engined Cessna, pick up three passengers [all that you could get into a Cessna] and then fly them over to a disused airfield in Norfolk where we'd drop them off before then taking off to return the aircraft to its legitimate home. The reward for each trip was to be six hundred pounds, cash – a vast sum of money in 1968.

This was a whole new world of experience for us two young men and we both beat the hastiest retreat that we could. The underworld was not one that either of us were anxious to join, far less the next world, which could soon follow on if things didn't work out. Fortunately neither of us had left any detail of our addresses, etc, with these people and so, back then, we were probably untraceable. No doubt just as well or we might well have each had a visit from the 'heavies' to warn us [at best] to keep quiet! This must have been very early days in the 'people smuggling' business and certainly neither of us had any idea that such nefarious activities existed.

A couple of years later there was quite a big story in the press; a light aircraft had landed in Norfolk in the early hours of the morning and been intercepted by a farmer up early and inspecting his crops. The four occupants had run off and the police were now looking for the suspected pilot, one Rafik Ashour – there was a mug shot of my former frying pan owning flying student colleague. The self same Rafik, was the man in the plan.

How someone as conscientious and as seemingly moral as the Rafik I'd known, and liked, had got himself tangled up in that kind of activity, I'll never know. I speculated that he'd eventually thrown so much money at trying to pass his flying exams that he'd finally run out of funds and in desperation, had allowed himself to somehow be dragged into the clutches of unscrupulous people who operated in this twilight world. Whatever, the story soon became yesterday's news and Rafik disappeared from view once more, still at large.

A few months later I read a small paragraph in one of our national newspapers; Rafik Ashour, who'd been wanted for questioning in relation to smuggling people into the country had been found dead in a flat in Paris, apparently shot through the back of the head.

How sad was that? In my eyes Rafik was just a well meaning young man with a burning ambition to make the grade as an airline pilot. Maybe he was over ambitious in his aspiration but his determination was admirable and no number of setbacks were going to dim the flame that burned within him. Somehow he became so obsessed that he lost track of his moral compass – but he never deserved to end up on that kind of scrap heap.

5. Scattering The Ashes

The flying course at Elstree was to take a year of tuition and flying training. During this time I lived in digs in a house, Letchmore Lodge, very close to the airfield. This was a property owned by the flying school and used as a dormitory for students who required accommodation at the lower end of the scale of affordability. There were probably about a dozen or so of us living there with two or three of us sharing each bedroom. I shared a room with two others. Fortunately the three of us got on very well.

One of these characters, Rod, was a year or two older than my other room mate, a student called Tristram. He, like me, had come into flying straight from leaving school. Rod on the other hand, had previously had an interesting job working as a steward on the private yacht Shemara, a 'super yacht' of its day and then owned by Sir Bernard and Lady Docker. The Dockers were a couple at the centre of high society in the 1950s and '60s and hosted many lavish parties on their well known and rather beautiful floating palace. Rod, whilst remaining discreet – he never named names – had many a lurid tale to tell about some of the shenanigans that had occurred during his time on board! The Dockers had recently decided that it was time to sell the Shemara and so Rod found himself out of a job and in need of another string to his bow, hence his presence at the flying school. He was to go on to forge a successful second career as an airline captain in a major UK airline.

Tristram and I were to become firm friends during that year of flying training and well beyond. He was a very lively character, full of curiosity, boundless energy and enthusiasm for anything and everything that caught his imagination. His family lived not too far away from Elstree and he went home most weekends, not least as his father was then rather seriously ill.

Another feature that seemed to mark Tristram out from the rest of us was that he always seemed to be the one student who was at the centre of some mishap or another. If ever there was a problem the chances were that Tristram would be involved in it somewhere. For example, a student getting lost in a small aeroplane whilst learning to navigate is not difficult and it often happens. But who was it who got lost and flew round in circles over Heathrow, thus bringing the whole airport to a grinding halt? Yes, you've guessed correctly! On another occasion, whilst carrying out his first 'solo' night flying circuit, a bat hit an important part of his aeroplane [the 'pitot' tube] which rendered his speedometer useless – not much of an issue for an experienced pilot but a nightmare for a student of the art.

Not long after leaving Elstree I had a call from Tristram. He told me that, sadly, his father had finally succumbed to his illness and that his last wish had been that his ashes be scattered over a particular Scottish grouse moor where he had spent much time shooting [he was a Knight of the Realm and had lived through prosperous times]. Tristram had 'borrowed' an aeroplane from a friend and the purpose of his call was to ask me if I'd fly this aircraft up to Scotland with himself, his brother and his father's ashes aboard so that the pair of them could scatter the ashes over the appropriate Scottish moorland. Needless to say, I was more than willing to carry out this sombre task for my friend and his family so we fixed a suitable date not too far ahead.

On the chosen day I drove over to Fairoaks Airport [near Virginia Water in Surrey] where I met up with Tristram, his brother, their father, Sir Robert, now in an urn in ash form and the borrowed aircraft, a single engined Piper Comanche. The aeroplane was looking spick and span and was full of fuel. It was the pride and joy of its owner and his only instruction to Tristram was that it should be returned in the same pristine condition and fuel state as when we collected it.

I flew us all up to Scotland where we landed at Inverness. There we met up with one of Sir Robert's old grouse shooting pals who identified the correct piece of moorland on a topographical map that I'd brought up with me for the purpose. We then retired to the airports 'Greasy Spoon' cafe for some lunch after which we removed a small hatch from the side of the cabin in the aeroplane so that the two sons would be able to empty the urn containing their fathers ashes over the moorland as I flew the aircraft overhead. This removable hatch had originally been fitted for the purposes of aerial photography but it would also admirably suit our purposes on this occasion.

Now fully replete and prepared, we took off on our planned mission. All went well – except that without the hatch fitted the aircraft was quite noisy – and it was now a bit draughty in the cabin as well. We soon identified the correct piece of Scotland over which Sir Robert had wished to be scattered. As I flew round in a tight circle above the target zone the two boys behind me started the process of scattering his ashes through the hatch.

At least, that was supposed to be how it worked. What actually happened was that one minute I was happily flying round in a circle with a good view of both the moor and the aircraft instruments and the next I found myself flying round in thick fog, unable to see either the ground or the instruments and also hardly able to breathe. Rather than exiting the hatch and floating down to his intended final destination Sir Robert instead was blown back into the aircraft and was now occupying the entire cabin.

Sad to say not too much of him actually ended up on his favourite moor. The now empty urn was almost the only significant artefact to achieve an orderly exit and reach the hallowed turf below. The bulk of Sir Robert instead settled all over the upholstery – and on every other surface inside the cabin. With nothing that could be done about this unfortunate development we beat a sober and rather silent retreat back to Inverness, although all three of us thought that this rather macabre turn of events was not without its own black humour.

Back on the ground again at Inverness we re-attached the hatch cover before refuelling for our flight back down south to Fairoaks and the safe return of the aircraft to its owner. Except that we now had a new problem. The strict brief was to return the aeroplane in the same pristine condition as we'd found it before our departure that morning – but how could we possibly claim to have achieved this when it's interior now looked like the inside of the flourmill from the Canterbury Tales? And what if Tristram's friend, the proud owner, was there to greet us on landing? There was only one thing that could be done. We borrowed the vacuum cleaner from the Greasy Spoon cafe and restored the interior of the aircraft to its former immaculate state of cleanliness on site at Inverness airport.

I'm still rather ashamed to have to report that Sir Robert was condemned to spend all eternity imprisoned in a soon to be discarded vacuum bag somewhere near Inverness. At the same time I draw some comfort from the fact that, if nothing else, at least we'd managed to get him back to Scotland – and he'd been pretty close to his beloved grouse moor for a final minute or two.

6. Why Jockeys Ride in the Grand National

The finish of my flying training more or less coincided with the effects of the aftermath of the so called Six Day War – when Israel and its middle eastern neighbours had a significant argument and came to blows. This had resulted in sky high oil prices which had a major and adverse impact on aviation – people stopped flying and airlines either re-trenched or, worse still, went to the wall.

My problem was always going to be that I'd find it a challenge to get a flying job because I didn't have any experience. The only way to get experience was to first get a job – classic 'Catch 22' territory! The present economic climate put me in an even worse situation than I should have found myself. There were now a lot of experienced pilots looking for work alongside me. What chance did I have, this very small fish, in such a large pond?

Needless to say I ended up working at the bottom of the food chain and at the bottom of the big pond. My first job [which I only won because no self respecting, experienced, pilot would touch it with a barge pole] was flying a small Cessna for a so called 'air taxi' company out of Teesside Airport.

It was run by a bit of a scallywag. Harry was actually quite a nice chap but was a rough diamond of the first order whose abiding creed was that rules were made to be broken whenever and wherever possible. This was partly as a point of principle but mainly because following them invariably cost money. He'd made a success of building up a taxi and coach hire business in Middlesbrough using this methodology and he applied the same 'rustic' approach to his fledgling flying business. The trouble was that I was the young pilot who'd be caught in the crosshairs if anything went wrong. I flew a lot of very marginally legal trips during my time there and was subjected to a steep learning curve but at least I was building up a bit of experience along the way.

At one point the little single engined Cessna was traded up for a slightly larger [6 seater] twin engined Piper Twin Comanche. This was a better aeroplane but it didn't last long as it was soon repossessed! However, I did a few charters in the Comanche whilst we still had it, one of which I remember very well.

The job was to fly a jockey, who'd had an early race at the nearby Redcar racetrack, up to Kelso [Berwick on Tweed] where he was racing again later on in the day. The time interval between his races was quite tight and not achievable by road, hence the need for an 'air taxi'.

The day of the race dawned with absolutely foul weather – freezing cold, rain, poor visibility and low, ice laden, cloud cover. Even the ducks stayed inside by the fire. This was not a day for messing about in an ill equipped twin Comanche light aircraft trying to fly into an ill equipped grass strip near a horse racing track. I contacted the jockey in the morning to tell him it would probably not happen. He wasn't at all pleased and said that he'd turn up anyway. He did.

The weather hadn't improved one jot and I told him that I'd have to cancel the trip because of the low cloud, etc. Neither the jockey – he wanted his race, nor my boss – he wanted his taxi fare, were at all happy. They both ranted and raved and thumped the table. In the end I said that if they were both that keen then I'd get airborne and we'd see how it went. If it looked OK I'd press on, if not I'd turn back. However, they needed to understand that even if we got up to Kelso, such was the low cloud that I was pretty damned l sure that we wouldn't be able to land. All in all it was likely that this would be an expensive and fruitless exercise. Undaunted, the jockey wanted to press on.

We did. Myself, my jockey friend [and his saddle] and the Twin Comanche departed and were almost immediately swallowed up in thick, low, stratus cloud. Before I'd even climbed up to 1,000 ft, ice had started to grow on the wings and airframe. This aircraft had no protection against ice – which gets dangerous if you accumulate too much of it [you end up falling out of the sky]. The only thing you can do in this situation – if you want to continue on – is to look for warmer air, either by climbing up out of the cloud or by descending below it. I couldn't go down as I would have hit the floor so I carried on up. As I suspected, there was no clear air higher up and the ice was getting worse, soon it would become concerning. I fairly swiftly decided to turn back to Teesside airport and I told my passenger.

"No", he said, "I'm paying for this, we'll continue to Kelso" he firmly countered. I pointed out that I was the Captain and that we were going back to Teesside and that was it and all about it. His response was as dumbfounding as it was immediate:-

"What's your problem, pal?", he said, "I'll have you know I've got fully comprehensive life insurance"!

At this point I suddenly understood why these jockey types climb aboard their highly dangerous animals – the fastest and friskiest of their type that they can find – a breed equipped with its' own mind but one lacking both brakes and steering – and then go jumping over high fences and great dykes, at lunatic levels of speed. To make matters worse, they first fit these beasts with steel capped boots so as to trample even harder on a fellow rider when he, inevitably, falls off. Not only that, the only thing that they provide themselves with, with which to hang on, is a flimsy bit of string tied to the horse's mouth! They're all insured – so they can walk on water!

My jockey friend was furious but I had more immediate problems to deal with, like getting us back on the ground before our mode of transport assumed the aerodynamic properties of an iceberg and fell out of the sky. It should all have been fine, I was tuned in to the instrument landing guidance system for the airport's runway and when I popped out of the bottom of the cloud the runway threshold would be right there in front of me. I left it quite late to extend the flaps and put the wheels down – I didn't want even more ice to stick to the aeroplane by exposing more bits to it. The flaps went down OK but the undercarriage didn't move.

This was not working out as advertised! I recycled the gear selector – still nothing. Landing with no wheels between the tarmac and the aeroplane was going to be noisy, expensive, embarrassing, inconvenient for everyone, uncomfortable and it could even be a bit dangerous on a bad day. On the other hand, climbing back up into the ice laden cloud wasn't much of a good idea either. I was between a rock and a hard place [almost literally!] but I chose the latter option, applied full power and climbed away.

The Twin Comanche's gear was operated by an electric motor which drove a set of steel cables to lower and lift the wheels. If the motor failed there was a long alloy bar stowed next to the pilot's seat that you could insert into a slot and push forward. This did the same job as the electric motor and would lower the wheels for you. Except that it didn't. It wouldn't move. I pushed harder, still nothing. Then I pushed very hard indeed. I was quite strong back then and at last the bar did move. But the wheels didn't, they remained stubbornly retracted. I had succeeded only in bending the bar – which was not designed to be forced, only to act as a substitute for a broken motor. I decided that the operating cables had become frozen in their sheaths and wouldn't move until they'd been thawed out.

This meant I'd have to now descend below the cloud again and then fly around at a very low level until the gear freed itself off. If it didn't break free before I ran out of fuel I'd have to land wheels up anyway – but that would be a last resort. Behind me my passenger was oblivious to all this, still chuntering on about his missed race and how useless I was. Happily It all ended well, the flying bit anyway. After ten or fifteen minutes of low level hedge hopping around the airfield the wheels finally co-operatively freed themselves and I was able to land normally.

And the jockey? I never saw him again and I'm sure he never knew that he'd been in a more parlous position in that aeroplane than he ever was on a horse over Becher's Brook – or anywhere else, insured or not!

7. Moving On

I hadn't actually planned to move on from my air taxi job. I was getting in a bit of flying , not a lot admittedly, there didn't seem to be as much demand as the boss had told me would be forthcoming when he took me on. But I was at least accumulating those all important flying hours that were a prerequisite to being able to move to bigger and better things eventually. I was also still somewhat grateful to him for the chance he'd given me to prove myself – despite the fact that things were habitually run pretty close to the wire and that it was demonstrably clear that it was a matter of pride to him that he continually strive to 'beat the system' whenever an opportunity presented itself.

When the little Cessna had been swapped for the bigger Twin Comanche I'd had to go down to Denham Airfield [just a little north west of London] to both collect it and to do a couple of flying tests in it – these allowing my licence to be signed up to prove that I was current on the type and capable of flying in cloudy weather and in controlled airspace [the aerial motorway system regulated by the National Air Traffic Services – or NATS].

My examiner for these tests was a chap by the name of Roxy Heart. The name kind of suited him, he was quite a character and was clearly of 'a certain age' – long past the first flush of youth and possessed of that confidence that told you he'd been round the block a few times and knew which way was up. He had a spectacular mane of silver hair, an enormous Burt Reynolds style moustache, with mutton sideburns to suit, and he had boundless energy. He looked rather like an archetypal silver haired Wild Bill Hickock [but without the gun belt]. He was also a bit of a wheeler dealer and had fingers in all sorts of pies, both inside and outside, aviation. I was to discover later on that he also lived in an enormous house on the banks of the Thames – which rather reflected both his character and his wheeling and dealing skills.

Anyway, Roxy adjudicated my flying tests, signed my licence and sent me on my way. I little thought that I'd see him again when I departed from Denham in the Twin Comanche. A few weeks went by and the new aeroplane was then 'repatriated', to be replaced with another single engined Cessna. I wasn't very pleased with this as two engines are always better than one from a flying perspective – and 'multi-engine' flying counts for much more on the C.V. too. To be relegated back to a single engined aircraft was definitely not a step forward.

One day, a few months later and out of the blue, I had a call from Roxy Heart. He had a proposition for me. He'd been retained by an American entrepreneur who was starting up a freight airline to be based at London Heathrow. It would be a big step up for me he said, flying a Beech 18 and being in this new airline at the start would stand me in good stead as it expanded with success. I had no idea what a Beech 18 was but even if only half of the picture that Roxy painted was true, it had to be a whole lot better than what I was presently doing, namely messing about in what was effectively a not much more than a below par flying club.

Roxy arranged a meeting for me with the aspiring airline boss in London. Steve Quinto was the man in question. He'd apparently made a lot of money in the American theatre, Broadway, etc, had an interest in aviation and he also flew himself. He wanted to start his own airline business in the UK. He'd identified a market in the air freight business, had the money to start the operation and already had a contract – flying English newspapers six nights a week, hot off the London presses, to Geneva for early morning distribution – no internet back then!

Steve was a typically laconic American, smoked big cigars [held between clenched teeth], had much enthusiasm for his project and was already operating his service with [an American registered] Beech 18, flying to Geneva and back himself – on all six nights of the week! He was currently the only pilot in the business and he needed a few more – a.s.a.p.! The plan was to put the Beech on the British register and run the whole operation under UK [CAA] regulations. Until the full UK paperwork was complete and approved, the airline would run under American [FAA] regulations. It all sounded pretty good to me and a month later I found myself back down south, living in Earls Court and working for Sagittair as Steve had elegantly named his fledgling airline.

In order to legally fly the Beech I had to first get an American Commercial Pilot's Licence [CPL]. In those days this was a simple process. If you held a UK professional licence it was just a question of filling in a few forms. No exams, not even air law, and no flying tests either. I applied for, and received, my U.S. licence before I'd even left my previous job. Unlike its rather fancy British cousin, the American licence was a very simple item, only a single postcard sized piece of paper. There wasn't much information on it either, just your name and one or two other details. The only striking thing I remember about it is that emblazoned boldly across the front of it was a slogan: –

"Safety is no accident, it must be planned".

An aviation truism, if ever I heard one – but a nice touch, giving a constant reminder of the stark reality and primary demand of our professional ethos.

My introduction to the Beech 18 was no more and no less than 'on the job' training. There was no real reference manual on flying techniques and no formal training process. The aeroplane was a big light aircraft – with a lot more knobs, dials and levers than anything I'd ever flown before. It also had its own set of challenges and required techniques – of which more shortly. Suffice to say that I flew a few trips to and from Geneva with the ubiquitous Steve before I'd mastered the basics and he deemed me fit to be let loose on my own with his favourite toy.

Once 'checked out' on the old Beech I thought that my life would be all plain sailing with routine trips to and from Geneva with an increasing variety of trips to different places as the business expanded.

The flights to different places was the only bit of my forecast that was correct. There wasn't much that was routine when flying that Beech and it was to provide me with a good few stories and a lot of experience in a fairly short timeframe, before I was to move on to pastures new.

Beech 18. American registered. N495F

8. Beech 18. Engine Fire

It was just another night. Harry, the laconic Australian ground engineer, had checked the plane in his usual laid back and inimitable fashion and I'd checked the plane too, as pilots do. Everything was good, as much as it ever was on a Beech 18 that was built before Pontius was a pilot. The fuel was loaded – avgas, otherwise known as 'petrol' – all tanks full to the brim, 240 gallons of the stuff. The engine oil tanks were full, there were no leaks that either of us had spotted and nothing was falling off. The cargo of newspapers was loaded, the paperwork was done and I would have to go.

I'd only been in the job a few weeks and already I didn't enjoy it. The aeroplane was noisy, it was old, it was cantankerous, it had no autopilot, it had few radio aids that functioned properly, it leaked water through the windows and it was cold; the petrol fuelled heater never wanted to work in the air. Not only that I was always tired. Night flying and I didn't get on too well together.

It was winter and I was, as usual, going to Geneva with tomorrows newspapers – hot off the press in London and ferried out to Heathrow by van for onward distribution by air – to be on the news stands bright and early the next morning. This was my routine, six nights a week, and departure time was 1am. Not a good time of day to start work at the age of twenty two, especially when there was a life to be lived outside aeroplanes.

At least this night the weather was good at both London and Geneva, clear skies, smooth air, no ice and an altogether straight forward run out to Geneva from my perspective. And my perspective was very important to me. Yes, I was a pilot but one with not a lot of experience. And this was a lot of aeroplane for a young whippersnapper to be driving around the place, especially when it was dark, mostly cloudy, turbulent, icy and altogether quite challenging – and all at the same time. Driving around the Alps was just an added pressure, mainly because there are a lot of hills around Geneva and most of them are significantly higher than the 7,000 feet of altitude above which the old Beech struggled to fly. Especially with a ton of newspapers weighing her down.

These things, together with the challenges inherent in operating the aeroplane itself, bothered me. Which was why my perspective was important – I wasn't ready to die just yet. You will already have deduced that I didn't, for otherwise who would be writing about it so many years later?

But these were the things that I thought about before a day's work then and these were the reasons that I already didn't much enjoy it. I should have done though because I came through it and hindsight is a wonderful thing, but this was my first 'proper' job in aviation. Looking back on it now, it was a great time; busy, difficult, challenging, fearful, all of those things and more. It shaped my attitude to flying, it gave me confidence, I learned about my limitations and I gained respect, for engineering, for air traffic control, for the power of the weather, for the frailty of humanity when set against nature and the laws of physics – and above all I gained respect for safety in aviation. No less importantly, in the short time that I flew the Beech 18 I gained a disproportionate amount of experience which was to serve me well over the rest of my flying career. It was just a bit of a tough lesson and a steep learning curve for an inexperienced and rather naïve young man.

Not much happened at Heathrow in the small hours of the morning in those days [we're talking 1969 here]. There was little 'traffic' then and the Sagittair Beech 18 operated on one of the few 'night slots' available at the airport [what would that be worth now?!]. The technicalities of operating out of Heathrow were altogether much less complex then than they were to become over the next thirty years.

That is more than can be said for the process of actually starting the two Pratt and Whitney Wasp Junior radial engines fitted to the beast.

To start an engine you had to pump neat fuel into the cylinders, press a button to make the plugs spark and press another button to operate the starter motor. We're already up to three hands being required here if you've kept up with the procedure so far. Then you needed to feed the fuel into the cylinders using the mixture control lever whilst controlling the engine speed with the throttle. We're now up to a requirement for five hands but there's only one pilot. Somehow or other it always worked and the engines would start in clouds of smoke, bangs and backfires before steadying into a rhythmical and satisfying sound of thrumping power [it's a boy thing that either you love or you don't – I did but my wife has never really understood!].

With all the formalities completed and with instructions from Air Traffic Control obtained I trundled out from the cargo area on the South side of the Airport to the beginning runway 27 Left – the runway in use for take-off this night [its 28 Left now but the variation was more in those days!]. Even taxiing the Beech was a bit of an acquired art. It had no steering wheel as there was no nose wheel to steer it with – it was one of those aircraft that dragged its tail along the floor – so to make it point in the direction you wanted to go you had to use the engines and/or the brakes to make it turn. Not too much of a problem once you'd mastered it but it could get a bit tricky when the wind was up. Whilst all this juggling of brakes and engines was going on you still had to talk to the air traffic controller, complete your take-off checks and make sure that the various engine oil temperatures and pressures, cylinder head temperatures and so on were 'within limits'. At the same time you had to check that you knew where you were going to go after take-off to stay clear of other aircraft and noise sensitive neighbours to the airport.

Such activity was all pretty routine stuff for a seasoned pilot but you needed to be awake to stay on top of it all in the Beech. This was because she had a habit of throwing a surprise at you from time to time – and always either when you least expected it or when it was at a most inconvenient moment because you were already occupied with some other important flying task.

This was particularly the case during the take-off when a lot was going on and concentration was required to get the best out of the old girl. The trick was to react fast and to make it smooth. The quicker you made a small input to correct a minor deviation, the smaller the correction you needed to apply. The bigger the deviation became, the larger the following correction needed to be. If you didn't get it right early enough it became a battle of wills between the two of you and if you were half asleep the Beech would always triumph. This was as embarrassing as it was unsatisfactory to a pilots self esteem. Any pilot will recognize this as a truism because the principles apply to all aircraft. The Beech though, required its pilot to elevate these skills to a somewhat heightened degree, with the emphasis being on ensuring that with maximum anticipation exerted, minimum input of effort would be required. Always the road to an easy life in aviation.

I was by now becoming reasonably seasoned but I was far from being the ace of the base. Every take-off was therefore an adventure, with me, the aircraft, my adrenaline and the newspapers all accelerating down the runway together. The adrenaline and the heartbeat were always going the quickest but somehow the aircraft was always at the front whilst my brain was bringing up the rear. That's the difference between an old pro and a beginner. As you become more seasoned you learn to train your brain to better take the lead. An experienced [and a good] pilot will always be ahead of the aircraft. That way lies both satisfaction and longevity.

With the appropriate clearance obtained from the air traffic controller I started the take-off run. The old Beech was not endowed with a massive amount of power from the engines. There was certainly enough power but not much more. Indeed, such was the design of the aircraft that in the event of one of the engines stopping the pilot's notes gave warning that you would be going down. If you had any load on board you'd be going down all the way to the ground. Not a happy prospect if you couldn't find a runway before you hit the floor.

We always had the maximum load of newspapers on board on the run to Geneva and the aircraft was, as usual, up to its maximum weight. The truth is that, in reality, it was almost always overloaded. The policing of such things were somewhat relaxed in those days and the contractors would always try and sneak on a few extra bundles of papers – sometimes quite a few and each bundle weighed a good number of performance sapping kilos. So departure was always more of a lumber than a real acceleration.

The start of the take-off was always a juggling act of flying controls, brakes and throttles to get the thing going forward in a straight line and down the middle of the runway. As the speed gathered the power could be increased. The engines were positioned close in on each wing and were pretty much in line with the cockpit so as the power came on the noise increased too, until once full power was applied, the volume was really quite deafening. This noise was made worse by the propellers cutting through the air. At full power and with the props set to 'fine pitch' the air at their tips was moved to supersonic speed. The whole thing amounted to a veritable cacophony of sound, exacerbated by the acoustics of sitting in a dustbin – with the lid on it and the engines in there with you. At 50 knots I lifted the tail in the prescribed manner and at 90 knots I eased her gently off the concrete and let her accelerate to 110 knots. Then it was up with the undercarriage and the start of the climb away whilst bringing back the power to the prescribed settings. The reduction in noise was as instant as it was welcome when climb power was selected.

With an uneventful take-off behind me, my ears no longer now ringing, everything under control and operating normally, I settled down to the business of the three and a half hour flight down to Geneva with a background of constant engine noise that would trouble the Health and Safety people more than just a little in this day and age.

The Beech was far from a modern jet. It didn't climb very fast and it didn't fly very fast either, so on a clear night you had a good and sustained view of the ground underneath. This night was such a night. The clear air produced a spectacular view of London and the South East as I turned on course. The moon was full and the night was light.

In forty years of flying such views never lost their appeal. I always felt it was a real privilege to be sitting in the best seat in the house, flying someone else's aeroplane, at their expense, and being able to marvel at the spectacle of a World unfolding before me.

The reflection of the moon as it cut across the twists and turns of the Thames emphasized the river's lazy meanderings through the city and the light constantly played over its dark water as every small movement of the aircraft shifted the reflections along its course. The great metropolis was asleep and I wondered, as always, what business was going on that required the few cars that were snailing along roads at that time of night. Surely all sensible people were now asleep? These drivers must be up to no good, returning from an illicit liaison, conducting a robbery, driving home drunk from a party, or otherwise involved in some nefarious activity. Maybe, like me, they were just in the wrong job and were having to work at the wrong end of the spectrum of the natural human circadian rhythm.

Such were my musings as I flew along. As I gained height, scanned the instruments and enjoyed the view, I made the first of the routine adjustments to the fuel mixture. Nothing was automatic on an aircraft this old and fuel delivery was no exception. As you climb the air gets thinner so you need to adjust the amount of fuel going into the engines to match the amount of oxygen available. It's a simple process of playing with a lever. On the Beech you just glanced through the window at the exhaust stubs sticking out of the engine cowlings and looked at the colour of the hot gas. What you wanted was a nice blue flame. Too much fuel and the colour would change to red, too little and it would turn white. It was important to get this right, partly because you didn't want to waste fuel by running too rich, and partly because if you ran with it set too lean the engines would overheat.

Adjustments made, I continued with the process of relaxation into the routine. That was where I made my mistake. I shouldn't have relaxed at all. The fickle finger of fate had alighted on my number on this night. When I next looked out of the left hand window expecting to see an efficient blue flame I saw flames all right, but they were angry, and red, and yellow, and streaked with black smoke, and they weren't coming from the exhaust – that was still burning a nice shade of blue. These flames were exiting from every orifice that the engine cowling possessed – except the exhaust stubs. In short the engine was on fire.

This was not good. Fire is not good on any aeroplane. An engine fire is not good either. An engine fire on an aeroplane that will only go downwards if an engine stops is definitely not good. I'd never had an engine fire before. The first thing you have to do if an engine catches fire is shut it down. I'd never had to shut an engine down before either. I'd practiced of course, and been trained to deal with these eventualities too. But those were all practices which isn't the same. This was real which is very different from the training and the practice.

Suddenly any romance there might have been in flying had lost its appeal. I'd rather have been on the ground, in one of those cars, a bank robber even. Anything but up here in an aeroplane on fire. That's another thing you learn about flying early on. There's no way out. You can't blame anyone else, you can't hide anywhere and you can't run away. You have to deal with it. If you don't you'll lose, sometimes pretty badly. Very occasionally and only for an even fewer, losing will be the last thing they ever do.

So I had to deal with it. I reverted to the training I'd had and I dealt with it. I shut the engine down and offset the swing of the Beech as the power on the left hand side disappeared. I increased the power on the other engine to compensate. Now the aeroplane wanted to descend and I had to let it do that thing. I marvelled at my composure but I actually felt anything but composed. This was new territory and it was territory that I'd rather not have been in. I looked out at the offending engine. The propeller was stationary and properly feathered but the fire was still there, as I knew it would be but hoped it wouldn't.

This old plane had but one fire extinguisher fitted to cover the eventuality of fire in either engine. Having shut down the offending motor the idea was that you then carefully selected either the port engine or the starboard engine on a selector switch. This selector governed to which of the two engines the contents of the extinguisher would be delivered. With careful precision, deliberation and I'm pretty sure, a shaking hand, I twisted the selector to the port engine position. There was only one shot available and I didn't want to get it wrong. When I'd checked that my selection was correct I pressed the button that fired off the extinguisher bottle. Then I looked out of the window at the offending engine and fire to watch for the result. The fire would go out wouldn't it? Nothing. I waited and watched. I had faith, but still nothing. After what seemed an eternity but was probably no more than a couple of seconds, there was a result!

The result was that the right hand engine started coughing and spluttering and the whole aeroplane started to shake and rattle in time to the coughs and splutters. My eyes swung round to the right. To my horror I could see foam and fluid oozing out of the engine cowls. The extinguishent had gone to the wrong engine and it was being choked to death. So now there were no engines and I was in a four and a half ton glider over London in the middle of the night. Not only that, it was filled with petrol – and paper – and me. I wasn't equipped to deal with this. This was outside any briefing in the text books and I would have to make it up as I went along if I was going to get out of this fine mess.

I wasn't that analytical about it at the time. I suppose I just reacted with instinct and a healthy desire to carry on living for a little while yet. I feathered the coughing engine – which meant stopping it with the propeller angled into the airflow to reduce its resistance – I knew it wouldn't run with the carburettor choked full of non flammable liquid. I also knew that the left engine had been running strongly even though it was on fire. If I could get that one going again then

I might have a chance of stretching the descent back to Heathrow for a safe landing. I tried it and it sprang to life. The engine noise I'd earlier merely tolerated now became sweet music. I'd not been airborne for long so I was still within a few miles of the airport and I'd made enough height to make the job possible. The issue now was how big a hold the fire would take on the engine or the wing. If that fell off or the fuel went bang I wouldn't have any more problems.

Somewhere in amongst all this activity I made my first 'Mayday' call to air traffic control. The voice that came back was calm and oh so cool, confident, unflappable and reassuring. The guy on the headphones at the other end was not only helpful and very professional but his tone and the manner of his delivery made me feel that he dealt with this kind of issue every day, this was just another walk in the park to him. Such was the tenor of our brief exchange, one stranger to another, that he gave me the impression that there could only be one outcome from this – and that was success. His voice told me this and I believed his voice. He didn't tell me this in words but he gave me confidence when I needed it. He instantly became my best friend. I never subsequently met that controller but he engendered in me the start of a feeling of great respect for his breed. Years later I was to forge a long and close working relationship with air traffic control in relation to Safety. That controller on that night sowed the seed that sparked that particular interest in me.

I turned the Beech back toward Heathrow, following the directions from my new found friend. The fire in the left engine began to look distinctly less healthy. Big flames became smaller, then they just flickered and then they went out altogether. The engine continued to run fine and fire was no longer evident. With the good visibility of the night I'd soon spotted the runway amongst the glitter of London's millions of lights. I had plenty of height in hand to make it and in no more than fifteen minutes I was back on the same runway that I'd taken off from a lifetime ago. Never was anyone more relieved than me – except maybe my friend the controller who'd handled my emergency.

I was followed down the runway by a posse of attentive fire engines. When I stopped they surrounded the aircraft and pointed their nozzles at me as if I were the target of a firing squad. Rather intimidating that was, for most of these trucks were bigger than the Beech, but at the same time it was also reassuring. It took a while to explain to the fire crews that I knew that the right hand engine was the one that was stopped but that it had been the left hand one, still running, that had been on fire. I'm not sure what they made of it all because the logic now didn't sound quite right and I felt a bit sheepish.

When we got the aircraft back to its allotted parking stand Harry the engineer appeared and prodded and poked. Both the cause of the fire and the problem with the extinguisher soon became apparent.

The fire had been caused by a broken fuel priming line. The first element of starting the engine is to pump fuel into it. This 'priming' exercise squirts petrol directly into the cylinders via a series of small metal pipes. One of these pipes had developed a leak and squirted fuel into the cowling, instead of into the cylinder. This petrol then soaked into all the oil and muck that had collected in the cowling over time. As the engine ran and the exhausts and other bits got hot it reached a point where it eventually caught fire. Once all the muck had been burned the fire went out. Wasn't I a lucky boy!?

The extinguisher had popped off into the wrong engine because whoever had last re-plumbed system had done it back to front. It had probably been like that for years and would never have been discovered until it was required. Wasn't I the unlucky lad!?

I went home to bed. Much older, much wiser and no more in love with the Beech than I had been when I'd last put my head on the pillow. At least I'd proved to myself that I could cope with an engine failure, and a fire. I now don't remember but expect I slept very well that night.

9. The Lobster Flight.

Working for Sagittair was many things but it was never dull. During my time there life was frantic, both in the office and in the air. In the office a bunch of us were working flat out to write and build up all the documentation required for the issue of a UK 'Air Operators Certificate' [AOC]. This was no easy task but was essential if the airline was to achieve approval to operate in the UK with British registered aircraft and pilots. Some of us, myself amongst them, were stupid enough to both work in the office and to fly the aircraft [a fine attribute, the stamina of youth, just a shame that it doesn't last!].

Until the UK flying approvals came through, we were operating this first [American registered] plane [a Beech 18] under USA regulations. It was not the best aircraft that ever flew. The VHF radio – there was only one – was unreliable. It was not connected to the aircraft electrical system but instead to a separate car battery that we carted to and from the aircraft when we were going flying. If the battery went flat in flight all communication with Air Traffic Control was lost. Not good if you were flying back from Geneva to Heathrow on a foggy morning. Not surprisingly, it caused chaos, the Heathrow controllers must have been tearing their hair out whenever it happened. These sorts of shortcomings with the Beech were relatively frequent and we pilots just had to work round them. The bigger problems came from unexpected quarters.

On one particular trip I found myself flying down to Portsmouth to pick up a cargo of a ton of live lobsters to then fly them over to Brest in sunny France where, presumably, the best of British would be distributed to myriad French gastro restaurants. There's actually nothing at all wrong with that – except that lobster is one of my favourite foods and I'd rather it stayed here for me and mine to enjoy!

I taxied up to the small terminal building on arrival at Portsmouth, shut down and was met by a handling agent and a salty south coast lobster fisherman. Inside the small terminal was a large pile of polystyrene boxes full of live lobsters packed in ice – my cargo, 1,000 kilos worth of them. I took the lid off one of the boxes and looked inside. Beautiful, large, blue, fresh lobster. How I would have liked to have taken one home to share with my fiancé. Alas, they were not for me, not unless I hijacked my own aircraft and flew the lot of them off into the sunset to an unknown, uncharted island not too far from the English Channel. Some chance, I didn't have the fuel to get as far as Necker [and I didn't know Richard Branson anyway. Probably he hadn't even been invented back then].

Back to reality and the job in hand. I set to, supervising the loading and the securing of this precious cargo. The polystyrene boxes were quite bulky, designed as they were to keep the cold in and the warm out. By the time the job was finished the entire cabin area of the aircraft was crammed full. There was only one access door fitted to the old Beech and it was at the back of the fuselage. I had to climb over the top of all the boxes to get back up to the flight deck. 'Climb' wasn't exactly the way to describe how I arrived up at the sharp end. It was more like an SAS commando worming manoeuvre – like they do on television documentaries when wriggling through one of those nets pinned to the ground on a training exercise. By the time I was seated in my 'office' my front was soaking wet, I stank of fish and I was panting heavily! Whoever had the idea that flying was a glamorous business?

I settled back into the flying routine, fired up the engines, ran through all the standard checks and taxied out to the beginning of the grass runway. It wasn't the longest strip in the world, but neither was it the shortest. At the far end, beyond the airfield boundary, was a rather large and solid looking warehouse building, reaching up into the sky. The performance calculations showed that, with the weight of cargo and fuel on board, with the current ambient temperature, with existing air pressure and wind conditions, more than enough distance was available for me to get the Beech to accelerate to take off speed, get it airborne and then to climb over all obstacles in our path – and all without any undue problem.

I lined up at the start of the runway and, with a final wind check from Air Traffic Control [ATC] and with clearance to take off, I opened up the power on both engines to go. We trundled forward, accelerating as we went. At some point along the way it dawned on me that we weren't accelerating fast enough. Visually it was beginning to look like there wasn't enough distance left for me and my lobsters [and the Beech] to all get airborne together and to miss the warehouse at the end of the runway before we came to some kind of collective and embarrassing grief. I looked at the engine instruments, they were telling me that both engines were working fine and were on full power. Maybe it was the extra drag from the grass? I'd not operated on grass before, maybe this was what was upsetting the calculations? There was not a lot of time left for me to make a decision. Either I took a gamble and carried on or, I closed the throttles while I still had time – and sufficient distance – to stop. Being a coward I made the latter decision. I closed the throttles and jumped on the brakes.

The aircraft stopped, with only a little room to spare but I was mystified and devoid of any idea as to why she'd not behaved as the books said she would. The only unknown was the drag from the grass strip. I convinced myself that this must have been the reason for failure. I told ATC that I'd retrace my steps and have another go. This time I taxied as close to the perimeter fence at the beginning of the runway as I dared before turning round to face the take off direction again. This won me a few extra yards of distance. Now tucked up right at the very beginning of the runway I applied absolutely as much power as I dared in one hit and again set sail down the runway, continually inching on as much additional power as fast as I possibly could as I went along and the rudders became more effective with the increase in speed. Again we only accelerated slowly and again I had to abandon the take off. I was now out of my depth, out of answers and out of ideas.

I trundled back to the terminal wondering what I was going to say, or even do. I slithered my way out of the aircraft and was met by a puzzled fisherman and a no less concerned handling agent.

"What's wrong?" they both chorused.

I don't know" I said, "It just wouldn't accelerate fast enough. Are you sure you only loaded 1,000 kilos?".

"Ooh argh" said Mr. Salt, "Your man said 1,000kilos tops, so I only got 1,000kilos of lobsters in them thar' boxes".

"OK" I said, with a vague penny now maybe beginning to drop:- "But what about the ice?", I queried.

"Ice?", said my friend Salt, "No none said anything 'bout ice. I got a contract for 1,000 kilos o' lobsters. I can't be payin' for ice an' all!".

Bingo! Now I understood. If I'd set sail on full power, by road, rail or sea, all the way from Portsmouth to Brest in southern Brittany, I would still not have had enough distance available to accelerate to take off speed! With all that ice keeping my best friends, the lobsters, happily asleep there must have been at least double the weight on board than the poor old Beech could possibly carry.

I ended up doing two trips but I never found out who paid for the second run, the poor fisherman – who knew no better – or our charter people, who must have had faces as red as the poor old lobsters after they'd been in the pot! Sometimes the left hand really does need to talk to the right!

10. Tales of the Unexpected

Flying the Beech was never dull. Almost every trip had some sort of surprise in store. Sometimes it was the aeroplane, sometimes it was the cargo. Sometimes it was just pure bad luck – wrong place, wrong time, the fickle finger of fate, etc. It wasn't only me who seemed to draw a short straw either, other pilots had similar 'happenings'.

Steve Quinto was quite right in his hunch that there was a market for a small aircraft that could shift loads of around a ton or so – and do so at short notice. There was a steady stream of both enquiries and work, with all manner of weird and wonderful items being moved around from A to B.

Beech 18 Flightdeck

One such trip, not flown by me, was to transport a pair of dolphins from Heathrow down to [I think] Barcelona where they were destined for life in a dolphinarium. This is not a particularly happy story and I would hope that in this day and age, some 50 years later, it would not be allowed to happen.

As an aside, I wish now that I'd kept a diary of my life and 'events' back then. At the time it was all pretty much every day stuff and didn't seem either that interesting or that important. Plus, I was always too busy enjoying life outside aviation to bother about writing anything down. All these years later it would be useful to have an accurate historical reference [memory is not always that reliable!]. Additionally, much of what was routine back then in the lives of pilots would hardly be believed by the generations now following along behind us. Some of our antics they'd find both foolhardy and fascinating. The world of aviation has moved on a mighty long way since I started out in the '60s.

Anyway, back to the dolphins. These two hapless animals had arrived at Heathrow, flown in from Florida strapped into specially made stretchers. They were accompanied by a handler and they were both covered in Vaseline to help stop them from dehydrating. When they arrived at the Sagittair handling agency at the airport they'd already been out of the water for a significant time and had also had to endure some seven hours or so of flight across the Atlantic. They may well have been sedated but they were still, understandably, quite stressed.

It was important to get the dolphins down to Barcelona as swiftly as possible to once again restore them to their natural marine environment. The Beech was no jet and the dolphins still faced another four or five hours, at least, before this could happen. There was a long hiatus whilst the stretchered dolphins were loaded into the aircraft. The rear door and the width of the fuselage were barely large enough to give the space needed for manoeuvring them into the cabin. Several attempts were made before both were finally in place, one on top of the other and with only inches to spare above the top stretcher.

At last everything was made secure and the dolphins, complete with handler, departed on the final leg of their journey. Sadly, it didn't go too well. On the way the dolphin on the top stretcher became very agitated and despite his best efforts there was little that the handler could do to calm or reassure the animal. The longer the flight went on the more upset the poor dolphin became.

Eventually the dolphin became so stressed that it started trying to thrash about, despite being firmly restrained. Little by little the restraining straps slackened off until eventually it was beating itself, with considerable force, against the roof of the fuselage.

Now there was real danger present. If any significant damage was done to the aircraft structure it could result in a failure from which recovery might well not be possible. And there was nothing the pilot could do about it – except hope. Even diverting to a closer airport would take time and such was the beating the roof was taking, time wasn't on his side. Fortunately the unhappy creature ran out of energy before the roof ran out of strength and the animal calmed down.

The rest of the flight was uneventful and the Dolphins went on their way, at last, back to the water in Barcelona. I don't know what the final outcome was for these two innocent creatures. I like to think that they both fully recovered from their ordeal but I have a vague feeling that I subsequently heard that one of them survived but the other didn't.

Either way, this episode reminds me of the rendition programme after the Iraq war. For dolphins substitute people. For zoo keeping entrepreneurs substitute Bush, Blair, Straw and co and for a pond in Spain substitute Guantanamo. Not my idea of the best way to go about engineering the preservation of species.

Another rather bizarre contract was the transport of a [so called] meteorological rocket up to Tromso in Northern Norway. Again, I wasn't involved in this flight but heard the story from the pilot who flew the trip. I remember it only because I've always thought that there was something not quite right about it.

The charterers had been keen to establish that the Beech had a heated cabin. Apparently this rocket powered weather probe had to be maintained at a temperature of + 10C. If the temperature fell as low as – 10C then it could spontaneously explode. Our sales people told them that the cabin was most certainly heated and so we got the job. The problem was that, whilst it was true that the cabin was heated, it was also equally true that the heater hardly ever worked!

We were always frozen when flying that aircraft and we dressed like Second World War bomber pilots so as to combat the problem; scarves, gloves, fleece jackets, fleece lined boots, etc, etc. Additionally, it was the middle of winter and Tromso is a long way up Norway which meant that weather conditions wouldn't have helped one iota in keeping the cabin warm, even assuming that, for once in its life, the heater actually had worked. It would also be a long flight in the Beech to get up there and there was only one real conclusion that could be drawn which was that the prospect of maintaining +10°C in the cabin was nil, whilst the prospect of hitting -10°C was pretty high indeed! An unintended explosion somewhere up at the top of the North Sea was therefore entirely possible, indeed even probable.

Undaunted, my pilot colleague pressed on with his trip. Happily this turned out to be uneventful. The aircraft heater had proved to be its usual unreliable self but, whilst it became undeniably cold in the cabin as the flight progressed, there was no explosion en route and both pilot and rocket arrived in Tromso in one piece.

Immediately on arrival at Tromso the aircraft and rocket were met by a very superior looking and unmarked white van which drew up alongside the, now silent, flying refrigerator. As the pilot stepped out onto the snow covered apron, so the back doors of the van opened to reveal a surgical like, and brightly lit, interior. The blast of warm air escaping from its heated heart hit my pilot friend as sharply as the temperature he would have felt if he'd thrown water onto the hot coals in a sauna. In no time flat the container, with rocket inside, had been transferred from the aeroplane into its new, warm and cosseted home in the back of the van.

Now, I know nothing about rockets or missiles – except that they're both powered by clever motors, fuelled with rather volatile liquids which are best kept in benign conditions, and that when launched, both climb skyward with great alacrity and into ambient temperatures that become significantly cold. So why all the clamour and effort to keep this bit of kit so warm whilst in transit? Was this item just a simple meteorological rocket, as advertised, or was it something more sinister? We were still in the middle of the Cold War back then. Nixon and his Generals were bombing [or trying to] the communists in Vietnam into submission and there was big rivalry between the USA and Russia in the 'Space Race'. If it was just a weather rocket why did it need to go all the way up to Norway – why not launch it from the top of Scotland?

Maybe I was just too cynical and full of conspiracy theories, even back then, but I've always wondered about that 'meteorological' rocket!

11. More Mishaps

As often as not, when flying the newspapers down to Geneva in the middle of the night, the sky was overcast and the flight progressed in cloud all the way. Not a problem as a rule, but if it was cold and wet as well, which it often was, especially in winter, then it was quite likely that ice would start accumulating on the wings, etc. Unlike the Twin Comanche I'd been flying in my previous job, the Beech was equipped with a de-icing system designed to cope with ice sticking to the wings.

This consisted of a pair of heavy rubber strips, one glued to the leading edge of each wing. These strips were actually tubes into which compressed air could be fed once a good crust of ice had built up on the front of the wings. The idea was that when the air was fed into them the front side of these boots would expand and so break off the accumulated ice. The air was then exhausted, the boots shrunk back down and the process could then be repeated as often as necessary. The trick was to make sure that there was a solid enough covering of ice before operating the system to break it off. Simple and effective and a system in common use on many aircraft fitted with piston engines – as opposed to jet engines – on which a hot air system is normally used.

Trundling down to Geneva one night, I was stuck in cloud and a fair amount of ice was building up on the wings. At regular intervals I was having to cycle the de-icing system and everything was working well. Life in the Beech was cold and normal. I was more concerned with navigating my way across France and into the foothills of the Alps to deliver the newspapers than I was about the ice.

Back then there was no G.P.S. available for finding your way around. Navigation was done by zig zagging along between various different radio beacons shown on purpose made charts. You tuned your navigational radio set to the unique frequency, published on the chart, for the radio beacon you were heading towards and were guided to it. Once over the top of the beacon you knew exactly where you were and you could then set course to the next one, having now had an accurate 'fix'.

On the Beech the radio aids were not exactly up to Rolls Royce standards. There were two sets, one worked on VHF frequencies – which meant' line of sight' only [if the beacon you were trying to use was over the horizon you wouldn't get a signal from it]. As the Beech didn't fly very high the range from these beacons [VOR] was quite short and there weren't then too many of them around either. The other type of beacon available used medium frequencies. These gave greater range but they were less accurate and more prone to interference. The big problem on the Beech was that the receiver for these beacons [NDB] was prone to overheating and would only work for 5 minutes or so at a time before having to be switched off for about 15 minutes to cool down again!

Thus, accurate navigation was not the easiest of tasks, especially in cloud. On a clear night things were much easier. Along the parts of the route where you were getting no radio signals for extended periods you could follow the lights of the jets flying past high up ahead of you – they had the kit and the accuracy! You could also see the lights of the large towns and cities beneath you which helped as well. In daylight you could follow the jet contrails. Nowadays none of this would be allowed and no professional pilot would accept that kind of flying. As I've said before, different days, different ways!

I was now approaching the beacon just to the north east of Geneva but wasn't certain of just how close I was. I couldn't start descending until over the beacon as there was a ridge of high hills running along the north side of the valley in which the city and it's lake sat. I needed to be sure I'd flown past this ridge before I started to venture downward. Still in cloud, I shone my torch out of the left flight deck window to check the wings for ice one more time. There was enough of a build up to clear off so I cycled the system and watched out of the window as the boot inflated and the ice was broken off. Except that it didn't work out that way this time round. Instead of expanding outward, the boot decided to peel itself off the wing and flail around in the air. It was immediately caught up in the propeller and in the blink of an eye the engine jammed up and came to a sullen and juddering halt.

Suddenly I had only 50% of my power left and I would have to let the aeroplane start to go down, there wasn't enough power available from just one engine to let me continue at the same height. If I didn't go down we would inexorably just lose speed until we reached a point at which the aeroplane would stall and then fall out of the sky. There was nothing I could do to stop this happening unless I started to descend, trading height for speed.

I was only about fifteen hundred feet higher than the top of the ridge. Had I passed over it already? Was I over it now? Was this ridge of hills still in front of me? I had no way of knowing. Should I press on in my slow descent in the hope that the hills were now behind me [and risk hitting them because I wasn't] or should I turn back because they were still in front of me [and again risk hitting them because I'd already gone over them and would now be turning into them!]. I didn't know – and neither do you! Proving that I was still a coward I made no decision at all – which meant that I simply carried on, descending in a straight line.

As history shows – for I'm still here – making no decision at all was absolutely the right decision! A couple of minutes later I was over my target beacon and I circled down, made my approach to the airfield and landed without further incident [and with great relief!].

I was now going nowhere in a hurry. Until I could find someone to effect repairs to my now stricken aircraft, I was stuck. Eventually, of course, repairs were achieved and I got home – but that's another story – read on!

12. The Gourmet Tour.

I was on the ground in Geneva with a broken aeroplane. Whilst my cargo of newspapers was unloaded I went off in search of a mechanic who might be able to do something about the tightly mangled de-icing boot that was wrapped around the port propeller and had created my problem.

An engineer willing to assist was located and came over to see what could be done. He prodded and poked and cut and hacked at the comprehensively destroyed, and surprisingly tough, rubber boot. Eventually he managed to unwind and remove it all and he then set about a more careful and detailed examination of engine and propeller, including a test run of the engine and the propeller pitch control mechanism. This concluded with him advising that he could see no further damage. By now it was daylight and the night time low cloud had lifted. With a much improved weather system now in play, all the way back to Heathrow, I was able to fly back without the need of de-icing protection.

After takeoff from Geneva it was necessary in the Beech, even with no load on board, to climb straight ahead along the valley to then circle over the radio beacon [about 4 miles beyond the end of the runway] whilst climbing up to gain enough height to clear the ridge to the north. I was just over this ridge when the left engine started to leak visible amounts of oil from somewhere at its front. I assumed that this was caused by secondary damage from the earlier de-icing boot incident.

At first the leak was containable but it very soon became clear that it was getting worse and that the engine would be running out of oil before too much longer. I had no choice other than to divert to a nearby airport. Dijon was my selected destination and I landed there before any further mishaps unfolded. Dijon was then very much a military airport and not normally available to civilian traffic. I found myself shuffled off to park a long way from the main heart of the place, in a corner where I couldn't see anything going on, other than a couple of bored French military manning a guard hut.

To be fair, the French military were very co-operative and they gave me access to the phone in the guard hut [mobile phones were still at least 20 years away!]. So there I now was, stranded in France, no money [credit cards hadn't been invented then either!], no transport, no engineering support available and with only limited communication via the guard hut.

I called the company back in Blighty, described the problem and the symptoms and in due course the boss, Steve Quinto, our Chief Pilot – we now had one [Bill Harvey was his name] and our, still laconic, Australian engineer, Harry Garside arrived on site with spares and toolkit. Bill, Harry, toolkit and spares were unloaded and Steve flew himself back to London. By now it was getting quite late on in the day and I was pretty exhausted. Bill decided that nothing much could be achieved before tomorrow and the best thing we could do would be to get a taxi into town, find a hotel and have a meal. He'd come equipped with bundles of company cash and we retired to Dijon for a bit of rest and relaxation.

Once established in a hotel in town we went out for a meal and I began to get to know Bill Harvey a little better. Like Steve Quinto he was a fellow American. He'd been around the block a few times and was both old and had a wealth of flying experience. He was also a man out of his time. He was a swashbuckling kind of guy who would have fitted seamlessly into the part of a wild west saloon bar gunslinger back in the days of the Magnificent Seven and the gold rush. He could certainly talk the talk anyway. Amongst many other things, for example, he would often claim that he'd previously been flying in Vietnam for Air America and working for the CIA – couldn't give us any details of course, you know, sworn to secrecy, etc. For all I know he could well have been telling the truth. A few years after I'd left Sagittair I heard that he'd ended up flying in some lawless part of Africa and was presently residing in a jail out there having been caught gun running. This may or may not have been true too but it wouldn't have surprised me if it was. Even if it wasn't I doubt that Bill himself would have denied the story – it played to the image that he liked to portray for himself!

It turned out that we'd hit Dijon at the right time. There was a high end, typically French, 'Fete Gastronomic' in full swing. Throughout our stay there, which was to become quite protracted due to various problems and delays to our propeller repair, we were treated to fabulous food in whichever restaurant we visited, on a daily basis. Bill was our banker and he made sure that we not only went to the best establishments but that we didn't go short on the quality of the wines that we drank either. It was all a culinary paradise but I would have enjoyed it a lot more if I'd not had an unwell fiancé in hospital back in London and I hadn't been so anxious to get home as soon as possible.

Harry the engineer was in charge of our oil leak repair, obviously! Looking back on it now, I think old Harry was somewhat past his sell by date. He should have retired years before he even joined Sagittair but he enjoyed his job and he was still full of enthusiasm for all things oily and connected to aeroplanes. The trouble was that he wasn't very organised, he was a bit slow and too often a job had to be done twice because there was a bit left over that shouldn't have been or the repair just hadn't fixed the problem.

From back in London Harry had diagnosed that the fault was that the propeller had been damaged in its argument with the de-icing boot on the previous flight and so he had arrived armed with a replacement. He set about removing the old prop whilst Bill and I watched and passed him the odd spanner. The propeller was a heavy item and a crane would be needed to effect the swap. Bill and I were tasked to find a crane. Not an easy job when on a military airfield in France. Bill spoke no French at all and my French language skills were then limited to not a very good schoolboy level. Eventually we were promised a crane and it would arrive to-morrow. And so another night in Dijon with a slap up dinner!

Tomorrow dawned and we were out at the airport bright and early. The crane driver, being French, was less enthusiastic and didn't appear until late morning. As soon as he arrived however, he announced that it was now time for lunch. He lit a Gauloise and then disappeared for his customary two hour break. The afternoon was spent watching Harry and Monsieur Crane battling together to get the prop and the aeroplane separated. This was quite amusing as Harry spoke not a word of French and did a lot of swearing [a skill at which many Australians excel] and Monsieur Crane spoke not a word of Australian and also swore with impressive frequency and fluency in his native tongue.

Eventually they succeeded and the old propeller at last swung free from the front of its engine. At this point Crane lit another Gauloise, said it was time for his aperitif and dinner and announced that he'd be back tomorrow to lift the new propeller onto the engine. We went back to Dijon for a third night and yet another evening banquet. The next day was pretty much a repeat performance of the day before, except in reverse, but by close of play the new propeller was secured in place and ready to go. We shook hands with our friend Monsieur Crane and he disappeared into the sunset with a pocket full of cash, a smile on his face and a cloud of Gauloise smoke trailing behind him.

Harry buttoned everything up so that we could start the engine for a test run. The propellers were of the 'variable pitch' variety, commonly fitted to all but the smallest aeroplanes. This meant that you could twist the blades to control the angle that they cut through the air as they turned – the aeroplane equivalent of a car gearbox. This twisting action was controlled by oil pressure, fed into the propeller from the engine. We started the engine and exercised the prop a few times. Both were working fine and we let the engine run for a few minutes more to make sure that there was no repeat oil leak from the new propeller. It wasn't long before we saw the first tell tale signs of oil appearing. The leak was back, and this time with a vengeance, it was pouring out of the back of the propeller!

We shut the engine down and Harry prodded, poked and scratched his head. He eventually concluded that the problem was that the new oil seals that came with the new propeller had been damaged during the battle of the refit. He then [rather too happily I thought] informed Bill and myself that he didn't have any spare replacements. So it was back to Dijon for a fourth night and yet more gastronomic offerings.

I'll spare you the detail of the rest of this saga, except to say that it was rather like Groundhog Day. It was to be fully 10 days since I'd last been at home and was next able to get back to visit my lady love in hospital. I was beginning to think that if my experiences in aeroplanes so far were typical of what lay ahead, then maybe I'd made a big mistake and was in the wrong career!

13. From Chaos Came Order

I was with another pilot on one particular flight, he was flying, and we diverted into Southend on our way back from somewhere in Europe with an engine problem. The Channel Airways engineer who came to our rescue told me that his airline were looking for pilots to fly their Viscounts. He suggested I apply. I still had very little experience and was sure that I'd fall well short of what Channel would be wanting but I sent in an application anyway. What was there to lose beyond the price of a stamp?

Surprisingly, I had a reply a week or so later inviting me along for interview at the Channel Airways offices at Southend Airport, from where the Viscounts operated. Even more surprisingly, a week or so after my interview with the Viscount Fleet Manage [a Captain Rod Taylor] a letter from the airline dropped through the front door of my flat in Earls Court, offering me a position as a Viscount co-pilot. This was fantastic news to me and a great break through. The Viscount was a 'proper' airliner and Channel Airways was a 'proper' airline with 'proper' terms and conditions. More importantly, my fiancé had by now become my wife and with that came responsibilities. The job carried a salary that was exponentially larger than anything I'd had before and this would help us tremendously.

I had to make this stick. It was a great opportunity to get somewhere at last and I could not afford to fail. There was a lot of work for me to do and much to learn. The Viscount was a serious bit of kit, four turbine engines and full of complicated systems: – pressurisation, hydraulics, electrics, propellers, avionics, performance, de-icing, etc, etc. Compared with the Beech 18, itself the biggest thing I'd flown to date [it would carry maybe 10 people if you put seats in it], the Channel Airways Viscounts packed in 84, plus crew.

This was a move to flying at a different level and I'd need to hone my skills to make it work. Not only that, I'd be flying with an experienced and beady eyed Captain sitting next to me the whole time and scrutinising my every move. There would be nowhere to hide and not only would I have to be up to standard, I'd need to watch my Ps and Qs as well – 'proper' airline captains wouldn't tolerate mistakes and I was sure didn't take too many prisoners either!

I served my notice with Sagittair and on the due date turned up at Southend for the start of my new job and training onto the Viscount. The training was to be a couple of weeks in the classroom, learning all we needed to know about the technicalities and operation of the aircraft. This would be followed by an exam to test our knowledge – set, invigilated and marked by the Air Registration Board [ARB] at Redhill in Surrey. The ARB was a rather forbidding Government agency which essentially policed the engineering side of aviation. Quite why they set exams for pilots I never could work out but they did. We would then have seven hours of flying training in the aircraft itself [no simulator for the Viscount so all training was done in the sky on the real thing] culminating in a flying test. Only once that flying test was passed would we be become licensed to fly the aeroplane. After that we'd face a further three weeks or so of flying under supervision before a final flying test had to be passed. All big hoops through which we had to jump.

There were only three of us on this course, a chap called David Carter who had a similar flying background to myself, a rather eccentric New Zealander called Maxwell Johnson who was also a qualified doctor and had a somewhat out of control beard that made him look like the Wild Man of Borneo, and myself. This eclectic band of brothers all set to in trying to absorb a never ending stream of facts, figures and information being relentlessly thrown at us. Every day a bucketful of fresh 'need to know' stuff came our way. Endless 'chalk and talk'. This Viscount was surely the most complicated aircraft on the planet. Somehow or other we all managed to make most of it stick and we all passed our ARB technical exam.

I actually think that these aircraft ground courses are the intellectual equivalent of a water boarding experience, as conducted by an unscrupulous military dictatorship [or the CIA!]. They're all the same; relentless, never ending and without respite. By the time I finished flying they'd become even worse. It was all 'Computer Based Training' [CBT] by then with precious little human interface at all, just rows of mindless students in a room, each sitting in their own cubicle, staring at a computer screen all day long. Their only activity being the clicking of a mouse – and much mental screaming! Hell on Earth.

Anyway, about half way through this torture regime in the classroom we were released from our dungeon and taken out into the daylight on the airport apron to have a look at a real Viscount. I have to say that I was impressed – and suddenly somewhat concerned that my new employers seriously expected me to be able to handle this beast! I'd flown in many aircraft in the past – Bristol Britannia, Boeing 707, Vickers VC 10, Douglas DC 8 to name a few [all quite a lot bigger than a Viscount] but I'd been a passenger in all of them, not a driver, their size had been of no relevance. Now, compared to the little Beech 18, the Viscount looked positively enormous, the diminutive Beech would have fitted under one wing! We toured round the outside of the aeroplane whilst our instructor pointed out all the hatches, access panels and other relevant bits that we needed to know about.

Then it was up the stairs and into the cabin. This too gave the feeling of being big, rows of seats stretching back into the distance, overhead luggage racks down each side of the cabin and each seat row with its own, large, pair of windows. We examined the fittings within, the galley, the toilets, the emergency windows over each wing and all the emergency equipment stowed around the place. It was somewhat daunting to think that this was shortly going to by my domain – assuming that I made the grade.

Finally I got to stick my head into the flight deck, my soon to be office – I'd be sat in the seat on the right hand side [Captains on aeroplanes always sit in the left hand seat]. I didn't know whether to laugh or cry. I vividly remember, to this day, being absolutely dumbstruck by what I saw. I knew, of course, that it would be busy in there, I'd been in airliner flight decks before and I'd been learning about this one in the classroom. But this was different. In this one I'd be using all this 'stuff' and I'd be the one doing the work, pressing the buttons and pulling the levers.

I'd never seen so many dials, switches, knobs, lights and levers all in one place at the same time before, they were everywhere. Stretched across the whole width of the flight deck in front of the two pilots seats, up on the roof above the seats, down the outside of each seat, between the two seats – and even behind the two seats. I needed eyes in the back of my head to do this job. There was no way on God's Earth that any human being could master this lot, far less me! My prospects of becoming a fully fledged airline pilot were suddenly in tatters, this was going to end in tears and humiliating failure and there was nothing to be done except to await my fate. I sat in the right hand seat – even that looked too complicated to operate and my feeling of panic was complete!

This abiding memory was to hold me in good stead in future years. When I started training pilots myself years later, and new and inexperienced students were my candidates, I remembered how daunting it had seemed to me and how I'd felt when I was first introduced to a big aeroplane. It was a great help in settling them into the learning process. Additionally, it helped me understand why, maybe, some people are scared of flying – how can such a big lump of metal fly through the air and how can the pilot possibly keep track of all those endless banks of instruments?

As I sat in that seat in the flight deck for the first time, trying to absorb it all I began to take stock. I began to think that maybe it wasn't quite as difficult as it first looked after all. The instruments in front of each pilot, the flying instruments, were duplicates of each other and were pretty much the same as those in the Beech and any other aircraft. The ones in the middle, between the flying instruments, were for the engines. There were four engines so there were four sets of the same instrument, one for each engine, all arranged in neat rows. Again not too complicated. Between the seats were the engine controls, again one for each engine. And so it went on. Certainly it was complicated but maybe I could master this after all!

And I did. A couple of months later I was a fully qualified and checked out Viscount co-pilot and released out into the big world of airline flying. My first flight on the Viscount once I was set free was with a captain called Alan Jarvis. Needless to say I was not totally relaxed when I went in to work that day. This would be the first time that I'd ever rub shoulders with a normal, experienced [and no doubt highly critical] airline captain without the protection of being 'under training'. Now I was fully qualified and there would be an expectation that I would be as efficient and competent as the next man.

I need not have worried though, Alan was as relaxed and friendly as they come and he gave me the impression that he could fly this aeroplane blindfolded, any mistake I made he'd correct in a flash and then carry on as if nothing untoward had happened. I was to learn fairly soon afterwards that actually Alan himself had only recently qualified as a captain – but he seemed a pretty seasoned operator to me! We were flying from Southend to Barcelona, quite a stretch for the old Viscount so we needed as much fuel as we could pump into the tanks [nearly 2,000 gallons of the stuff]. We also had a full load of 84 passengers and so the aircraft was as heavy as it could be for us to lift off safely from Southend's, not over long, runway.

Alan was flying the aircraft and so my job was to hold the four throttles in the 'full power' position once he'd opened them up and then to monitor all the instruments, etc, as we accelerated down the runway. If anything was to go badly wrong then [in simple terms] my job would have been to close the throttles and call 'Stop!'. Alan's job would be to apply the brakes, keep the aeroplane on the runway and bring us to a halt before we fell off the end of the tarmac.

Nothing did go wrong of course, except that about half way down the runway the whole engine instrument panel fell out on top of my left hand – which was holding the throttles open – and jamming it where it was. Technically we should have stopped but I couldn't move my hand to close the throttles. I didn't really know what to do so I just uttered a short expletive at which Alan laughed and said 'carry on'! We did, uneventfully [probably the safer option anyway] and once we were safely airborne I was able to lift up the panel and re-attach it in its proper place.

This experience gave me a bit of a fright, it wasn't something that the text books talked about but I learned a lot from Alan as a result that little event. He analysed, almost instantaneously, that it was a 'no threat' issue and he remained totally relaxed and calm, even finding time to chuckle at my obvious discomfort. If I could ever reach that level of calm reaction when something went wrong, I thought, then I'd be doing OK.

The rest of that first flight went fine – life was then great!

Channel Airways Viscount [812 series] at Southend.

The Viscount Instrument panel that overawed me on first sight.

14. Structured Recruitment Process

I'd now been flying my first 'proper' airliner [the Viscount] – as a First Officer with Channel Airways – for long enough to be comfortable with it rather than overawed. We'd bought a house in Malden, Essex, near Southend from where I was working. We couldn't afford the mortgage but we at least had the house! We were happily content and life was sweet and untroubled. We weren't looking to move anywhere and I had settled into working on the Viscount more easily than I had thought I would, despite one or two embarrassments along the way showing my inexperience.

One of these occurred early on in my flying training process. I was teamed up with my boss, Rod Taylor and we were going to Jersey [the airline wasn't called Channel Airways for no reason!]. One of my jobs was to check the weather before departure and as we were training Rod accompanied me to the briefing room to see how I got on.

In those days airports provided proper meteorologists and us pilots were treated to one on one briefings from these specialists [now it's all done 'on line', another big change in working practices]. Anyway, the met. man gave me a report saying that Jersey had a 30 knot wind with 200 metre visibility in fog and the sky was obscured. Now, when I had been at Elstree studying meteorology, we were taught that for fog to form there had to be next to no wind, anything over about 4 knots and the fog would dissipate in the mix of the air. So, as a professional pilot, I told the met. officer that this couldn't be right, there was a mix up somewhere. Rod and the met. man looked at each other and both smiled indulgently,

'Ah', said Rod, 'But this is Jersey. Jersey is different. In Jersey you get high speed fog!' I'll spare you the explanation but I felt my cheeks glowing red from having challenged the met. officer and so comprehensively shown my ignorance!

As I was saying, I had not a care in the world until I came home from work one day and switched on the [black and white] television to watch the 6 o'clock news. Half way through the broadcast they announced that Channel Airways had called in the Receivers. I was stunned. Not an hour earlier I'd been in the office at Southend and no one had said anything at all gloomy or had even looked at all perturbed. The crew room of any airline is a veritable crucible for the production of rumour and scuttlebutt. Ours was no exception but there hadn't been any of that either.

I was due to be flying again bright and early the next morning too but more importantly I was now worried that I had been told by the BBC that I was out of a job before my employers had had the courtesy to do so. I called the office to find out just what was going on. All a big mistake they said, the BBC was talking nonsense [what's new?!] – turn up as normal tomorrow, all will be well. I did and my Captain, Alan Jarvis [the same friendly Skipper from my first flight with the company] and I flew our morning scheduled service from Southend to Rotterdam and back without incident. Only once we'd landed back at Southend did we discover that the airline had indeed gone bust the day before! How different these things were back then – clearly things like 'HR' and man management hadn't yet been invented.

With my head in a spin I wondered how I was going to break this devastating news to my wife. How would we manage without an income – we now had a mortgage? Channel was a big player in its day and there would now be a lot of pilots suddenly looking for a new job, most with considerably more experience than I had, how could I compete? These and many other questions with no answers raced through my mind as I pondered what the future would hold for us. And then I had a sudden thought which gave me hope.

I'd heard that British Midland Airways were in need of Viscount pilots. If true, this might be the olive branch that I needed, I thought.

I might not have much experience but at least I was qualified on the type. This would help make it both quicker and cheaper for the airline to get me up and running as a productive pilot – if they liked the cut of my jib and took me on and, if indeed, they really were looking for Viscount co-pilots. I decided not to stop to make an appointment with anyone [no mobile phones back then either], I just drove straight up from Southend to the British Midland offices at East Midlands Airport near Nottingham. Once there I knocked on their door, introduced myself as a qualified Viscount pilot and asked to speak to their Viscount Fleet Manager. I wanted to be the first in the queue if there were to be any job slots at all available.

Fortunately the secretary to whom I spoke was in a good mood, as was the Viscount Fleet Manager himself and I soon found myself seated in front of him at his desk.

It sometimes proves to be a small world and here was evidence of just how small it gets every now and then! It turned out that the pair of us had met before. I was face to face with one Captain David Court. The last time I'd seen him he was an examiner with the Civil Aviation Flying Unit [or CAFU], that much feared branch of the Civil Aviation Authority [CAA] who sat in judgement over student pilots taking their flying tests. On their say so hinged your future as a professional pilot. The standards were high and these guys didn't take prisoners. As it had turned out, when Capt. Court stepped up to judge my flying test performance he was generous enough to tick all the boxes for me. Happy days.

As luck would have it, British Midland were indeed looking for Viscount pilots, lots of them. They'd recently acquired seven Viscount aircraft from South African Airways and so now needed both the pilots to fly them and the routes on which to operate them. This sudden and unexpected demise of Channel Airways was a godsend to BMA and the answer to both of these problems. It offered a ready qualified bunch of oven ready Viscount aeroplane drivers, all anxious for fresh employment and it made available a batch of, now vacated, profitable routes. British Midland grabbed both, with alacrity [and I dare say, with much relief].

If it was good fortune indeed for British Midland then it was even more so for me too as Dave Court offered me a job on the spot. I've never been more relieved than I was at that moment. As suddenly as it appeared my crisis had just as rapidly disappeared – and all because of a spur of the moment decision to take a chance drive up to the midlands!

I doubt that Dave Court took me on because he was impressed with my flying prowess [although as he'd endorsed my basic flying standard a year or two earlier by allowing me to pass the initial flying test he could hardly turn me down on that score]. Rather, I suspect that I was taken on solely as a matter of expediency, speed and economics – I had the type rating, I'd be cheap to train and I was there. The real bonus in all this for me was that the new job [doing the same work but now limited to a maximum of 600 hours a year by contract] came with quite a significant pay rise as well as much more generous terms and conditions! I wasn't yet out of the woods though, I still had to pass a few 'in house' exams – both flying and written – before my longer term employment with British Midland could be assured.

15. Stringent Flying Training

Having been made redundant when my previous employers, Channel Airways went bust, I'd fortunately been able to get my foot in the door with British Midland Airways [BMA]. Given the importance of our need for me to find a job, I wasn't about to let the olive branch of being able to carry on paying our mortgage be snatched away by me showing myself up as no use when it came to the routine operation of the aircraft. I was therefore more than determined to succeed.

Even though I'd been flying the Viscount for a while there were still hoops through which I had to jump before my new job was secure. These consisted of a string of flying tests and a ground exam set to demonstrate my technical knowledge of the Viscount. There was no law that said I couldn't fail and a lot of traps and curved balls remained that could yet catch me out. I would not let this happen.

My first day with BMA saw me and a dozen or so of my former Channel Airways colleagues in a classroom at the company's East Midlands Airport offices.

Unlike the airliners of today, which are all built with almost identical instrument layouts and systems, no matter which airline is buying them, back when the Viscounts were built in the late '40s and through the '50s, the instrument layouts were to a great degree dictated by the company buying the aircraft rather than by the manufacturer. Thus, although the aeroplanes performed in the same way, the detail of operating them could be very different from one aeroplane to another.

We were assembled in the classroom to undertake a 'Differences Course' – designed to teach us the technical differences between the Viscounts that British Midland operated and those that we'd been flying whilst with Channel Airways. The trouble was that our instructor was no more familiar with the Channel Airways Viscounts than were we with those operated by British Midland. The result was that we found ourselves in a classroom where the blind were leading the deaf and where no one knew what to teach us and we didn't know what we were supposed to be learning either!

Us new recruits all thought this was rather amusing [strength in numbers usually helps!] but our British Midland ground school instructor was a bit highly strung and he wasn't at all impressed – which rather made the situation all the more comical! We ended up laboriously going through the various different aircraft systems – electrics, hydraulics, pressurisation, etc, etc, and came to the happy conclusion that both sets of aircraft were remarkably similar. This was good because we then had to sit the technical exam for the BMA aircraft to show that we were au fait. Fortunately no one was disgraced and we all passed this exam.

A particular detail that I remember from this 'Differences Course' was occasioned by one of Channel Airways ex Comet pilots who also joined Midland when I did, John Murphy his name was. John had been flying the Viscount with Channel but then had moved on to fly the Comet jets that Channel operated. By way of background John was a pure bred pedigree Cockney. He hailed from London's East End and he spoke with that perfect cockney twang. He'd started life as a conductor 'on the bleedin' buses' but somehow or another had managed to claw his way into the world of professional flying. However John had made this transition, as impressive as his effort was, he hadn't lost a single ounce of his cockney background, or his accent in the process. He was quite a character.

Immediately before the lunch break our intrepid ground instructor announced that we'd be going over the 'Smiths Flight System' when we got back together in the afternoon. The 'flight system' was a gadget, built into the flight instruments, designed to make it easier for the pilot flying the aircraft to operate it more smoothly and efficiently that when using just the basic instruments alone. There were three or four different systems in existence, each did the same end job but had different presentations and different controls. One of the British Midland aircraft was fitted with a 'Smiths' system so we had to know about it. It was a really clunky bit of kit to use, not at all intuitive and altogether a rather oddball device. It worked well enough once you knew what you were doing with it but it was a bit of a weird and wonderful invention that few pilots would select as their weapon of choice.

Anyway, as soon as our instructor made his announcement John stood up and said, "If it's all the same to you guv', I won' bovver turnin' up after nosh. I didn't understand the bleedin' Smiths System on the Comet and I won't understand na'r either". And with that John disappeared for the rest of the day! Our instructor was somewhat nonplussed but he didn't say a word!

Another little snippet about John was that for years he rented a room in Nottingham where he would stay when he was working. He commuted to and from Southend where he lived on his days off. I was forever telling him that he should buy a house locally but he wasn't having any of it. Then one day he accosted me in the staff car park,

"…'Ay Jim," he said, "I've gorne an' dun it, I've bought a bleeding 'ouse!"

"Great John, where is it?"

"Bleedin' 'ucknell," said John.

"Excellent," I said, "Well done!".

"Don't know 'bart that," he replied, "It was dark when Ah looked rand it an' I thought that it looked art over a fairground 'cos there was a Ferris wheel there an Ah like Ferris wheels. Trouble is, now Ah've moved in, turns art that the Ferris wheel is a bleedin' colliery, Ah'm right next to the bleedin' coal mine!"

As I say, John was a bit of a one off!

Next up was a flying test. There was no simulator available for the Viscount at that time so the flying test had to be carried out in the aeroplane [with no passengers on board!]. This was both an expensive exercise for the company and a serious test for both candidate and examiner. It wouldn't do to fail this test; having to go through it all again would make it doubly expensive for the airline and the examiner would not recommend a second attempt unless he was pretty sure that a positive outcome was more than likely.

For my sins I was selected as the first candidate from our bunch of recruits to face this challenge – the test to be taken as soon as we'd finished in the classroom on our first day. Needless to say I was somewhat nervous, a lot was riding on this for me and as I was the first candidate I'd got no feedback on what to expect!

I found myself in a briefing room with my examiner, a Capt. Jim Shaw. He was friendly but thorough in his briefing of what he wanted from me. The test lasted roughly an hour and a half and consisted of various exercises during which I had to demonstrate my competence on a raft of flying skills. I don't remember the detail of it all except to say that it followed a pretty standard set of exercises and there were no big surprises. Jim made me feel relatively relaxed and at the end of it all he pronounced me fit to continue with the airline to the next stage.

As I came to know Jim Shaw later on I was to discover that he was both an exceptional pilot and an exceptionally likeable individual. Having made it through as a Spitfire pilot at the backend of the war, he'd then moved into civil aviation. Jim had accumulated a wealth of experience and many anecdotes along the way. He should have written an autobiography, it would have made for a fascinating read.

16. An Unusual Training Captain

The last link in the chain of my apprenticeship with British Midland was what they call 'Line Training'. This is a series of flights, now with passengers on board, but still with a Training Captain overseeing one's flying. It's designed to ensure that you both adapt to flying the aircraft to the expected standard operating procedures, as detailed by the airline, and also that you continue to demonstrate a consistent standard of basic flying and airmanship skills. In other words you have to impress your instructor over a series of flights by getting everything pretty much spot on, on every flight – to the point where the trainer finally signs you off as being OK.

I started this training on day two of my employment with BMI. I was to go up to Teesside airport in a taxi to fly our scheduled service down to London from there. We'd operate this route for a couple of days and then taxi back to East Midlands. That evening I had a call from the Training Captain who would be supervising me for these next few days. Would I mind if we went up to Teesside in his car rather than by taxi, he asked? I said that would be fine and he told me to meet him in the staff car park at 10 a.m. tomorrow, he'd be in a Morris 1000 Traveller, he said.

I wanted to impress and was at the car park with time to spare. 10 a.m. came and went. Eventually a car appeared. It was a Morris 1000 Traveller, but not as you'd know it. This was the most dishevelled contraption you've ever seen, covered in dust and muck. Straw protruded out from under the doors and tailgate and amazingly, this aberration was being driven by an airline pilot in full uniform!

'Surely not?', I thought, 'It can't be!'

But it was. The car stopped and my mentor introduced himself. I opened a back door to stow my suitcase and came to a sudden stop. You won't believe this, I know, but I was now face to face with a real live goat!! Not any goat either, this was a massive goat with a beard, and horns, and bits and things.

"Ah" said my man, "I maybe should have mentioned the goat, we're dropping him off at Thirsk on our way up – for breeding you know!"

I couldn't decide whether I was joining an airline, a madhouse or a circus! To cut a long story short, once I'd got over the goat, and it's endless flatulence, the rest of my week went well. I soon worked out that as long as I tuned one of our radio navigation systems in to The Archers at 7pm every evening for him, my Training Captain would be happy. After our stint up at Teesside he judged me to be a suitable candidate for BMA and so started a job that was to take me through the next 36 years of my career until retirement beckoned.

During our two days of flying together my mentor mentioned that he lived in a small village that I'd never heard of, a place called Diseworth. I didn't know it at the time but we were to move to Diseworth ourselves a year or two later and he [and his wife] were to become longstanding and lifetime friends.

I cannot possibly divulge his name of course but he walks amongst us. To protect his identity I'll just give him an arbitrary Christian name – let's say Dave. I'll pick a random surname too – Moores [for no particular reason]. Only the names have been changed to protect the innocent, the story itself is true!

Another little anecdote about Dave occurred years later. By then I was a manager and traded under the title of 'Fleet Manager – Viscount'. This meant that I was responsible for the operation of our Viscount fleet of aircraft and for the pilots who flew them, of which Dave was one.

Dave was flying one particular week-end, hopping to and fro around the Channel Islands from East Midlands Airport. On landing at Guernsey, one of his cabin crew came into the flight deck and advised him that a passenger, sitting on the starboard side of the aircraft, had "seen something fall off when they came in to land". Dave and his co-pilot both ventured out to have a look. They soon spotted the problem; one of the guide bars that controlled the flaps [the planks at the back of the wing that extend for landing and take-off] had broken and was hanging down with a part of it missing. A consultation with our Engineering people elicited the information that if the offending part was removed altogether and the flap was not extended beyond a certain value, then he could continue to fly the aeroplane. This would not present any problems for the rest of the flying planned for that day so Dave had the broken part removed and he then carried on to Jersey, his next port of call and only a ten minute flight away.

I should perhaps say at this point, that it is highly unusual for bits to break and fly off aeroplanes, normally all the bits stay attached and fly along quite happily in harmony with each other and in close formation. In all my flying career on airliners, I don't ever remember any part of my aircraft parting company from its immediate neighbour. Dave was just a bit unlucky that day!

Anyway, when he landed at Jersey and his passengers had disembarked, bounding up into the flight deck comes our resident engineer – big Jim Peacock – who'd already been advised of the missing flap guide rail: –

"You ain't goin' nowhere Dave", says Jim, "You've lost more than your bleedin' guide rail, the whole bloody jet pipe's missing!".

This was a serious bit of news, the jet pipe really isn't supposed to go missing. The 'jet pipe' is effectively the entire exhaust system for the engine. It guides all the hot exhaust gas out of the back of the engine and clear of the under surface of the wing [which is full of fuel, pipes, wires, etc, etc]. On the Viscount, the exhaust burns at nearly 800 degrees centigrade on engine start and at 730 degrees in the climb and cruise. To have no protection from these sorts of temperatures is not a good idea. Luckily Dave's trip between Guernsey and Jersey was very short so no damage was done – but it could have been a very different story if it had been a longer flight. As it was the next fight from Jersey was up to East Midlands, an hour's trip in the Viscount and quite long enough to cause huge damage, if not disaster.

Incidentally, this purveyor of bad news – Jim Peacock – was the same engineer who'd acted as the catalyst to me applying for the job I had landed with Channel Airways and which kick started my airline career, now a good few years earlier.

What had happened was that it was the jet pipe that had let go on the way into Guernsey, it had struck the flap guide and broken it on its way past. To be fair to all who'd inspected the aircraft in Guernsey, it's easy to understand why it wasn't spotted. They simply saw the broken guide bar and concluded that this was the culprit. The jet pipe itself is a big black tube of metal that looks like a big black hole and it sits inside a big black hole. As one big black hole looks much like another – and you've already got an explanation for your problem – why delve any deeper?

Anyway, Jim had spotted it so all was well on the safety front but now there was a logistical issue or two. Clearly the flight could not depart in that condition with passengers on board so another aircraft would need to be found to get them home. Further, the aircraft was needed back at East Midlands – which was also the best place to repair the damage and replace the missing pipe.

The Viscount could be flown on three engines, without passengers, so this was obviously the way forward to get it back home. To carry out a 'three engined ferry flight' the operating Captain was required to get a full briefing from the Fleet Manager as well as written permission. In the case of Dave this was a bit of a joke and rather unnecessary – he had taught me the art when I joined the company – but we went through the motions anyway and I sent him a fax by way of 'permission in writing'.

Jersey wasn't the longest runway we flew from and a take-off with three engines required a much longer length than when all four were working – with or without passengers. It was, in fact, a bit of a marginal do and required some careful performance calculations, as well as favourable wind and temperature conditions, etc, to ensure that it would be safe in the prevailing conditions.

My fax gave Dave the permission he legally required but I also added a strict instruction – in the event that he failed to get airborne and instead went into the sea at the end of Jersey's runway, he wasn't to emerge again from the water until he'd found his missing jet pipe! Happily Dave was more than thorough, as well as competent and professional and he remained both dry and unscathed and of course he got the aircraft home.

17. My First Flight with British Midand.

I'd not yet been with British Midland for a week and already I found myself processed through the system and churned out at the other end as a fully qualified First Officer with the airline, judged fit to be let loose with any of the airline's unsuspecting captains. Happy days, it doesn't work like that in this day and age!

Nowadays all airlines really do have a structured recruitment process with formal interview panels, 'Human Recourses' inputs, psychometric testing, flight tests in simulators, even background checks for criminal activities, etc, etc. No way could an airline pilot find himself/herself fully processed, trained, licensed and 'checked out' in four days. Quite right too, it's just one of very many reasons why flying has moved on in the last 50 years from being safe – to now being extraordinarily safe. But that was back then and this is now.

Anyway, I was indeed checked out and I was now rostered to fly [even though I'd not yet been issued with a pilots uniform], after five days into the job, on my first unsupervised trip with the airline. This was to be the East Midlands to Belfast [and return] service. My Captain was to be a Captain Mike Tracey. Mike and I had never met before of course and I was a little apprehensive as to what was in store for me, not least because there I was, presenting myself for work and wearing a jersey and a pair of jeans!

Captains could be rather fierce and forbidding in those days, especially with young and raw first officers, what would he think of one of these not even dressed properly?! I needn't have worried though, it turned out that Mike, like most of his fellow captains in the airline, was a perfectly reasonable chap who knew what he was doing and who didn't get too exercised if I made the odd mistake. He was maybe in his mid thirties and wore a dark navel styled beard, a bit serious looking at first sight but his personality soon shone through.

All went well on my first flight. I did everything that I was supposed to do – the procedures and processes that BMA used on their Viscounts were very similar to those I'd been used to with Channel Airways – and Mike was a relaxed and professional operator so we got on fine on our trip across the Irish Sea.

At Belfast, then in the grip of the earlier days of 'The Troubles', the Authorities had not yet got round to building up a complete security system with full perimeter fencing, etc, around the airport. Aircraft on the ground were instead guarded by soldiers – armed with menacing looking automatic guns which they slung from their shoulders and then swung around, with purposeful and steely eyed intent. Both threatening, for those with evil intentions, and reassuring, for those of a nervous disposition. There were two soldiers assigned to each aircraft, one for the left side and one for the right.

With the passengers disembarked and led away to the terminal building by the ground staff, I did what all dutiful and keen First Officers were supposed to do. I leapt [with alacrity] from my seat to check the outside of the aircraft for any leaks, damage, etc, and to organise the refuelling – whilst the Captain [of course] relaxed in the cabin with a leisurely cup of tea and in the company of the air hostesses. All normal, routine stuff.

The Viscount had four engines [with propellers] and the main undercarriage was housed in a nacelle [a pod] under each of the two inboard engines, one each side of the fuselage. When the wheels were extended [for landing – obviously!] a pair of doors on the bottom of each side of the nacelles first opened before the wheels were lowered from their respective housings under each wing. These doors then remained hanging down whist the undercarriage was extended. Inside these wheel bays were a veritable tangle of hydraulic pipes, fire extinguisher bits, wires, cables, etc, etc, and part of the First Officers job on each turn round was to check that this lot were in order. Checking these wheel wells entailed ducking under the dangling undercarriage doors and standing up, head and torso inside the well, checking for leaks, condition, etc. This meant that from the outside only a pair of legs could be seen, from the knees down.

So there I was, dutifully doing my duty, checking inside the port undercarriage bay for leaks, etc, when I felt a sudden – and none too gentle – prod in the small of my back. It was a very solid prod and it stayed there, digging in, small, hard and round. A very cockney voice said:-

"Your 'ands on your 'ead mate – and step out slowly". I did. The soldier then stepped back, a couple of paces away from me.

"Turn round!" he ordered. I did. Now I could see him. Piercing eyes, alert, unblinking, clenched jaw line, his gun, three feet away and pointing straight at my stomach, finger on trigger.

"What d'ya think you're doin'?", he demanded.

"I'm the co-pilot" I said, probably rather weakly.

Only then did it dawn on me that he could now properly see me too. A very young man, hardly old enough to have finished school, never mind be one qualified to fly – long hair, wearing jeans and a jersey and claiming to be the co-pilot of an airliner. I may have imagined it but I'd swear that I saw his finger tighten on the trigger. His colleague on the other side of the aeroplane had seen what was going on and he too was now pointing his gun at me and marching over.

"Ay, Fred", said my soldier, "This bloke reckons 'e's the co-pilot!"

At this precise point my rescue party arrived. My Captain and best friend Mike, with his serious beard, appeared at the top of the steps leading up to the open rear door of the aircraft, flanked by two air hostesses. The soldier saw him at the same time as I did.

"Ay, Skipper, this bloke reckons 'ee's your co-pilot!" says my captor. Without hesitation and with total conviction Mike called down:-

"Never seen him before in my life!"

I could almost feel the bullets ripping into me! Both these soldiers at that point must have thought that I was the real McCoy, that they'd actually caught a proper terrorist red handed. They were probably almost as frightened as I was, where there was one bad guy there were usually several! Their rifles both raised even more menacingly at me. They both stood there, silent for a second whilst they wondered what to do next.

The tension was broken with a sudden outburst of haughty laughter and giggles as Mike and his two female 'would be' collaborators came bounding down the stairs to proclaim me as actually being one of their team. It took a moment or two before my two guards accepted that Mike's response had been a joke and then all five of them were laughing, the two soldiers with relief as much as anything I suspect. It took me a little longer before the adrenalin subsided but eventually I saw the funny side of it too!

Although I'd only met Mike the once so far I told him that he now owed me a beer, an apology and a new pair of underpants. I don't recall any part of my demand as ever being honoured!

18. Not My Favourite Captain.

When I was interviewed for my job with British Midland Airways it was for a First Officer [co-pilot] position to be based at Teesside Airport , near Darlington in Yorkshire. However I spent my first few weeks working from East Midlands Airport and so rented a flat in Breeden On The Hill [over a butchers shop run by a jolly and genial chap called Les Fisher] along with another refugee from my previous company, a Captain called Neil Bromley. Neil had been the Chief Pilot at Channel Airways and I got on well with him so the arrangement worked out fine for both of us.

After a month or two I was then sent up to work from Teesside, as per my contract. This was fine by me but the pilots union [BALPA] took a different view. I hadn't appreciated it at the time but our terms and conditions required us to be paid a per diem allowance whenever we worked away from our assigned base. The union pointed out that as I was technically based at Teesside, I should have been in receipt of this allowance for the entire time that I'd spent working at East Midlands Airport. Our Fleet Manager, Dave Court, being very much a 'company man' had apparently 'overlooked' this minor detail. I didn't want to rock the boat – I was very much the new boy on the block and would have preferred to keep a low profile – but the union argued that the rules were the rules and I'd have to be paid every last penny of these allowances. Reluctantly Dave had to concede and I received quite a good wodge of unexpected [but very welcome] cash.

All that has nothing to do with this particular story but it was indicative of the laissez faire way that things worked back in the early 1970s. Nothing was particularly formal and there was little by way of strict compliance with correct industrial procedures and protocols – which is probably one [of many] reasons why there was so much strife between management and unions in those days.

Anyway, I was one of five co-pilots working from Teesside but it was a new base for the company and we had no Captains up there to work with us. Captains were sent up from East Midlands and would spend a few days at a time doing their bit before then returning down south. Pretty much all the Captains I flew with were both pleasant people and also, unsurprisingly, good pilots but there's always one exception, isn't there, there just has to be!

In my case it was one individual, Derek, who was to become my bête noire. In those days the Captain was God. His word was law and he could do no wrong. Co-pilots on the other hand, were mere bag carriers and wobetide any co-pilot who questioned or challenged his Captain, their life would be made more than miserable. Happily, the world has now moved on a very long way from those days – and just as well too.

The first time I flew with Derek all was well and there was nothing untoward to indicate that working with him would be any different to working with any of the other Viscount Captains on the fleet. However, as the week progressed I began to get an inkling that life under Derek would not be a bed of roses. He was really quite rude to pretty much all the ground staff and cabin crew and often pretty short with them too. He was also impatient, rather arrogant and to cap it all, his flying was surprisingly sloppy – not dangerous but lazy and none too accurate – and without any hint of mechanical sympathy or finesse.

Over the summer weekends we used to run a service from Teesside to the Isle of Man and back, an easy day's work. One weekend my best friend Derek and I were teamed up to operate this trip. All went well [in other words he was his usual obnoxious self] until we arrived back at Teesside where Derek carried out the landing. Very soon after touch down there was a loud bang from the starboard side of the aircraft – which sounded like a tyre bursting. There had been nothing wrong with the landing per se, it was perfectly normal in every way. We rolled down the runway with the aircraft seemingly unaffected [there were two tyres on each undercarriage leg]. I said I thought that a tyre had burst. My remark was very shortly followed by the air traffic controller advising us that there was a lot of smoke coming from the right hand undercarriage which kind of confirmed my suspicion. He asked us to stop on the runway whilst they sent a fire truck out to inspect – which any sane and normal pilot would do anyway. Derek told me to tell the controller that he'd continue to our parking spot, he didn't want to alarm the passengers! I protested but he carried on anyway. Short of wrestling the controls from him there was nothing I could do and he continued taxiing.

Once we'd parked a fire engine drew up next to us. Derek opened the window on his side of the aircraft and told the Fire Service to 'Go Away' [except that his language was significantly more colourful] and he proceeded to let the passengers disembark. This was madness. Tyres can explode if they get too hot and the wheels on the Viscount were made of a magnesium alloy – which would burn spectacularly if they got hot enough [I'd seen this happen at Southend when a wheel had caught fire on a Channel Airways Viscount on landing at night. The light generated by the burning alloy was so intense that it turned the whole airfield into bright daylight!]. There would be severe danger to anyone near the wheels if that happened.

Happily, nothing untoward did occur and all ended well, except that I suspect neither ATC nor the Fire Service people would have been impressed with us, the British Midland crew. It turned out that the burst was caused by a faulty brake which had locked the wheel – nothing to do with Derek at all, or the quality of his landing.

I was appalled and embarrassed by this episode. I knew both the Fire Service people and the ATC controllers and had no wish to be associated with the singularly poor airmanship displayed by my Captain on that day. As far as I was concerned this was the straw that broke the camel's back in my relationship with this Captain. But what to do? As I've already said co-pilots didn't hold any sway and anyway, I'd only been in the company for five minutes, what weight was carried by anything that I said?

I wrote to our boss and described both the event and my concerns about Derek's cavalier attitude. I did this in fear and trembling. It was not smart for a very junior co-pilot to criticise a Captain. Even so, I finished my letter off by requesting that I never again be programmed to fly with Derek and I posted it, fully expecting to be summonsed down to head office to face the Sword of Damocles.

A few days went by and nothing happened. Then a few more, still no message summonsing me down to face the music. Then my next roster appeared. Captain Dave Court, the boss himself, would be coming up to fly with me in a couple of weeks time. Now I knew, that's when he'd deliver the news about the termination of my employment.

I was not looking forward to Dave's arrival up at Teesside but eventually the fateful day dawned. I turned up to face the music... but there was none. Dave was perfectly pleasant and we flew a perfectly routine series of trips. I assumed he'd speak to me after our days work but he didn't. He merely bid me au revoir and went off to his hotel. I then thought that he'd deal with me tomorrow. To-morrow came and went but it was the same story again and nothing was said. The next day was to be our final days work together, Dave was going back down to East Midlands after we'd finished work. Now I knew it would all be over after our final landing back at Teesside. The day's work seemed to drag on for ever and I was becoming ever more anxious in contrast to Dave who didn't seem to have a care in the world. He's a hard man I thought, knowing what he's going to tell me shortly!

Come the end of our flying day, my heart was pumping as we completed the last bit of paperwork. Any second now, I thought. Finally Dave spoke,

"Well Jim", he said, "Thanks for a pleasant few days, see you next time I'm up here". This was just too much for me!

"Dave", I said, "I wrote to you a few weeks ago about Derek, did you get my letter?"

"Ah yes", he replied, "I vaguely remember".

"Well", I said, "I asked not to fly with him again".

"Yes", said Dave, "Join the queue!". And with that he was gone!!

As I said at the beginning, life was much more laissez faire in those days. Luckily for both Dave and myself, the problem of Derek was resolved shortly after this episode by the man himself. He inherited a large lump of family fortune and left the company to pursue other interests.

19. Boeing 707 Course

British Midland Airways had a couple of long haul [world wide operation] Boeing 707s when I joined the company in 1972. The rest of the fleet, and the company's operation was all short haul, [domestic and European flights] and consisted of a couple of jet BAC 111s and a dozen or so turbo props – Viscounts and Heralds. I was taken on to fly as a co-pilot on the Viscount fleet.

The Boeing 707 was the cream of the airline's aircraft and the star attraction. Only the most senior and best pilots got to fly them – not only did they carry more 'kudos' – these were shiny jet aeroplanes – not noisy old propeller jobs. More importantly, they carried a higher salary grade which was also an added incentive and so most of the pilots wanted to fly them – for these reasons amongst a host of others.

I, of course, would have no chance of getting to fly the 707 for a long time. I was right at the bottom of the pilot seniority list. Pilot seniority, based purely on length of service, determined the pecking order of everything in the world of piloting in those days and obviously therefore I hardly even featured. In any event, I hadn't yet racked up much overall flying experience, another consideration for getting to fly this machine.

So, for these two reasons, and also as we only had the two aircraft, my prospects of promotion to the type were about zero [on a good day!]. There were never likely to be any vacancies for 707 pilots created other than when [and if] a current incumbent voted with his feet and left the company for pastures new – or the company expanded the fleet. This latter eventuality was not considered to be particularly likely to happen any time soon.

All this meant that I was quite content with my present situation and status. I was now enjoying secure employment along with a stable lifestyle and living in a pleasant neck of the woods to boot. On top of that, I was beginning to really rack up that all important ingredient of an accumulating increase in my total flying hours and at the same time I was gaining greater experience. Both good things to be able to add to the CV when it came to exploring future prospects.

Although it had come as a big shock to us and it had been quite an upheaval to have to re-locate from the South of England to Yorkshire following the collapse of Channel Airways, my previous employer, we were now quite happy to be up there. We'd let out our little house down south, so that was more or less looking after itself, we were now renting a house up north and, all in all, life was being kind. This happy state of affairs continued for the next eighteen months or so without interruption.

Then it looked like our tranquil and contented lifestyle was about to change somewhat. Out of the blue one day I had a phone call from work. It was Captain Bert Cramp, then our Operations Manager. Bert didn't call me every day, I was far too unimportant, and I wondered what he wanted. Whatever it was I assumed that it wouldn't be good news! Obviously, if a senior manager telephoned a pilot at the bottom of the company food chain it had to be only because there was some sort of bad news to be imparted. I steeled myself for whatever hammer blow was to follow. Formalities exchanged Bert cut to the chase: –

"How would you like to go on the 707?" he said.

I was even more shocked I think, than I would have been if he had indeed telephoned to deliver bad news! This was good news, in fact this was very good news, except that I couldn't quite believe what I was hearing. How could this be happening? I'd only been in the company eighteen months or so and there were still many co-pilots much more senior than me – how could I possibly leapfrog all these people?

"Well", I said, "Yes, I'd love to fly the 707 but I haven't got the seniority, there are loads of co-pilots more senior to me, how can I jump ahead of them?"

"That's not your problem" said Bert. "Not all of them are suitable and not enough of those who are want to relocate to Stansted [where the crew were based]. We're buying another aircraft and so need six new co-pilots. Do you want a slot or not?"

"Well, yes please" I said, "I'd love one!"

And so, very suddenly and unexpectedly, out of nowhere, I was somehow especially selected to fly my first pure jet aircraft! Not only that, this flying would be based at Stansted, not much more than a stone's throw from Maldon [Essex] where our own house was. We'd be able to move back down south and into our own house again. Very much an added bonus.

A few weeks later I found myself down at our company offices at East Midlands Airport and starting on my ground course, learning all that needed to be known about flying the Boeing 707. Our instructor for the course was Jim Shaw, the same Captain who had conducted my initial flying test on the Viscount when I'd first joined the company.

Compared with the Viscount the Boeing 707 was a big, and much more complicated, aeroplane altogether, in fact it was in another league and of another generation in the evolution of aircraft development. It was a pure jet so it was much faster, it was also mechanically more complex too and so it carried a Flight Engineer as well as two pilots. It also flew all over the world so the navigational management was more involved and we carried [back then] a navigator as well. It all started off looking pretty daunting but Jim was as good a ground instructor as he was a pilot and training captain and he made it all seem less difficult than it might have otherwise been. This classroom work was scheduled to last two weeks, then we would be subjected to a dozen or so sessions of simulator training and only then would we get to fly the real thing.

My fellow students on this course were all pilots based at East Midlands and so they went home after each days tuition in the classroom. I, on the other hand, being based up at Teesside, retired to a local hotel, booked and paid for, by the company. Here I spent my evenings studying before retiring to bed each night with yet another dose of numbers and technical jargon spinning around in my head.

There was a lot of work and a lot of studying to be done to learn all that needed to be known about this aircraft. Not only was every day a 'full on' bombardment of new information, the evenings were taken up with homework and/or consolidation of that day's classroom work. Thus, by the time I finally put my head on my pillow each night I was more than ready for immediate sleep.

The trouble was that this sleep was always late in arriving. The hotel selected by the company as my 'digs' for the fortnight of this course was not exactly a high end affair. The powers that be in British Midland were a bit parsimonious when it came to looking after the comfort of us pilots and no more was spent on accommodation than they thought was the minimum that they could get away with without the Union kicking up a fuss. Thus this hotel could be described as 'adequate' but that was about all. The biggest drawback was that the bedrooms had fairly thin walls which were not exactly fully soundproofed – in fact, far from it.

I probably wouldn't have noticed this defect in hotel construction if it hadn't been for the unfortunate fact that for the entire fortnight that I was housed in this establishment there was a rather enthusiastic couple in the room next to mine. I never saw these people and I have no idea what they were doing [outside their bedroom] that required them to be housed alongside me in this hotel but it was the same every night. And every night they kept me awake, for what seemed like hours.

Not only did I have no idea what they were doing outside their bedroom, I also have no idea what they were doing inside it either. I suspect that I understood the general principle of what was going on but such was the noise and the long and gradual build in the tempo of activity that by the end of it all I was totally baffled – and exhausted

– and I was only listening! As I say, it was the same every night and it always ended in the same way too. Lots of noise and banging and squealing and grunting to be followed by an endless series of 'Yes... yes...yes...yes' from the female of the species. So loud and prolonged that I felt like shouting back from my side of the divide:-

"For pity's sake, stop asking her binary answer questions!".

I now think I remember more about these interrupted nights than anything I learned about the Boeing 707 on that course

Following this ground course and the subsequent simulator and flying training my further advancement on this aeroplane was to come to a grinding halt fairly quickly. The third aircraft that we were purchasing – to fulfil a contract to fly for an emerging middle east airline that had been signed – suddenly fell through at the eleventh hour. The purchase was therefore postponed and having hardly tasted the joys of flying large jets to exotic locations I found myself back flying the Viscount just as fast as I'd left it. Nothing is certain in life!

20. The Mysteries of Promotion.

There's nothing especially clever about being a pilot. A lot of people think there is though, probably partly because pilots are a fairly rare breed and most people don't know one, partly because flying is a strange and not altogether relaxing thing to do for a lot of people and it's all a bit of a scary mystery. Not many people understand how it all works and they're baffled by that seemingly formidable array of knobs, dials, switches, lights, levers and instruments in a pilot's office. So people think we pilots are something a bit special. Mistake! We're not, we're 'ordinary', just like everyone else. The difference is that the job we've chosen to do is considered more 'scary' than most other peoples is, that's all. There is sometimes another difference though; some pilots actually do think that they're a bit special and a cut above the rest of us, these people are probably best avoided, poor souls!

That's what I think anyway which is maybe why I always seemed to be taken by surprise when a promotion came my way. The first time this happened was when I was offered a chance to train as a co-pilot on our Boeing 707 aircraft. This was way out of left field and I jumped at the chance. My time on the 707 didn't last long however and I very soon found myself back on the Viscount as the Boeing vacancy evaporated just as fast as it had appeared in the first place.

The next surprise came not too much later and was an offer to train for a command with the airline. Again, I had no idea that this might happen. I was a pretty junior First Officer having been with British Midland for less than three years and this alone put me way down the queue for promotion. Even assuming that one was considered a suitable candidate, these things were decided strictly on seniority and I had precious little of that. Also, there was a minimum level of experience required before promotion to command could take place. This was set at 3,000hrs for the Viscount aircraft that I was flying. I was well short of that with only 2,400hrs under my belt – at least another years flying in those days. On top of that, I only had a Commercial Pilot's licence. To be a Captain you had to first upgrade your licence to the level of Airline Transport Pilot's Licence [ATPL]. I'd done the exams for this but I hadn't yet got the all important piece of paper – that was going to cost me a large fee to acquire and since there was no chance of me being made a captain in the short term, plus, I didn't have the spare cash, I hadn't bothered. I was happily content with my lot and being made a Captain was far from top of my thoughts at this point.

The 'phone rang. It was Bert Cramp, then our Operations Manager. He didn't ring me every day and my first thought was "What have I done wrong this time?"

"Have you passed your ATPL exams?", asked Bert.

"Yes", I said, "But I haven't actually applied for it to be issued".

"Well get on with it then, you've now got a choice. You can go back on the 707 as a co-pilot or you can have a command on the Viscount. Which do you want?"

This was a 'no brainer', as they say. Much as I would have loved to get some long haul experience on the Boeing 707 there was only one way to go and that was to move to the left hand seat [i.e. take the command].

"Well, I'd love to take the command", I said, "But I've only got 2,400hrs!'".

"Never mind that, we'll sort that out with the CAA".

"What about seniority?".

"Don't worry about that either, I'll deal with the union, leave it to me".

And so it came to pass, somehow or other I became a Captain, way out of left field.

The next promotion, again out of the blue and a couple of years down the line, was to the position of becoming a Training Captain. It had never crossed my mind that I'd ever be considered for this role. I was chuffed to bits, it meant that the powers that be thought I was actually a reasonably capable driver of aeroplanes.

A year or two later I had yet another seminal call. This one from our now Flight Operations Director, one Dave Court.

"How would you like to be Viscount Fleet Manager?", he asked. This was indeed a lightning strike. It was an offer that would take me into a 'proper' management role. The Viscount at that time was the mainstay of our short haul operation and our largest fleet [we had 14 of them then]. I had had no idea that anyone would consider me to be 'management material', I'd always seen myself more as a bit of a rebel. When I'd recovered my composure I asked to first discuss this with my wife [it would mean some changes at home – more work and less time off]. It was really another 'no brainer', and having consulted the Boss, I accepted. Dave explained that as I had no previous management experience he'd arranged for one of our more senior and experienced pilot mangers, a certain Jim Shaw [a wonderful man] to show me the ropes for six months, after which I would take over the full reins.

The three of us, Dave, Jim and myself met the following Monday to run through the details. All Fleet Managers [we had 4 different fleets] had company cars. Jim asked what car he could have. Dave explained that as Jim's role was temporary he wasn't entitled to a car. Jim explained, somewhat emphatically, that if he couldn't have a car, then he wouldn't be showing me the ropes. He left the building.

Dave looked at me:-

"Well", he said, "Looks like you're the Viscount Fleet Manager, you better go and order yourself a car!"

A week or two later we had a Viscount aquaplaning off the runway at Leeds Bradford in horrible weather and breaking a leg, its right undercarriage. Talk about a baptism of fire, you couldn't make it up!

My next big surprise followed on after a further two or three years.

It started with a pretty big falling out between my immediate boss and myself – to the point that I decided that I could no longer work for him. I wrote my resignation letter and the next morning , on my way to do some training work in our simulator, I left it on the desk of my bosses boss [Dave Court]. This was not a smart career move; many a former manager had found themselves out of the door altogether. I was expecting a call.

Sure enough, halfway through my training session I had a message to 'attend Captain Court's Office' when I'd finished my training detail. This did not auger well. With beating heart I knocked on his door. I was ushered to the chair in front of my hatchet man's desk.

"I got your letter this morning" he said, "Were you serious?". Here was my chance, an escape route, an olive branch!

"Yes", I said. Why? What on earth was I thinking? I had a wife, children, a mortgage. I needed the salary, not the dole!

"I see", he replied. He then paused and allowed what seemed like an endless silence to follow. I said nothing. At last he said: –

"How would you like his job?"

Just how do these things work?!

21. The Turdicle Issue

In an earlier story I wrote about my flying instructor. A lot of water under the bridge later, I was now a Training Captain on the Viscount aircraft with British Midland Airways. My original flying instructor from my flying student days at Elstree aerodrome, one Dave Rowley, had by now become only a distant memory. The last time I'd seen him he was on his way to start a new job flying with the British Antarctic Survey.

My next week's roster appeared and I noticed that I was scheduled to do a series of 'line training' flights with a new recruit, a First Officer D. Rowley ['line training' is that advanced part of teaching a pilot to fly a specific aircraft type once he/she has mastered the basics and is now safe to fly with passengers but not yet sufficiently fluent to be released without supervision]. It couldn't be the self same Dave Rowley who taught me all those years ago could it? Unbelievably, it turned out that it was that very man. I don't know who was the more surprised, Dave or myself!

So here we now were, the tables turned. Me now the instructor and Dave the student. Now it was my turn to give him a hard time, the poacher turned gamekeeper – what goes round comes round. This was delicious irony, I was the boss and he was my bag carrier!

Of course, the reality wasn't like that at all, Dave was an experienced and very capable pilot and he breezed through the training process with no trouble at all – and with a few beers along the way. He was now married and, like me, had a young family. He soon settled into the airline and subsequently moved his home and his family into the area. Our two families became firm friends, even on occasion, holidaying together.

Dave had a good sense of humour and a rich fund of stories and jokes, some of them very ripe. He was also a good raconteur. I remember flying with him on one particular day and him telling me his story of 'The Turdicle'.

"Any day now", he announced out of the blue, "An iceberg made of human excrement will be released into the South Atlantic and become a hazard to shipping!". This statement was delivered with triumph, with authority, with finality, with a large grin and in a tone that indicated that it was a categorical fact and couldn't be challenged. Needless to say, I had no idea what on earth he was talking about and I queried both his sanity and the logic of his pronouncement [which was actually a little more earthy and less refined than the version I've quoted].

Then came the explanation. Apparently the system of toilet construction on the British Antarctic Survey expedition then [I don't know what they do now, if anything different, this was all forty years or more ago!] was to dig a very deep hole in the ice and place a couple of planks across the top of said hole, the complete assembly housed cosily within a portacabin. This created both a perfectly workmanlike loo and also a foolproof sewage disposal system. All in one easy step, a deep freezer with no electricity required. The deposited product would freeze immediately on impact at the bottom of the pit. There was therefore no health hazard and no offensive aroma either. Further, once the first pit was full, a fresh one could be dug close by and so the system continually repeated itself. A simple and neat solution to an otherwise difficult problem that would have required an expensively engineered piece of hardware needing constant maintenance.

There were however, two consequences to this approach of waste disposal control. The first was that the science of dropping matter down a freezing hole, from the same starting point on every occasion, would inevitably result in the formation of an overly long stalagmite. Not a problem in itself but eventually this stalagmite would grow in length until it reached a point [literally] where it would threaten to rise above the level of the planks that spanned the pit. This was not good for toilet users and a resolution was required.

The solution was simple – but it involved an unpleasant spell of manual labour which took the form of a 'Turdicle Party' – and there were never any volunteers. A turdicle party was a team of two volunteered men whose job it was to attack the giant stalagmite with ice axes and to chip it away so that it no longer existed and was instead evenly spread across the bottom of the pit! This surgical solution had the double benefit of both removing the threat to human posterior as well as optimising the useful life of the pit, a win, win solution, [unless you were a turdicle party member of course]. Volunteers were selected by the short straw method.

The second consequence of this toilet system construction took a lot longer to manifest itself but it had a greater potential impact on the world outside the immediacy of the toilet requirements of the British Antarctic Survey members.

As most of us know, icebergs are formed by great chunks of ice breaking off from the edge of the ice platforms that cover the Arctic and Antarctic. The ice platform migrates towards the sea a little bit every year as fresh snow and ice builds up behind it. Thus, the toilet system employed by the Survey team also slowly moved seaward a little every year. Eventually it was going to break off from the edge of that continent and set sail all on its own.

By Dave's reckoning, on the day he made his sudden and unexpected announcement high up in the sky, the original sewage storage system created by the British Antarctic Survey people was about to cut loose and drift off into the South Atlantic sunset.

Dave swore that this was a true story. I'm not so sure but it makes for an amusing tale. If it was true then no doubt there were some happy and replete 'bottom feeders' in the South Atlantic at that time – no pun intended.

22. The Embarrassing Lawnmower.

Our first child arriving, moving into a house of our own and getting my first command, all arrived pretty much at the same time in my life – an exciting, if exhausting time. With our new house came a lawn. A lawn needs cutting and I didn't have a lawnmower. What's more, such was the size of our new mortgage that I couldn't afford one either.

Amongst the small band of pilots in the airline based up at Teesside along with myself at that time was an old Captain, I'll call him Gordon. I say he was 'old' for that was what he seemed to be to me at the time – I was still pretty young then. In fact he must have been under 55 as that was the age at which pilots 'retired' in those days, so he was then at least more than 17 years younger than my age now. How time flies!

Gordon lived in the most rundown and decrepit old caravan that you've ever seen and he drove the most decrepit, run down and colourful car ever seen on public roads too – a little old Simca on which every panel and door was of a different colour, each one having been rescued from a scrap heap because the original had either been badly dented or had rusted away.

Why on earth did Gordon, a fully fledged and long time airline captain, live like this? Because he was the stereotype caricature of an airline pilot, a Lethario too easily led into temptation, unable to resist and unable to distinguish between love and lust. Thus he had been married six times, was now again divorced and he lived alone in his disintegrating caravan. Not surprisingly Gordon had no money, he had a veritable army of former wives to maintain instead. He kept his caravan in the grounds of a disused farmhouse on the edge of the airfield boundary where he tended the garden of the abandoned farmhouse as if it were his own – a noisy place to live, an airfield boundary but the advantage was that he paid no rent for the privilege, instead he acted as the guardian of the disused house.

I digress, but I was once flying with our boss [or Chief Pilot to give him his official title] between Teesside and London – up and down the spine of England six times a day for five or six days in a row. Dave kept looking out of the window at the landscape, a long way down underneath us.

"Somewhere down there' he said, 'Is Gordon, towing his decrepit caravan with his decrepit car all the way down to Newquay in Cornwall! When he gets there I'm going to have to phone him and tell him to drive all the way back up again. We were going to have pilots based down there for the summer and Gordon had volunteered for a posting but we've now decided not to continue with that plan!".

No mobile phones then – poor old Gordon!

Despite both of us being Captains, Gordon and I were still teamed up to fly together from time to time. As we trundled along on this particular day, up and down England's backbone as usual, we chatted about this and that between bursts of flying 'work'. We got on to the subject of houses, gardens and lawns. I told him about my lawnmower problem and he said that he had a petrol mower which he'd happily lend me. We arranged that I'd go round to his caravan tomorrow to collect it. What a nice chap!

We landed at Heathrow and set about preparing for our return fight north. We were told that we would have a 'stretcher case' on this trip back to Teesside. A 'stretcher case' involved an injured individual, not surprisingly, lying on a stretcher which was then strapped across the first row of seats in the cabin. No big deal, it happened from time to time. It turned out that this particular casualty was a not unattractive young lady, in her twenties, with a broken leg – which was sticking up in the air from under a blanket and was encased in a full plaster cast.

Not too long after we'd taken off from London Gordon announced that he was going back to 'check on the casualty'. He was gone for some considerable time but did return for the final bit of the flight. We finished our day's work, bid each other farewell and went our respective ways.

Tomorrow dawned a bright summers day and after a leisurely morning I determined that I would take Gordon up on his lawnmower offer so I trundled over to his caravan, only a few minutes drive away from our shiny new house with its overgrown grass. On arrival, Gordon's car was in evidence, parked up next to the caravan, the pair of them well matched in their decrepitude, but there was no answer to my knock on the caravan door and no sign of the man himself. Maybe he was in the old farmhouse?

There was a hedge between house and caravan so I opened the gate set in the hedge and stepped through with the intention of checking the house. And then I stopped in my tracks! There in front of me, no more than three yards away, was a veritable sight to behold. Lying on a blanket spread out on the lawn in front of the farmhouse was a plastered leg, sticking out from under Gordon's little white torso! I froze and, as delicately and quietly as I could, I selected reverse gear and backed out. The only detail I noticed was that Gordon had a neat little dimple on each of his exposed, and very white, cheeks! Fortunately, the happy pair were so engrossed in their fresh discovery of Nature's bounty that I hadn't disturbed their activities one jot.

I drove away with a quiet chuckle and in awe of Gordon's chutzpah. It was a hot summers day with not a cloud in sight and I wondered whether or not he'd get sunburn on his petite derriere if he tarried for too long.

I did manage to successfully borrow the mower from Gordon a few days later but I never did tell him that my grass could have been cut sooner – diplomacy and tact dictated otherwise. The story had a happy ending too. Gordon and his new friend became 'an item' and eventually the young lady became his seventh wife. I know not what happened to Gordon. He could, just possibly, still be going but I rather suspect that he died happy – and of exhaustion – some time ago now!

23. The Garage Door

I was alone at home and I was flying early in the morning. My wife had decamped with our young baby to spend a few days down in Kent with her parents. My alarm went off and I wandered into our kitchen to put the kettle on. To my surprise, when I looked out of the window I saw that it had been snowing. Not only that, the snow had settled and at the precise time that I was gazing out on this landscape a fox trotted across our lawn and disappeared from view.

Fascinated to see where Rex had gone, I opened our kitchen door and stepped out to have a look at where his tracks went. There were three consequences to this hasty and ill thought through action. The first was that it woke our dog, who had been asleep under the kitchen table. He decided that he needed to visit the scenery and so dashed out through the open door. The second consequence was that on his way out he caught his backside on the door which, as it opened inwards, then swung shut behind him. The third consequence was that I was outside, stark naked and bare footed, and as the door was on a Yale lock I was now marooned in the snow with no way back in! The only consolation was that as it was deep winter, at least it was still dark outside.

I had to resort to finding a brick to break the glass in the door window to regain entry. Not very satisfactory but at least I was back in and out of the cold! Somewhat cross with myself [and our innocent dog!] I proceeded to prepare myself for work and then went out, for a second time. With the car now out of the garage I went to close the garage door. This door was of the slatted roller blind type and was made of aluminium. There was a toggle on a rope on the door, used to pull the door down to close it. I remember the previous house owner telling me to always use this toggle to close the door [but he didn't say why]. For some reason, on this particular morning I ignored his sage advice and instead of pulling down on the toggle as usual, I reached up, grabbed a convenient gap between the aluminium slats of the roller then and pulled down.

The immediate, and obvious, consequence of this action was – searing pain! It was never going to take a rocket scientist to work out that as the door rolled down, so the slats would close up – tight. I had simply put my fingers into a vice and then proceeded to tighten it up! I now found myself, not only in extreme pain, but with my fingers stuck tight in the grip of the closed metal slats.

Unfortunately, the handle to open the door was at its base and my fingers were now stuck at a point that was too high up for me to reach down with my free hand to the handle at the bottom! There was no one I could call to help and I had no option other than to grit my teeth and physically wrench my trapped fingers clear, which I did. There then followed another episode of extreme pain but fairly soon this second instalment began to ebb away and I was able, somewhat chastened, to drive off to work.

By the time I arrived at the airport things were more or less back to normal and I was left with nothing more than a bit of a throbbing finger and a very dark and angry blood blister under the nail. Beyond that I was otherwise none the worse for wear after this rather unfortunate start to my day.

Flying with me was a co-pilot called Klem. Between us we carried out all our flight preparations as per usual and, passengers aboard, we then took off to fly down to Heathrow. I had recounted my sorry tale of earlier woes to Klem during our preparations and he had been very amused by the saga but not at all sympathetic – typical First Officer!

On this particular trip I was doing the flying and Klem was manning the radios and looking after all the other 'stuff'. Once we'd climbed up to our cruising height and were trundling happily along minding our own business, my bruised and battered finger began to remind me that I'd not looked after it particularly well earlier in the morning. Soon the throbbing sensation under my fingernail started to become quite strong and it was not long before it started to transition over into becoming ever more painful as we flew along.

It wasn't difficult to work out why I was increasingly feeling this pain now. What was happening was that as we'd gained altitude and the air pressure decreased, so the pressure exerted by the blood blister under the fingernail was proportionately increasing, thus exacerbating the pain [hindsight is a wonderful thing!]. Although the aircraft was pressurised, we flew with the cabin set to a pressure altitude that was higher than that on the ground. I couldn't increase the pressure inside the aircraft any further as we were already at the maximum level allowable. If this went on much longer and the pain in my finger got any worse, then I'd have no option other than to descend to a lower level so as to be able to increase the air pressure to relieve the pain.

Not many more minutes passed before I reached the point of no return as the pain was now becoming close to agony. I decided that enough was enough, we'd have to descend. This was quite a bit earlier than we would normally have started down but down we had to go. "Ask ATC for descent Klem", I said, "I can't stand this pain in my finger!"

"Ha-ha!", said Klem who clearly didn't believe me and thought it was a great joke.

"No, I'm serious!", I said, "Get descent".

Klem thought I was still playing around and so did nothing – except to laugh even more. By now I was becoming a bit desperate. I knew [from the radio calls being made] that there was no one immediately underneath us so I just disconnected the autopilot and started going down. Klem looked at me, suddenly rather startled, but at last he got the message, asked for descent clearance and we were soon going down to an approved lower level. As we descended, so the pain in my finger eased and the rest of the flight went without any further hitch.

There was no way I could have flown the return flight back up to

Teesside with my finger in that state. We had about 45 minutes on the ground so I decided that I'd have to visit the Medical Centre in the Queens Building [now demolished and just a piece of history] to have the offending blood blister lanced. I briefed Klem accordingly and off I went to be attended to whilst he prepared for the return trip in my absence.

I must have been in more of a state of shock than I had realised. I remember walking into the Medical Centre one minute and then the next thing I remember is waking up on the reception floor with a sea of faces looking down on me! Goodness knows what all the poor, and presumably under par, passengers in there awaiting treatment thought – an airline captain in full uniform, gold braid, stripes, et al, strides into the Centre and immediately collapses – like a pack of cards – in front of them! They must have all hoped to high Heaven that I wasn't destined to be their driver!

I was soon ushered through into a cubicle and then shortly attended to by a rather fierce looking nurse. I explained my predicament and she said that she could happily deal with it and provide a solution. She disappeared but was soon back with an electrical device that she plugged into the wall.

This was a soldering iron type machine that had a needle on it which glowed red hot when switched on. I was asked to put my hand on the table, fingers spread and the nurse then explained that I was to let her know when I was ready and that she was going to burn a little hole through the fingernail to relieve the pressure. It would hurt while she carried out this procedure she said but she wouldn't do anything until I was ready. I was about to reply when I felt the most almighty hammer coming down on my already delicate finger and I nearly jumped into next week! She had done the deed even before I'd had time to show any cowardice!

Immediate relief followed of course and I was soon released and back on my way to my return flight, which passed [as usual] without further incident. All in all, a day to remember!

24. House Move

In 1976 British Midland introduced the Douglas DC 9 jet into service. This aircraft was to eventually replace the venerable turbo-prop Viscount aircraft that had been the backbone of the company's short haul operation for so many years.

These shiny new jets were inevitably going to be flown by the most senior pilots in the company and the first service on which they were to be deployed was our Teesside – Heathrow route as this was the company's most profitable at that time. Back then Middlesbrough, despite not being the UK' most prosperous city, had a plethora of big companies – ICI, British Steel, Black and Decker and several others, all needing international connectivity and keeping our aircraft seats full with their requirements for fast transport to and from London – and beyond. There was also a big demand for seats for oil rig workers who regularly commuted between their homes in the north east and the big world of oil to be found beyond Heathrow.

This was unfortunate for us pilots then based up at Teesside, of which I was one. We were all very much down the pecking order in the seniority stakes which meant that if we wanted to keep our jobs we'd have to up sticks and move down to East Midlands. My wife and I were sorry to leave the North East, it was a great place to live but necessity meant that the move had to be made – paying the bills and supporting the mortgage were high on the priority list, I couldn't afford to vote with my feet and walk away from a position that I'd find virtually impossible to move into with another airline. Even if I did leave Midland, we'd still have to move house as there were no other airlines operating from T'side in those days to whom I could jump.

We ended up moving to a small village called Diseworth in N.W. Leicestershire. This story has nothing to do with flying aeroplanes – except that the job was the reason that we ended up living in this village – where we've remained for the last forty years. I recount it here only because it makes for an amusing story with a very tenuous link to aviation!

One of the reasons we've stayed put in our little rut is that we live in a community of characters who create an atmosphere that doesn't leave room for a dull minute in our lives. I can perhaps best illustrate this by telling you about the first conversation I ever had with a Diseworthian, a conversation I remember well to this day. It took place on the day we bought our house in the village. All will be revealed – but first some background:-

The house we wanted was to be sold at auction, the auction to take place at the property itself. No one knows how old the house actually is but the Estate Agent's blurb said 'Dating from the 16th Century'. Anyway, not to put too fine a point on it, it was old and it was in a mess. It was old enough for the Council to have put a Preservation Order on it and it was in sufficient a state of disrepair that they'd also put a Condemnation Notice on it as well. So we couldn't live in it and we couldn't knock it down and start again either – not that that was what we wanted to do anyway. Far from it, our plan was to restore and renovate but that's another story.

None of this bothered us then, we were young enough to have the energy and naive enough to have the imagination to see [eventually] a habitable home for our children and ourselves. In short we could see the potential and we were possessed of the arrogance of youth that told us that we could complete the job.

Come the day of the auction I turned up to bid and it wasn't long before my heart sank. We had but a limited budget and the place was heaving with people. It only took a couple of seconds before I had convinced myself that my mission was doomed to failure, competition would be fierce and we'd be outbid. Before we even got started the price would have shot past our predetermined maximum ceiling.

As it was, it turned out there were only a few serious 'buyers' in amongst this throng. We won the battle and I stepped forward, a stranger in the crowd of onlookers, to pay the obligatory deposit to the auctioneer. The crowd, I was to later discover, comprised almost entirely of Diseworthians who had turned up, only out of curiosity, to see who would buy 'Old Ted's place'. [We never knew him but the former occupant of the house was one Ted Howe. By all accounts Ted had been a veritable character and reputedly, in his day, was known to be the best poacher in the whole of Leicestershire].

That evening I came back to Diseworth [we were then living in Castle Donington, an adjacent village] to sample the delights of one of the two pubs in the village. I chose the Bull and Swan, for no reason other than it was closest to our 'new' abode. The pub was pretty full and as I stood at the bar to order my beer I caught the gist of the conversation. It was all about the auction that morning. I listened with wry and growing amusement – and said nothing. What idiot had bought it? Where did they come from? Why would they want a wreck like that? Didn't the fool know it was condemned? Didn't they know it was falling down? Must have more money than sense, etc, etc.

As I stood taking all this in a small lady perched on a stool the end of the bar and with a kindly, smiling face caught my eye. She leaned towards me and said:-

"Hello, what brings you to Diseworth, who are you?".

"Hello" I replied, "I'm the idiot they're all talking about" said I, "I'm the fool who bought the house at the auction this morning".

"Ooh!" she said, "Are you going to live in it?".

"Yes, eventually, when we've done it up".

"Ooh, good", she said, "My name's Dolly and I need to ask you a question!".

"Hello Dolly, I'm Jim. What's your question?".

"Well", said Dolly, "When people in this village die, I'm the one who lays them out. So what I need to know from you is; Do you dress to the left or do you dress to the right?"!!!

And that, dear reader, is the kind of village in which we live.

Sadly, Dolly, passed away a few years ago now, like too many other colourful characters from Diseworth with whom we've rubbed shoulders since 1978.

As a footnote of possible interest to visitors to our sanctuary, Dolly transferred her allegiance from the Bull and Swan pub to the Plough a year or two after our initial introduction to each other. A part of her memory lives on still in the Plough. If you look closely at the small table top, between the windows to the left of the bar, you'll see a small inlaid brass plaque which simply says 'Dolly's Shelf'. There she sat every evening drinking her half pint – no doubt at the same time conducting, from her vantage point and between sips of beer, an intimate appraisal of every male she encountered. It's a sobering thought that without Dolly around to look after our best interests, we males in the village can no longer be assured that we'll have a comfortable eternal rest when our time is up.

25. Reality Check.

The first aircraft I flew for bmi – or British Midland as it was known, was the venerable Viscount. It had four engines so pilots liked it and it had big windows so passengers liked it too. It also had two toilets, but these were fairly early days in the context of sophistication and the two loos were furnished with buckets which had to be removed and emptied on a regular basis, a bit like the loo in an old caravan. Although the Viscount was still flying as late as the mid 1990s, it was designed immediately post war and first flew in 1948 – hence the none too modern toilets!

Anyway, we did a regular service from East Midlands Airport [with some passengers on board] which called in first at Birmingham where we picked up more passengers. From there we flew down to Guernsey where some of the passengers got off and some got on. Then it was across to Jersey where again, some got off and some got on. From Jersey we went on up to Southend in Essex where all the passengers decamped. At Southend we then refuelled before collecting a fresh set of folk and retracing our outbound route to eventually arrive back at East Midlands.

On this particular day I bowled in to work in a bit of a rush and hadn't had time to fully complete the morning ablutions. The consequence was that we left East Midlands on time but I was already in need of a visit to the boy's room. It was but a short hop across to Birmingham from East Midlands so I couldn't leave the flight deck. We were only scheduled to be on the ground at Birmingham for a few minutes so the same constraints applied there, I was too busy.

Then it was on to Guernsey. Again, not a long flight and too much going on for me to find the time to do what needed to be done to clear the tubes. By the time we landed at Guernsey my life was becoming a bit uncomfortable but we weren't scheduled to stop long enough for me to find an opportunity there either. Life was beginning to become just a little strained. The hop across from Guernsey to Jersey was barely even ten minutes and the time we had on the ground there was not much longer so the same time issues intervened.

The next leg, up to Southend, was a bit longer and I was confident that I would be able to find a resolution to my little private problem. It was not to be however. I don't now remember why but it was a busy flight and again there was no time to leave the flight deck. What I do remember is that each passing minute made matters worse and I was having to concentrate as much on my personal discomfort as on the professional job in hand.

Southend was not the easiest airport to land at smoothly in a Viscount, the approach is flown in over a railway line and the runway was not too long [it has been lengthened since my flying days there] so you needed to get the thing on the tarmac pretty pronto, which didn't leave much room for finessing the arrival. The result was that a landing at Southend often ended up being a bit of a thump onto the ground. I was desperate to make it a smooth arrival this time, a heavy landing could have been disastrous in the underwear department. We'd now been on the go for a long and increasingly uncomfortable [for me] four hours or more since I had first felt the need to answer to nature's demands.

The landing was good, good enough anyway, and happily there was no embarrassment. I knew that relief was close at hand. In ten minutes we'd be parked up, the passengers would have disembarked, the co-pilot could supervise the turn round and the refuelling and, best of all, I could do what needed to be done before we re-boarded.

And so it was. It seemed to take an age for everyone to get off and I was by now really desperate but at last they were all gone and I dashed back to the loo. What pleasure, what bliss, I have never been so comfortably seated! I'd just passed the point of no return when there was a loud and urgent knocking on the door and a dismembered voice said:-

"Oi, 'ooever's in there, there's no bucket"!

"Too late" I called back.

Quelle horreur, the cleaners had already taken the bucket out to 'refresh' it and I had now left a message on the floor! Life is a great leveller and none of us are immune!

But it gets worse. The rest of my crew fell about laughing as soon as my little faux pax was revealed and any respect they'd had for their Captain had now left the aircraft along with the contents of the bucket. Happily, the damage was soon repaired, the next set of passengers boarded and the senior stewardess started her welcome speech over the tannoy: –

"Ladies and Gentlemen…" she said, "…Welcome aboard this British Midland Viscount flight to Jersey and Guernsey. On behalf of Captain Crapper and the crew …etc.…"

Every time I spoke to the passengers on each sector for the rest of the day I had to introduce myself as 'Captain Crapper' – and that's what I call a reality check! [All due to Jenny and Gail, the two cabin crew involved!].

The story found its way into the folklore of the airline but fortunately for me the nickname didn't! It's a happy coincidence that this all happened in a Viscount registered as G-AZLP, the very same flight deck that now resides in the Brooklands Museum. The bucket and the loo might now be long gone but it amuses me to think that the site of my torture and humiliation still lives on in the safe hands of the museum.

The Viscount was a great aeroplane to fly [even if it had lousy toilets!] in an era when it was all still fun and before it all got too serious and too technical. By the time I retired, the aircraft I last flew didn't even have a control column and its toilets were controlled by computers – I've no idea what the computers did for the toilets but

I'm sure it was useful! The bottom line [no pun intended] of the story is that in 40 years of flying this was the most serious 'accident' I ever had. That being the case, I can happily stand a bit of humiliation every now and again!

26. No Hiding Place.

In the days of my Viscount flying when we operated the schedule service route between East Midlands and Frankfurt, as I've described in an earlier tale, we had a long 'day stop' in Frankfurt before then flying back to East Midlands. However, in the earlier days of operating this route and before we had a 'rest room' supplied at Frankfurt, we'd fly the aircraft out to Frankfurt in the morning and then spend the rest of that day and the night in a hotel in town. The next day we'd operate the return trip, departing mid afternoon and arriving back at East Midlands around 8 p.m. – an easy two day's work!

The hotel which the company had especially selected for us to stay in [as usual] was not exactly one of Frankfurt's finest. Rather, it was down at the lower end of the scale of what was considered to be acceptable but it was not unpopular with the crews. The staff were friendly – some more so than others – [more of that a little later]. It was also situated on the edge of a respectable part of the city so it had restaurants and cafes that were quite decent without being overly expensive.

Back then our Boeing 707 crews used to use the Lufthansa simulator for their training but they used to stay in a hotel closer to where the 707 simulator was housed as it was a fair hike away from our accommodation. We therefore didn't bump into them too often and generally speaking, we'd only see them when they were commuting to and from Frankfurt as passengers on our flights.

Back to the Frankfurt hotel. As I say, it wasn't the most salubrious joint in town but everything worked as it should, it was clean and the staff were always helpful and accommodating. Also, the hotel bar was well stocked and they served bar meals which were none too shabby either.

The key player at this hotel was, as with all hotels, the manager, it's always the hotel manager who dictates the ambience and the mood of the establishment. In this case the manager was actually a manageress who went by the name of Eva, a lady maybe in her mid thirties, quite attractive and endowed with a good figure. Eva was also a total Anglophile, spoke very good English and spoiled us British aircrew something rotten – with big discounts on our bar tariffs and on the bar meals we consumed. More than that, Eva was single and was always keen to let any British aircrew member know that this was the case and that she was also available. In this context, over the time that we spent staying in her hotel, Eva 'interviewed' a fair number of our pilots!

The odd thing though, was that Eva was very particular as to who might knock on her bedroom door. This was not the way it was done, she was more discreet than that. All her visitors had to enter her abode via a window at the back of the hotel. Her rooms were on the ground floor of the hotel but even so her visitors had to climb up onto the top of a dustbin to gain access through said window. As far as I'm aware, this dissuaded none of her suitors. In fact, one of our brave pilots was so enamoured with Eva that he used to take himself off to Frankfurt on his days off to make sure she stayed happy!

On one occasion I was operating the return flight from Frankfurt to East Midlands so had stayed the previous night in the hotel [without incident and, I might add, without Eva!]. We reported for our flight in the afternoon as normal and eventually the passengers boarded and we were ready to go. Unfortunately, the engines wouldn't start. There was an 'emergency' electrical system fitted to the aircraft – in case the main electrics failed – but this could, on occasion malfunction and drain the aircraft battery. To guard against this eventuality when you shut the aircraft down with no further flying to be done for a few hours the crew were supposed to trip the circuit breaker governing this system, to provide further protection. On this occasion the inbound crew had forgotten to carry out this little drill, the battery had drained and so we found ourselves unable to start. This was a blow, we would now have a long delay whilst an engineer was summoned to rectify the problem. I clicked on to the passenger address system and advised our passengers accordingly.

A few seconds later a head appeared at the flight deck door, 'Hello' it said, 'Can I do anything Jim?' I turned round to see who it was – Neville, now one of the flight engineers on our Boeing 707s. Neville had previously worked on Viscounts as a ground engineer so knew the foibles of the aircraft. I explained our predicament and Neville disappeared down the aircraft steps and into the bowels of the beast where he fiddled and furtled to fix the problem. A while later he was back up top, the problem was solved and we were soon on our way. Certainly we were running late but by not too much – and it could have been a lot worse.

We didn't get to see much of each other as a rule – the 707 operation was very different and distinct from the rest of the airline and mostly they operated out of Stansted so it was rare that we'd meet up. Neville stayed up in the flight deck for most of the trip back as we chewed the cud and caught up with each others news. Neville was a very likeable character, friendly, affable and a good engineer. He was also married but [like most engineers] still had a roving eye and a voracious appetite for the ladies.

Neville had been out in Frankfurt for his six monthly simulator check he said but the hotel they normally stayed at was full so they'd instead used the hotel we used and were there the previous night where he and his lot had spent the evening, in the bar where they'd also had a meal. Strange that we hadn't met up but maybe we'd chosen to go out somewhere else for a change. Anyway, Neville then went on to tell me about his good fortune with one of the staff in the hotel.

"You haven't been climbing over dustbins to meet Eva have you Neville?" I queried.

"How did you know?", he replied, sounding rather surprised and shocked.

"Neville", I said, now moving into gear on a bit of a mischievous wind up mission, "I have to tell you that every man and his dog has been there. Are you going home this evening?".

"Of course", says Neville, "Why?"

"Well", I said, warming to my sadism, "I suggest that you stay well away from any canoodling tonight and you get yourself down to the clinic first thing tomorrow".

Neville was horrified to discover that he was but one of many. Not only did he shoot off to the clinic the next morning, he apparently confessed all to his wife when he got home that evening into the bargain! Not really what I'd intended to happen but ... if the cap fits...it's not compulsory to wear it! He did tell me later that he'd gone down to Leicester [less local so more discreet] to the clinic there and when he walked in and sat down, sitting directly opposite him on the other side of the room, was one of our Boeing 707 captains. It's a small world with few hiding places!

Another Neville tale is worth telling. I didn't witness this event myself but it was relayed to me via reliable sources.

We did a lot of flying on our Boeing 707s for newly independent countries who wanted their own national airlines and for these to be flying shiny jet aircraft, not old prop jobs. We filled a gap for these airlines with our Boeings whilst they awaited delivery of their own new aircraft. Consequently, the service on these flights was top notch, designed to complete with the best that existed in the already developed world. Thus, our aircrew on the Boeing fleet had become used to being served First Class standard food.

On this particular flight though, on which the unfortunate Neville just happened to be the Flight Engineer, there had been a bit of a mess made with the catering provided for the trip. When Neville decided that he wanted his 'crew meal' he pressed the call bell to summon the stewardess to the flight deck to ask her to bring up his food [all normal routine stuff].

The stewardess in question on this flight was one, Paula. Paula was a seasoned campaigner and an experienced cabin crew member, she'd been around a while, she knew what was what and she was also bright and not bad looking either. Not only that, she was also wise to the ways of too many pilots [and even more so flight engineers] and she knew all about Neville and his ever wandering eye also. It would not be wise of Neville to try it on with the redoubtable Paula. Unfortunately, Neville kept his brain in his trousers and he lacked the logic and ability to be able to exercise restraint.

When Paula returned with Neville's meal she presented him with a sort of Caesar's Salad but with a cold sausage presented as it's centre piece, the offending dish offered on a paper plate as well! This was not at all what Neville had been expecting. Paula executed a quick u-turn and vanished before Neville could say anything. He stared incredulously at this apology of a meal, not knowing if it was for real or whether Paula was trying to wind him up.

Not to be undone, Neville had an idea. He removed the sausage from the salad, tore a neat little hole in the base of his paper plate, unzipped his trousers, pulled out his favourite boy's toy – which he then neatly threaded though the hole in his plate. He then put the plate on his lap and neatly re-arranged the leaves, tomatoes, cucumber, etc, around his pride and joy. Once he was satisfied with his artistry he re-summonsed Paula to the flight deck. The two pilots flying the aeroplane had seen what was going on and waited with incredulity and baited breath for Paula's return.

In she came. "What do you call this?", exclaimed Neville in tones of feigned disbelief that she could have given him such mangy salad. Paula, being the woman of the world that she was, glanced down and immediately recognised it for exactly what it was. With complete composure and a totally unchanged complexion, Paula did no more that pick up Neville's fork and give the sausage a very healthy stab – at the pointy end too! And with that she turned on her heel and marched out! Neville hit the roof as he jumped up, clutching himself in agony whilst bits of lettuce and tomato flew everywhere. The two pilots both collapsed with laugher, tears rolling down their cheeks, partly from the laughing but also, possibly, in sympathy with Neville's pain.

Neville learned his lesson that day though. Don't mess with seasoned cabin crew members and certainly don't mess with the likes of Paula!

27. The Ultimate Benefactor

Most of us know people who are especially generous with the time and effort that they're prepared to give to others who need a helping hand, sometimes quite frequently. Maybe, just once or twice in a lifetime, you'll come across someone who makes a real sacrifice, more than just time and effort, in order to help someone else go forward. One such in my line of life was a pilot by the name of Bill.

Bill was a solid, steady, dependable captain, he'd been flying a long time and was an experienced aviator, with what you'd describe as a 'a safe pair of hands'. Most of all he was a very pleasant individual, quiet, friendly, good company and an all round decent chap. He was also a well respected Training Captain on the Viscount.

I was now the Fleet Manager on our Viscount Fleet, my first management position, and I'd only been in post for a couple of weeks so was still pretty green around the gills working at this level. Anyway, I had a phone call one evening from our Operations room. One of our Viscounts had gone off the runway at Leeds, the starboard undercarriage had collapsed and the passengers had been evacuated. Thankfully were no injuries and everyone had walked away. It was a foul evening, lashing horizontal rain, a howling and gusty wind and low cloud. The captain on this fateful flight was, of course, the unfortunate Bill. His co-pilot was young and not very experienced. Both in the wrong place at the wrong time!

This sort of incident – where an aircraft is damaged, even if no-one is hurt – is classified as an 'accident' and this triggers a whole set of protocols and required procedures, not the least of which is that the airline is required to notify the CAA [Civil Aviation Authority] and the

AAIB [Air Accident Investigation Branch]. We had our own defined process for dealing with such an eventuality and our Ops. people were busy running through the checklist of all these requirements – and very efficient they were too.

Somewhat out of my depth already, I met up with our own company Accident Investigator, a Captain Roger Wise, as well as with our Director of Operations, Captain Dave Court and we drove up to Leeds to do what we could to assist with the aftermath of this accident and the forthcoming investigations. These couldn't start until the AAIB people arrived and as the crew involved were 'quarantined' pending interview with the AAIB [i.e. we couldn't talk to them ourselves] there wasn't much that we could do save have a look at the damaged aircraft – itself also quarantined – from a distance.

It really was a dark and stormy night and not much had changed when we ventured out into the driving rain and howling gale, quite late on in the evening, to inspect the damage. The aircraft had been landing from North to South and had left the runway on the right hand side, not too far short of the end of the tarmac – which was just as well as almost immediately after that end of the runway there is a very steep and long drop. Had she overshot the end of the strip it would have been a very different story – so we could at least be thankful for small mercies.

As it was, there was a concrete drainage culvert just off to the side of the runway and the right hand undercarriage had caught this obstruction and hence had collapsed, tearing a hole through the top of the wing in the process. Had that concrete block not been there the whole thing would have ended up with the mere embarrassment of the aircraft being stuck in the mud – still not good but a far more benign outcome. That's the bit called 'Sod's Law'.

The next morning, with the AAIB now on site, the investigation got under way in earnest. They soon had the two flight recorders removed from the aircraft and dispatched for analysis. Then they wanted to know about our checks, procedures and techniques for landing the Viscount. These were all pretty simple and straight forward – and common to most turbo prop aircraft of the period.

There was little in the way of automatics on the Viscount, it was all manual hand flying. Basically one pilot flew the aircraft and the other operated the radios, flaps, undercarriage and other ancillary systems. One of the more unique features though was the 'Ground Fine Lever'. This was a lever that controlled the propellers to give much of the braking power available on landing. Once the aircraft had touched down the pilot flying would call for 'Ground Fine' and the non flying pilot would pull the lever back to provide propeller braking. This was because the pilot flying didn't have enough hands to both control the aeroplane and to pull the lever himself. You needed one hand to steer the nose wheel and the other to keep the wings level. All pretty routine and straight forward stuff.

Once familiar with our techniques the AAIB went off to interview the two pilots and to get their explanations as to what had gone wrong. We met up with them an hour or two later and they were scratching their heads.

Bill himself had been flying the aircraft with the co-pilot doing the radios, etc. It was indeed a dark and stormy night with a lot of rain and a gusty wind blowing, as confirmed by the weather history available from the Air Traffic Control Tower. Even so, assuming the aircraft had touched down where it should have done and that the pilots had operated in accordance with standard operating procedures then they should have stopped well before the end of the runway.

Bill's explanation was that he was late calling for 'Ground Fine' so they simply didn't slow down fast enough and it was all his fault he said. He also said that he was forced to put the aircraft onto the grass near the end of the runway to avoid going over the end and down the slope. Clearly more analysis would be required – maybe the flight recorders would yield something giving better and more definitive information.

Our own further discussions with the two pilots got us no further forward and both the AAIB and Roger and myself remained mystified.

The runway was plenty long enough, even in those conditions – maybe they'd aquaplaned or perhaps they'd landed too far down the runway and were hiding it [or something else?].

A few days later I had a call from the AAIB lead investigator – could I pay a clandestine visit to Farnborough, he wanted me to listen to the Cockpit Voice Recorder [CVR]? This was a highly unusual request. There had been a long and difficult negotiation between the Authorities and the pilot Unions about the installation of CVRs. The pilot and Union concern was that it was the thin end of the wedge in terms of 'the spy in the cab'. One of the resolutions to this debate was that 'Airline Management' would be barred from access to the content. [All this happened many years ago now so I hope no one will, all this time later, find themselves in any hot water!].

Anyway, I turned up for my meeting [that never happened] and duly listened to the CVR. What I heard astounded me! All was revealed. Not only had Bill been a bit economical with the truth in claiming to have been 'late' calling for 'Ground Fine', he'd called for it not once, not twice but three times – before finally selecting it himself! Now at least I understood how the aircraft had run out of runway and why Bill had been forced to put it on the grass. The unfortunate and inexperienced co-pilot had simply frozen [or, just 'not heard' the calls] presumably being somewhat overawed by the gusty and turbulent landing conditions. In any event Ground Fine [i.e. braking] had not been selected when requested. As a result none of the most effective form of braking, whilst at high speed, was applied until way too late.

What I didn't understand though was why Bill had rigidly stuck to his line about not calling for Ground Fine until too late when, in truth, he'd called for it three times – and still didn't get it. It made no kind of sense to either me or my AAIB co-conspirator.

My problem now was that I couldn't let it be known that I knew the real explanation. To do so would reveal the sin that I'd actually heard the recording. This would have caused an almighty row across the industry, possibly even resulting in the removal of CVRs from flight decks – putting accident investigation back years.

The innocent man would be found guilty unless the dilemma could be resolved. The only men who could do that were Bill himself and/or his co-pilot – by coming clean. Sadly this didn't happen and eventually I had to hold a 'Disciplinary Hearing' with all that that entailed and implied.

Bill stuck rigidly to his original line and, given the only explanation that was on the table – that he had not called for Ground Fine soon enough – l was left with little choice. This, despite my hinting as strongly as I could [several times] that I knew the truth of it – meant that I had no option other than to dismiss him.

I felt very trapped and no less mystified by this outcome. Doubtless however, I didn't feel as bad as Bill. He loved his flying and now, simply because of some reason that I couldn't fathom, it had been taken away from him. His chances of finding another flying job, certainly in the airline world, were pretty slim – not too many pilots come back from having been blamed for an accident – even if no one was hurt.

A couple of hours after this uncomfortable encounter I called Bill and asked him to meet me at a local hostelry that evening for a drink and a chat. We met and I told him, off the record, that I knew exactly what had happened – and how I knew. I asked him why he felt it more pressing to sacrifice his career than to reveal the full story. His explanation was as simple as it was extraordinary and it takes us back to the opening paragraph of this tale: –

"Well", Bill said, "The thing is I'm now pretty much near the end of my career but young Fred [we'll call his co-pilot Fred] is just starting out. If I explained what actually happened it would wreck his career before it's even really got going – and I wouldn't want that".

How selfless was that?

Actually, although it was an act of undoubted selflessness, I also thought it was a little misguided. I have no idea what happened to "Fred" and his career because he followed in the same footsteps down the road as poor Bill but if he couldn't cope with a bit of a 'sporty' approach and landing on a day of challenging conditions then maybe he was in the wrong profession anyway. Plus, what sort of man hides behind his colleagues chivalry? I hope Fred took many positives and salutary lessons from his experience on that day and that Bill's benevolence and example to him wasn't wasted.

Sadly Bill passed away a year or two ago now. I was proud to have known him and to have been at his funeral.

28. The End is Nigh

After many years – and hours [nearly 10,000 of them] flying Viscounts, the time finally arrived when I had to move on. The Company was replacing these old turbo prop aircraft with Douglas DC9 jet machines. Additionally, I had a new management role in the company which meant that I was now responsible for all of our short haul aircraft fleets. This required that I had to finally part company with the 'Queen of The Skies' and convert to our short haul DC9 jet.

Although our 'new' DC9s were far more modern than the old Viscounts, they were still second hand when we acquired them. Even so, they were a quantum leap forward from the Viscount in terms of their technological sophistication. One major difference was that they flew a lot faster and lot higher than the old Viscounts did. Where the venerable Viscount trundled along at 18.000 ft. altitude at a speed of some 4 miles a minute, the DC9 cruised at 35,000 ft and chewed up about 9 miles a minute. This meant that they were a lot more sprightly and we pilots had to adapt to these changes in speed and range of operation.

Another big difference between the two types was that whilst the Viscount was pretty heavy on the flight controls and required a bit of muscle power to make it point in the right direction, the DC9 was as light as a feather, a bit like the difference between driving a lorry from the 1950s as opposed to a modern car fitted with power steering, servo brakes, etc. All in all, one an agricultural tractor, the other a sleek sports car.

The conversion course for the DC9 followed much the same pattern as any other at the time; a fortnight of classroom work, a written technical exam and then another couple of weeks of simulator training before finally moving on to flying the real thing.

The classroom work, or 'ground school' as it was called, was always a fortnight from hell on any type conversion. Endless facts and figures that had to be committed to memory, huge amounts of important technical information that had to be absorbed and a whole lot more besides. No one, except perhaps the most committed masochist, ever enjoyed the purgatory of ground school. The enjoyable bit started when training reached the simulator stage of the programme. Nothing was different with the DC9.

Back then the simulator we used belonged to Finnair and was based up in Helsinki. Finland is a very cold place to be in winter – and it always seemed to be winter when we did our training. And so it was when I went up there to do my conversion training. Absolutely freezing. In fact, I don't think I've ever been anywhere as cold as Helsinki in winter.

I was teamed up with a likeable fellow pilot called Barney, he hailed from Rhodesia originally but had moved on from there and re-settled in the UK. Over here we had Arthur Scargill so it must have been a bit of a tough call for him back then to stay put but then they'd had Ian Smith out there so maybe the UK wasn't quite such a bad place after all!

The instructor detailed for our simulator training was to be Captain Roger Wise. Roger was a senior and long serving pilot, a wise old bird, an excellent and very experienced instructor and he was also our DC9 Fleet Manager. We went straight over to the simulator after landing at Helsinki for our first four hour session of how flying the DC9 would feel.

Roger gave us a thorough briefing as to what elements we would be covering during this detail. The first element of the process was fairly simple – get airborne and fly the thing around for a bit to get the 'feel' of it all before settling into the greater detail. Roger, who himself had done a lot of flying on the Viscount, was very clear in emphasising that we'd find that the DC9 was "very light on the controls" so we'd need to make sure that we didn't 'over control' the thing and in doing so make accurate flying difficult for ourselves. Small and delicate control inputs were to be the order of the day if we wanted to avoid fighting the aeroplane.

With this advice uppermost in our minds as Barney and I seated ourselves in the flight deck. Me, the captain, sitting in the left hand seat with Barney next to me in the right seat. We started by running through all the necessary pre-flight checks, which took quite a while as this was all new territory. Roger was at his place in the instructors seat behind us and he guided us through this laborious process. At last we had the engines started, were sitting at the beginning of the runway and were ready to take off on our first flight.

I was handling the aircraft for this first foray and before we started the take off run, Roger again reminded me to remember how light the controls were and to make sure that I didn't overdo my inputs on the control column. With this advice ringing in my ears we set sail – full power on and accelerating down the runway. At the appropriate speed Barney called 'Rotate' and I pulled back on the control column to lift the nose and get us airborne, consciously making sure that I didn't pull too hard and so jerk us uncomfortably into the air.

Nothing happened! The aircraft continued to accelerate down the runway, chewing up the tarmac with its nose still firmly on the ground. I pulled harder but still nothing happened. Barney and Roger could both see what was going on and I had their full attention!

"'It ain't half heavy, Rog!", I said through clenched teeth and I then positively heaved on the control column at the same time as playing with the electric trim control – a sort of 'fine tuning' system for controlling the angle that dictated the pitch of the aeroplane. At last the nose lifted and we rose into the sky. As the nose continued to go up so I checked forward to hold it at the correct angle. Again there was no response and the nose continued to rise alarmingly. I pushed for all I was worth and managed to reverse this new trend, again messing around with the electric trim. No matter what I did with pushing and pulling on the elevator controls I couldn't stabilise the aeroplane, it was either pointing at the ground or pointing at the sky.

I could see an increasing look of concern on both Barney's and Roger's faces. Barney because if a senior and experienced pilot [i.e. me] couldn't properly control this machine, then how was he going to get on with it when it was his turn? Roger, because it wasn't supposed to be like this, experienced captains just didn't fly as badly as this, especially fellow management pilots and training captains. I could sense that he was perplexed – and without any ready advice coming from him I didn't feel any better either!

I kept saying that the controls were heavy but Roger was now lost in his own thoughts and concerns. I was a senior pilot manager and an experienced captain. Not only that I was also now technically his boss. If I carried on flying like this the result would be that he'd end up with no option other than having to send me home – having first pronounced that I was unable to master the DC9. This was not working out very well! Eventually Roger said:-

"OK, put the autopilot in and let it settle down, you'll need to trim it properly".

I didn't think much of that by way of helpful advice, I'd been franticly using the trim controls to try and stabilise things from the start but to no avail. Even so and with some relief, we selected the autopilot anyway. The aeroplane settled down and flew straight but I really didn't think tinkering with the trim was the issue. If it was, then I was in trouble and maybe this aeroplane was too much for me! After a pregnant silence of some duration Roger then said:-

"I know what the problem is, you haven't got your seat adjusted correctly!"

Now I knew that I was indeed in trouble – this was nonsense and a great example of clutching at straws! If Roger couldn't explain my non performance [and I certainly couldn't] then there was no hope, I'd be on the next flight back to the UK and my flying career would be in tatters. Even so I fiddled about with my seat to satisfy Roger's fantasy, the autopilot was switched off and the whole pantomime repeated itself. Me unable to properly control the aircraft and Roger unable to explain what I was doing wrong. At this point I think all three of us knew that I was on my way to being consigned to history.

Roger decided that enough was enough. "Let's put this thing on the ground", he said, "And then we'll go and talk about it over a coffee".

I was doomed! Somehow or other I eventually managed to land this uncontrollable beast and we shut it down.

We stepped out of the simulator to make our way to the canteen for our promised coffee and my certain execution, the mood quiet and sombre. Roger no doubt wondering how he was going to break the bad news to me. Barney no doubt equally concerned as to how he was going to make the grade and me, wondering how I was going to cope with this humiliation.

The next thing that happened was that we found ourselves out of the simulator and splashing about in a sea of hydraulic oil covering the entire floor of the simulator unit! It turned out that a pipe carrying the hydraulic fluid [which operated the flight control systems and the hydraulic rams that gave the simulator its motion] had burst and dumped its life blood all over the room. I'd had no elevator control at all whilst I was trying to, ever so delicately, fly this 'very light on the controls' DC9. I'd actually been flying a brick with only the electric trim control available to me and with which I'd managed to get airborne and eventually, to get back on the ground! I felt a bit better after this technical failure had been discovered.

Saved at the eleventh hour! Once the leak had been repaired, we returned to the simulator and all was well – for all three of us. I could [after all] fly a DC9 as well as the rest of 'em! As a footnote, Roger was right – the DC9 was indeed very light on the controls!

As some pilot wag once observed of the rivalry between the two great American plane manufacturers Boeing and McDonald Douglas: – "Boeing build bombers but Douglas build fighters".

A young author at the controls of a Douglas DC 9 [Dash 32 series].

29. J.T.W.

Many of my anecdotes involve, in on way or another John Wolfe, otherwise known as J.T.W. John was one of the shareholders in British Midland and he had a very hands on approach. He was also my ultimate boss. I got on well with John but we also crossed swords on several occasions and he gave me many sleepless nights. Sadly John passed away in 2015 and I was asked by his family to give a eulogy for him at his funeral which I felt privileged to do. I reproduce it here because I like to think that it reflects the flavour of the character of the man. It also goes some way in explaining the culture and ethos that pervaded the airline:-

"In the many years that I worked for British Midland Airways and knew John, I never thought that I'd be standing to see the day when he finally ran out of fuel. Such was John's stature within British Midland that I suspect that most of us assumed that he was invincible.

As I speak, John will have arrived at that ultimate Airport Terminal Building in the sky. If I know him as well as the rest of you here today, I'd bet that he'll have got himself a prime time departure slot to get there too. He'll have somehow then jumped to the front of the immigration queue, successfully negotiated his political asylum and visa, been chauffeured to head office, in a Jaguar, and he will now be on the golf course… having first blagged himself a lifetime membership… and a permanent seat at the clubhouse bar.

To use an old cliché, John was a Marmite man… either you got on with him or you didn't. He came from the school of hard knocks, he was driven to succeed and driven to make British Midland successful.

His work rate and his stamina were little short of awesome. His eyes and ears were everywhere, he never shied away from the hard decisions and he took no prisoners. He was a hard man with whom to do business – which undoubtedly made him seem difficult on occasion – but which was also one his greatest strengths. John never asked for respect, he deservedly earned it and that respect ran across the airline and translated over to those elsewhere in the industry with whom he dealt.

He also had another, pretty unique, quality – no matter how much research you'd done before pitching an idea to him, no matter how many answers you'd prepared for the awkward questions that you knew would follow – John had an uncanny and unswerving ability to ignore all the positives and to go straight to the one aspect that you hadn't fully considered – and to which you had no ready response. Always the killer question… from a clever and intuitive mind.

John liked a game of cards. As many of us know to our cost, he wasn't, by any standards, a bad poker player. He played with a steely eye and a straight face. He gave nothing away – and he didn't very often lose. John used these same strategies in British Midland – not the gambling – but the steely eye and the straight face. You never quite knew what was coming next but whatever it was, it was always pertinent, perceptive and it was invariably a challenge. He was direct and straight talking. What you saw was what you got, and mostly, he held all the aces. He set high standards and he wanted those standards delivered – usually by yesterday – seldom easy.

Once he'd made up his mind, John was not one to be confused by the facts. On the rare occasion when you thought that he hadn't got it quite right, disagreeing with him was a fraught business and never the simplest of tasks. However, those who were brave enough to take him on, usually found that behind that tough exterior, there was another side to him: – he was always prepared to be persuaded – if the logic was there – and he had a great respect for those who were willing to try.

John was one of the three partners, Stuart Balmforth and Michael Bishop [later Sir Michael and now Lord Glendonbrook] being the other two, who, all those years ago now, took over British Midland and succeeded in transforming it from a small, provincial airline, into one that became a major force and a key player in UK aviation. Theirs was an airline with a truly international scheduled service route network, a reputation to match and one with a significant presence at Heathrow. A formidable achievement by any standards and one which took great courage, vision and fortitude. John played his full part in that evolution and he took us willingly on the roller coaster journey with him – and his fellow partners.

To John fell the responsibility of overseeing the day to day running of the airline. The integrity of its engineering and maintenance, its flying and flight operations, its ground operations and all the other aspects that made it happen, that made it tick, that kept it safe, that made it punctual, that made it appealing, that helped secure its reputation. An airline willing and able to rise to the many significant challenges along the way. Challenges created by both expansion and by recession – two distinct sides of a very sharp double edged sword – neither of which were ever easy to conquer. These were John's hunting grounds.

Whether it was overseeing a rapid expansion of the airline fleet, generated by the never ending perseverance of Sir Michael in his dealings with the political game changers, or responding to the effects of, yet another upset in the Middle East – sending fuel prices soaring, yet again – and generating another inevitable recession, John managed both within the airline, with a resolute determination, with unstinting effort and without fear or favour.

John was not one to stand on ceremony. If you fell foul of him, the subsequent interview was always short – and generally pretty one sided. As a 'victim', you didn't get to say very much in your own defence. I well remember one such occasion. I had displeased him once too often and the outcome was inevitable. He sacked me from my management position without much ceremony. Not ten minutes later, as I cleared my desk, he 'phoned me to demand a further meeting. This one in the pub, where he bought me many beers. Happily, I was rehired a few months later, John never held a grudge and he had a very human side behind that seemingly tough exterior of his.

John had an ability to recognise expertise in others. He was able to build a team of players around him who also recognised the demands and the responsibilities he faced, who were good in their own fields of expertise, who rose to the challenges – and challenged him too when necessary – and who were able to implement the solutions required, be they opportunities or reversals. The way it worked was quite simple:-

John would say "Jump".

We would say "How high?"

To which he would merely respond "Very". And people did.

Some might call such a management style autocratic. John would have disagreed. He had a more analytical approach to a problem and to its solution. He didn't do 'agonizing'. He would distil the pros and the cons of an issue until he'd boiled it down to a simple case of black and white. And then he'd act... decisively. Whether the solution was easy or difficult was never an issue for John. If it had to be done he had the chutzpah to see it carried through. That attitude, I believe, is what will generate Johns true legacy to the world of aviation and it will be how he will be remembered by all of us who worked for him, and with him.

The brand of bmi, British Midland may now no longer be around, the airline having been absorbed into British Airways. But its reputation remains hugely well respected. Its spirit – and the positive attitudes it generated – will live on for many years ahead. The tentacles of the work ethic, the expertise and the professionalism of its people, spawned and inspired by John's example and drive, have spread across the globe. Many of the World's airlines now have ex British Midland people in senior positions and many of these people learned their skills in British Midland at the hand of J.T.W. and his appointed lieutenants.

John was a key player in an airline that grew to change the face of British aviation. He's up there on the Pantheon with the rest of the greats in the airline business. To his partners, to the airline and to its staff, John provided the real 'Diamond Service'.

To Jo and the family we say "Be very proud".

To J.T.W himself we say simply:– "We salute you John. They were the best of days".

30. When Airport Security lost the Plot

Immediately after 911 the world of aviation changed very significantly. Incidentally 911 is either a German motor car made by Mr. Porsche or a date in November. What it most certainly is not is a date in September. Not on this, the civilised side of the pond anyway. That aside, airport security was, not surprisingly, pretty sensitive – too often almost to the point of absurdity. The day after the horrors of the event itself for example, such was the heightened awareness that we airline pilots were stopped from flying if we had so much as a bank card in our pockets – difficult if you were about to launch off on a two or three day trip, or longer, away to somewhere foreign!

Anyway, a few weeks after this new [and ever evolving] 'Post 911' regime of airport security came into play I was rostered to fly our early morning 7.30 a.m. scheduled service from Teesside [Yorkshire] to Heathrow. Teesside Airport is a lovely little provincial airfield with a pleasant and uncomplicated terminal and it was never very busy at all. In fact, ours was the only airliner on the apron first thing in the morning and the only scheduled service departure due out so nothing was likely to be too arduous with the check in process – or so you would think!

As usual myself [and crew] arrived an hour before our due departure time in order to complete our initial flight planning work before then venturing out to our aircraft – via the security process – the same as that to which our passengers were subjected – to continue our pre-flight preparation on board. We joined the queue at security and awaited our turn at the x-ray machines for both man and baggage.

Our crew that morning were all based at East Midlands [Leicestershire] so had spent the previous night in the airport hotel,

The George, which had originally been the Officers Mess in its previous life when the airport was first built for the RAF in WW2.

My overnight bag sent the x-ray machine into panic mode and so I was asked to present it for inspection. The Security Officer rummaged about, pulled out my wash bag, opened it up and triumphantly produced a pair of nail clippers.

"You can't carry these clippers through Captain", he said, 'They're dangerous'.

Somewhat taken aback I paused, for a moment rather lost for words. Half of me thought that he was winding me up but the other half disagreed. This security man looked more like a 'jobsworth' traffic warden type than he did any kind of comedian. Standing there in my full Captain's uniform, gold braid et al, with a now attentive audience of passengers queued up behind me and somewhat annoyed with Jobsworth, I decided to play hardball:-

"Well", says I, "I'm not prepared to hand over my clippers and I'm not leaving without them. If you really think they're dangerous call your supervisor over so that we can escalate the debate to a higher, more sensible, level".

"I am the supervisor!" responded Jobsworth [rather too smartly I thought] and with a very smug expression on his face. Stalemate.

"In which case", I said, "I have to repeat that I will not be leaving here without my clippers. I have at my disposal a forty ton guided missile, capable of speeds somewhat in excess of 600 miles an hour, which I can navigate to an accuracy of 2 feet. I can deliver it – and 11 tons of explosive kerosene – anywhere I wish. I do not need a pair of nail clippers to make a nuisance of myself! If this flight is delayed by your petty mindedness, questions will be asked and you will have to stand to account for your actions".

Jobsworth hesitated for a second and then he capitulated. With smug satisfaction now no doubt showing across my face, I departed to our aeroplane, in tandem with both nail clippers and a feeling of well being.

Thirty minutes later, with passengers now on board and all checks complete, we were just waiting for the final bits of necessary paperwork to appear before departing when bounding up the stairs and into the flight deck came Mr. Jobsworth, the security man. This time he was acting as a courier and was carrying a rather fancy leather bound box.

"Excuse me Captain", he said, "But can you carry this box down to London? It belongs to one of your passengers".

"What is it?", said I.

"Tools of the trade", Jobsworth advised, "He's a chef and we confiscated this from him at security".

I opened the box. Inside was a full set of very sharp, and obviously very expensive, shiny kitchen knives, ranging from about 4 inches in length through to the full Monty carving knife at 10 inches or so. There was also a heavy meat cleaver in the set! Given the fact that we'd clashed over 'dangerous' items only thirty minutes earlier, I could hardly believe the brass neck of the man! How did he reconcile giving me a whole set of kitchen knives on the flight deck when he'd been trying to confiscate my nail clippers only minutes before!?

We carry, amongst other things, an axe in the flight deck. This is provided to help us hack through tangled metal, etc., in the event of not being able to open the door after a bit of an accident [I've always thought that this was a very pessimistic provision, thought up by some 'expert' somewhere!]. The closest I ever came to using this 'axe of pessimism' was now. With as much contempt as I could muster, I slowly and deliberately addressed Jobsworth:-

"You see that axe down there?", I said, pointing to the axe stowed behind the co-pilot's seat. He nodded. "If you don't get out of my flight deck right now I'm going to bury it in your jolly head!!"

He fled.

Of course I took the chef's knives down to London with us. I never saw Jobsworth again – but I still have my nail clippers and I dare say that my passenger chef produced some good food – and never knew the story behind how close he came to losing the tools of his trade!

31. A Life Changing Trip

Sometimes the stories aren't so funny and the flying element of the tale is merely incidental to the main event.

The Berlin Wall came down in November 1989, marking the end of the so called 'Cold War' and the resumption of open access for travel between East and West for the first time since probably the Russian Revolution. Not too long after the re-opening of borders we had a one off charter flight to take a group of American Jews to Krakow in Poland so that they could visit relatives and a homeland they'd not seen, presumably since they or their relatives had managed to escape from the country circa 1939 or thereabouts.

I was the Captain assigned for this trip. In those days charter flights were not permissible from Heathrow so we had to position the aircraft [empty] from Heathrow to Luton where our passengers would join us. In the meantime these self same passengers flew into Heathrow from the good old US of A and then, all eighty five of them, came up to Luton by coach, or rather two coaches. I expect we watched their inbound Pan Am flight land at Heathrow as we queued for take-off at the end of the runway to go to Luton! You couldn't make it up, no wonder we now have a global climate change crisis! From Luton we flew out to Poland where we would be staying in a hotel in Krakow for two nights whilst our customers went about what would no doubt be an emotional 36 hours of making up for lost time and re-visiting a painful history.

Eastern Europe was now beginning to emerge from years of Soviet repression but it hadn't yet had much time to start clawing its way back into the second half of the 20th century of Western society. Krakow was then the most bleak and desolate concrete jungle I think I'd ever seen. Every building was just an anonymous grey concrete block, with grey doors, grey windows and grey everything. If Poland had been given paint during the Soviet occupation it had been made available in any colour that the proletariat wanted, as long as it was grey. I don't remember seeing any trees as our taxi took us to the hotel but if there were any they must have been grey too.

Our hotel was no different from the rest of the city. Another grey building in another grey part of a grey town. It was hardly any more welcoming inside in terms of either decor or amenities but at least the staff were friendly and some of them even spoke English which, for some reason, was mildly surprising to us. We had a night to spend here, followed by a full day and then a further night. We had a grey evening meal in a grey dining room in our grey hotel, there was no point in going out as there was nowhere to go.

As I put my head on my grey pillow in my grey room I wondered what on earth we were going to do to occupy ourselves for a full day tomorrow in this featureless, colourless place with no cafes, no restaurants, no shops, no entertainment and not even, seemingly, any historic buildings, churches, museums, etc, apparent anywhere that might keep us busy for even an hour or two, never mind occupy us for the full day in front of us.

I awoke the next morning without much enthusiasm for the day ahead. This was surely going to be one of the most boring days I'd ever spend in all the stopovers I'd experience in my entire flying career. We'd arranged to meet up as a complete crew for breakfast and to discuss what we might do with our time for the day. I wandered over to the reception desk to ask – without much hope of any positive suggestions being forthcoming – what distractions Krakow might have to offer.

Sure enough, I was not disappointed. As we all know, these days every hotel in every town in every country is stuffed full of leaflets designed to entice tourists to one local attraction or another. Not so in Poland in 1990. I was met with a shrug of the shoulders and a few 'errs' and 'ums' before the receptionist finally said: – "You can always go to Auschwitz if you like".

Auschwitz? I'm not sure that back then I even knew that Auschwitz was in Poland, far less that it was near Krakow. Even so, it wasn't exactly at the top of my bucket list of places to visit and it certainly hadn't crossed my mind that it would be an option on this trip. There didn't seem to be much else on offer so it looked like it was going to be Auschwitz or nothing. I reported back to the rest of our little entourage. Like me, they displayed the same lack of awareness and the same level of enthusiasm for the project. However, the general consensus was that as Auschwitz seemed to be the only game in town we would go.

I ordered a taxi for us from reception and we set off. Auschwitz, unsurprisingly, is not that close to Krakow. In fact it's quite a long way out of town and no doubt, quite deliberately, was built not near anywhere.

I've had some pretty lively taxi rides in my life from some of the worlds' most notoriously bad drivers: – Greece, Belgium, Cyprus, Vietnam, India, Uganda, Mexico, Italy, to name but a few. However this journey turned out to be probably the worst white knuckle taxi ride I've ever experienced anywhere on the globe. Our Polish chauffeur must have thought that his was the only car in existence in the entire country. He used both sides of the road, clipping the apex of every corner we came to like a formula one racing driver, quite perfectly, left or right, it made no difference. Traffic lights, cross roads, give way signs? They were all studiously and routinely ignored – as were my exhortations for him to slow down – he spoke no English and my Polish was as good as his driving. He can't have been all that wrong though as we didn't meet anyone coming the other way and we finally arrived at our destination in one piece and unscathed, even if somewhat unnerved.

I can't now remember the detail of how the Holocaust was seen in the '80s and early '90s. Certainly we knew about it and about concentration camps too but I don't think there was the same wider knowledge and public exposure that prevails today. Looking back, the more immediate and higher profile public debate about prejudice and bigotry at that time, I seem to remember, was apartheid and the focus of Nelson Mandela as the champion of Freedom in South Africa. Now that we've had 30 years or more of access and exposure to these dreadful places in Eastern Europe I think people probably have a better idea of what to expect when they visit these concentration camps and of what went on in them.

For me this single day, which had started so casually and with so little thought or concern, this visit to Auschwitz, originally designed simply to pass the time, was to turn out to offer one of the most profound and salutary experiences of my life. I don't remember ever being so moved, before or since, than I was by what I saw and experienced that day.

The detail of what went on at Auschwitz and the other camps are now quite well known and are often described, or even shown, in articles and through television documentaries. But in 1990, as we toured around this camp, much of it was new to us and all of it was shocking in the extreme.

I was particularly awed by the scale of the place and the detail of the planning that was applied to its' construction. Serried rows of barrack blocks, each entered through an etched glass panelled door, with an etched glass panel above each of these doors announcing the nationality of the occupants; German Jews, Austrian Jews, French Jews, Italian Jews, etc. What sick mind could sink to that kind of perverted detail and have it first designed and then manufactured and then, finally, built into each door?

Especially moving was each central corridor of these barrack blocks. The Nazis had been particularly Teutonic in their efficiency at keeping records and had taken photographs of each and every prisoner entering the camp. Post war, the Russians [who had 'liberated' Auschwitz] had preserved some of the camp and had turned it into a museum. They had then lined the corridor walls of these barrack blocks with thousands of photographs of the victims of the camp and its atrocities, row upon row of them. What was particularly moving was the fact that as we walked down various of these central corridors the sun shone on the glass of the photos and revealed lip mark imprints of relatives who had embraced these pictures of loved ones whom they had lost. All that was left of them – fathers, brothers, mothers, sons, daughters, cousins, et al.

I stood in front of a particular brick built wall between two of these blocks where prisoners, having first been made to strip naked, were then made to queue up in line to stand in front of the wall, in pairs, to be shot. Some 6,000 people were said to have been executed in this way. Mans capacity for evil to his neighbour screamed at me and pierced my very soul.

There was no redeeming feature at this desolate place. It was a sunny spring day but there was no bird song, no spring flowers, no colour, no warmth, no grass and no trees. The only signs of life were the smell of a fetid cancer of depravity that lurked in every corner along with the bent and broken ghosts of the shuffling victims imprisoned in this empty desert. The only view was of barbed wire and railway lines, gas chambers, barrack blocks and desolation, lined up like rotten teeth in a mouth full of halitosis.

There was much more I saw and much more that I could describe but none of it is new all these years later. In 1990 the general knowledge was there but seeing the detail was a huge and sickening shock, to me anyway. How anyone can claim that Auschwitz [and the other camps] are the product of mere propaganda defies all credibility. Equally, I find it hard to accept the line that the good and the great knew nothing about it until after the event. The scale, the meticulous planning, the detail, the numbers of people needed to design, to manufacture, to police, to patrol, to operate this vast and efficient factory of death, the tentacles spawned by these camps reaching out into each of the occupied European countries, all these factors expose the weakness of that defence.

That people survived this carefully manufactured hell and then went on to live a full and happy life is testament of true courage and fortitude. That many even found it in their hearts to forgive their oppressors is a demonstration that not all humanity is evil – but these people are better men and women than I, a mere second hand spectator with an easy way out. That generosity of spirit would have been way beyond me had I had any direct involvement.

All of us who visited Auschwitz on that day were affected, as I'm sure are all who visited before us and after, have been. There was little banter in our taxi on the way back to the hotel.

I can write about this experience because I sit alone, but to this day I still cannot speak about it without showing profound emotion. And I was only there for a few hours and all the time with the knowledge that I had a time and a place to rendezvous with my taxi to take me away. How anyone could endure that place as an inmate, knowing that there was no way out, was then and remains now, quite beyond my powers of comprehension.

Having been exposed to the detail of this architecture of death and the meticulous fashion of its construction – by many skilled and evil minds – I made a resolution that has stayed with me ever since. If those poor victims could endure Auschwitz, knowing the horrors of what lay ahead for them and that they could do nothing about their fate, then I would have no need to worry about anything ever again. My problems could only ever be insignificant by comparison.

It has been a creed that has served me well [even if I've sometimes broken it!]. As I said, some of my stories have no real connection to aviation – and are not especially amusing.

32. Playing Away

One of our more senior Management pilots – to be christened 'Rob' for the purpose of this story – was an incorrigible individual when it came to accommodating the young ladies. He had a track record second to none in this regard and was well known throughout the airline for his weakness and his ever roving eye.

The extraordinary aspect of this instinctive trait in Rob, which clearly rendered him incapable of helping himself – was that he had a record of almost infinite success with these self same [and otherwise worldly wise] eligible young ladies. This, despite the fact that his antics were more than well understood by our female cabin crew – who were all anyway wise to the predatory attitudes and wandering hands of too many pilots. As a consequence of this, there was hardly ever a trip away where Rob failed to suitably impress one or other of the female contingent of his crew. His good looks and suave charm were seemingly too much for the natural female inhibitions of those he seduced to resist. To be fair to all, the art of seduction was made more easy for Rob's type by the very nature of the job of being a pilot.

Every time he strapped himself into an aeroplane and took off into the wild blue yonder, he carried with him a bevy of beautiful women. At the end of the day's work there was always a hotel in which to stay – provided and paid for by the company, there was invariably a bar in the hotel [as often as not providing subsidised drinks to aircrew]. There was, in most cases too, a swimming pool, warm weather and sunshine. Back in those days there was also almost always plenty of time off 'down route' in which to visit the sights, laze around and generally to relax and get to know your fellow travellers.

Throw in a good looking, red blooded male, equipped with a smart uniform, all the right patter and a double bedroom [paid for by the company] and what could go wrong? – it was all manna from heaven if you were that way inclined. Throw in an attractive lady of similar disposition [and there were many] and the sparks would soon fly. Suddenly there was no spare minute and no boring interlude for the entire trip. Once back at base it was a case of 'butter wouldn't melt' and 'what went on tour, stayed on tour'. And everyone understood the rules and the protocols.

Thus Rob happily navigated his way through life, working hard and playing harder. Rob did have a little problem though and his problem was that he was already married. Not only was he married, he'd been married before, this marriage was second time round. More significantly, Rob had met his current wife whilst he was flying. She too had been working as cabin crew and so she knew only too well how the system worked, what her husband was like, how he behaved when he was away and so she kept a close eye on him.

To further compound matters, Marie was also a formidable lady in her own right, she could give it out just as well as take it and Rob knew only too well that he'd be in very deep doodoo if he ever got caught out being a naughty boy. Rob always therefore, took great care to ensure that there were never any telltale signs of shenanigans when he arrived back home from a trip. His tracks were always carefully covered and he was a seasoned expert in this dark art.

As ever with such subterfuge, there was going to come a day when the inevitable happened and the whole facade of Rob's impression of leading an honest and upright life whilst away from home would crumble. His carefully constructed persona as the ever loving husband, with eyes only for his beloved wife would all be snatched away from him in the blink of an eye. Rob would be cruelly exposed as a philandering no hoper and he would be left only with his lack of morality nakedly visible to all – and most especially to his wife, whom he feared more than anything, or anyone, else.

It all finally went horribly wrong when Rob was away flying a particular trip to some far off land. As usual Rob had carefully briefed Marie as to when he'd be back home. His mistake was that he hadn't checked that Marie had made a note of this date in her diary.

He'd been gone four or five days when he was finally exposed. The good Marie couldn't remember what date Rob had told her that he'd be back home from this specific cycle of work. She needed to know in order to make some plans to suit their domestic agenda. As she'd got nothing written in her diary to tell her when her ever loving husband would return, Marie did the sensible thing and she telephoned the company to find out when he'd be back. Once put through to our Crewing Department she asked the question. The conversation was fairly brief: —

"Hi", she said. "Marie here, when does Rob get back from his trip?".

"Just a minute Marie, let me have a look…[pause to rustling of paper]…er,… he got back yesterday" came the reply!

"I see, OK. Thanks". And with that – and in icy silence – Marie hung up.

Oh dear, poor Rob was at last undone. All that work and effort invested in the subterfuge and the deceit – over so long and now all to no avail. Rob had been caught and well and truly hoist by his own petard and – best of all – he didn't even yet know it! Marie now had ample time to prepare her dish of revenge, to be served very cold [except that it wasn't!].

What had actually happened was that Rob had indeed landed the previous day, back at Stansted. However, before he'd left home he'd told Marie that he wouldn't be back until a day later. This was the bit of the jigsaw that Marie had missed and Rob hadn't properly secured. His reason for this economy with the truth was because he had a 'friend' who lived near Stansted and he'd planned to visit the lady in question, a previous but still interested conquest, on his way back home for a bit of 'rest and recuperation' and to spend the night [as merely 'a guest' you understand]. This time it was one lie too many. He had no idea that Marie hadn't made a note of his return and had called the company to ask the question – he was clearly getting careless! The chickens were now soon to be coming home to roost.

Bright and early on the fateful morning Rob disentangled himself from his temporary host, made his excuses, dressed in his uniform and drove home. He arrived a couple of hours later, parked on his drive and marched up to his front door – fully regaled in his pilots uniform, dapper as ever, and carrying a couple of plastic bags with his 'duty free' goodies inside – acting just as though he was fresh off his flight back into the UK and had driven straight up the motorway from work. He was just about to insert his front door key into the Yale lock when the door opened in front of him and there stood Marie – with a face like thunder. She looked Rob straight in the eye and said, with as much menace as she could muster [which was quite a lot]:-

"Why didn't you come home yesterday?".

Suddenly Rob knew the awful truth – he had been undone. He didn't know how, or when, or by whom or even on what scale. He just knew that he'd been well and truly kippered, the facade had crumbled. For once Rob was rendered completely lost for words. Marie just stared and remained silent, waiting for an answer that wouldn't come. Eventually he spoke. His reply was the most pathetic, weak, unimaginative, stupid and meaningless response ever given by anyone caught out as he had been. He simply said, in a very forlorn and small voice, not even worthy of a young schoolboy having been caught out scrumping apples:-

"I forgot!"

That was the best that he could muster. You couldn't come up with anything either more pathetic – or more hilarious, than that mouse like admission of guilt – wonderful!

But it didn't end there. Rob, having had a long trip away, burning the candle at both ends throughout, had then returned back to the UK for a further night of activity and not a lot of sleep. He'd then driven up from Stansted to the Midlands and was now in great need of his bed. Marie announced that this was fine, he could sleep for as long as he wanted. However, she said, just as soon as he was in full deep slumber she would be boiling the kettle. She would then pour its contents over the entirety of his wandering bits. Marie was not one for making idle threats and Rob knew that he could not now go to bed.

Happily Marie forgave her wandering husband. He, in turn, learned his lesson and the pair of them ended up with a close and enduring marriage that was to last for the rest of their days.

33. The Broken Window.

British Midland Airways, or BMI as it was to become known, was a company run on pretty autocratic lines. Certainly managers had discretion and a degree of autonomy, as in any other organisation, but this independence only went so far. When one of the shareholders issued an instruction there was no discussion and a manager who questioned such a dictate usually had a fairly limited lifespan, however well intentioned the intervention.

The co-owner who oversaw the operational side of the airline was John Wolfe. He was a complex – and much feared character. He worked all Gods hours, had spies everywhere, and had an unswerving ability to sniff out any problem, almost before those responsible even knew that the problem existed. In short, he was a clever man and he seldom took any prisoners once he felt he'd been let down. John's approach was all well and good but the trouble was that he wasn't always right and neither was he a pilot or an engineer. This meant that he didn't always understand the complexities that surrounded the business of flying aeroplanes but it didn't stop him getting involved in the detail of technical flying issues. Very much a case of a little knowledge being a dangerous thing.

I was in my office one winters afternoon when I had a call advising that one of our flights from London to Edinburgh was diverting into East Midlands Airport with a cracked windscreen. This was no problem in itself and East Midlands was a pretty good place for one of our aeroplanes to divert to because we had a big maintenance facility there. It would be easy to replace the screen without too much trouble and to also conjure up a replacement aircraft pretty quickly to minimise the resulting delay.

I knew that John would want an account of the detail of this little incident – it would cause a delay and also cost money – both issues that were close to his heart and for which he would demand censure if there was any culpability. I decided to go up to the Airport and meet the crew flying the aircraft in and to inspect the cracked screen for myself so that I would be fully equipped with all the information required at the inevitable inquest the next morning.

The first thing I noticed when I went into the flight deck was the co-pilots windscreen [the main right hand front screen]. Usually when a windscreen breaks merely a couple of hairline cracks appear, rather like a stone chip in a car window that then grows. This screen however was hardly recognisable as a windscreen at all, it was completely opaque. I'd seen a few cracked screens in my time and had had a few fail whilst I was flying myself but I'd never seen one shatter in the way that this one had.

Aircraft windscreens are laminated – just like a car screen – only they are much more substantial and they're heated to stop condensation or ice forming. On most aircraft types it's acceptable to have a crack in the inner pane of glass but not in the outer – but this presents a problem, especially when the screen cracks and you're up at 30,000ft. Firstly, it's very hard, if not impossible, to tell which bit of the screen it is that's broken, inner or outer pane? Secondly, if you don't know which half of the sandwich is at fault you won't be able to work out whether or not you'll be able to operate the next flight without first having it fixed. Thirdly, if the screen is cracked you have to switch off the screen heating system which means that if you get condensation or ice building up you'll have to carry out your landing using only Braille – which is not a good idea and has seldom proved successful.

There was a fourth issue with this particular screen too. Had I been the co-pilot on this flight I would not have wanted to be sitting three feet behind this window for more than one minute longer than was necessary. I would have wanted the thing back on the ground a.s.a.p. – never mind any of these fine niceties about inner or outer panes of glass or anything else. The preservation of my good looking face would have been significantly more important to me than any other consideration. Besides which, this winters evening was normal for Scotland – poor visibility with low cloud full of ice and rain. Not a smart place to be in an aeroplane when looking for the end of a runway through a blanket of condensation and thick ice.

I had a chat with the two pilots, I forget now who the co-pilot was but he was flying with a captain called Peter, a very pleasant individual and a more than competent airline captain. I came away perfectly happy with the way they'd handled their problem and with the actions they'd taken, it was operationally and logistically the right thing to do. More importantly, given the visual state of the screen and the weather prevailing in Scotland, it was the safe and prudent thing to do.

I was not much surprised to receive the call bright and early the next morning from John Wolfe's secretary, the great man wanted to see me. I was pretty sure I knew the reason why and I had all the necessary answers. Immediately I set eyes on him though I knew I was in for a rough ride. Absent was the usual friendly greeting I [mostly] received from John. Instead he wore his other look, the one that told me he was displeased, that he had smelled something bad, that he had made up his mind [in advance of having all the facts] and that he was going to demand that blood be spread on the walls. Once John had adopted that kind of perspective it was always difficult [and dangerous] to diverge from his view. To do so meant that you were likely to get caught in the crossfire.

I was not wrong. He launched into an attack on Peter, the captain of last night's windscreen damaged aeroplane. It was an inner panel that had failed and that was allowable, [he'd checked this with the engineers, he said]. Why had the captain diverted , he should have carried on? The weather at the Scottish end wasn't that bad, the freezing level was at 1,000ft, etc, etc. I listened with sinking heart. There was a fork in the road looming ahead and I would have a binary choice to make, turn left or turn right. Either I adopted John's stance and pilloried Peter – unfair but at least I'd come out of it with a whole skin. Or, I defended Peter – fair but I would probably become a casualty as a consequence, along with Peter.

I explained my perspective to John and said that I'd make further enquiries and get back to him before any final decision was made. This wasn't particularly well received and it was clear I'd already put myself on sticky ground. I beat a hasty retreat before I'd dug a bigger hole for myself.

But what to do next, how was I going to get Peter off this hook and retain my own skin at the same time? I made a positive decision and that was to make no decision, I sat on my hands whilst I ruminated. In the meantime poor old Peter was half pilloried anyway, his immediate line manager had no option other than to send him on gardening leave until John Wolfe's wrath was quelled.

After a couple of days I had a bright idea. I phoned our engineering people and asked them if they still had the damaged screen that they'd replaced a couple of nights ago? Yes they had, they said. Could they please bring it down to my office [about 5 miles from our engineering base at the airport]? They weren't too happy with this request but I was insistent. When the screen arrived a couple of hours later I understood their reluctance to move it.

I'd been looking through aircraft windscreens for twenty years or more but had never before realised just how big these things are when not in situ. They're enormous, at least half the size of a big front door. Not only that, they're incredibly thick, at least 3 inches [7.5cms if you're a Remainer] which makes them incredibly heavy too. Anyway, two engineers staggered into my office carrying this screen.

"Where do you want it?" they asked.

I hadn't expected it to be so big and hadn't made any room especially available for it. I glanced around the office seeking a suitable spot.

"Lean it up behind the door" I said.

Depositing the screen behind the door hadn't been a part of my master plan but it was to prove beneficial. They deposited the screen as requested and left. I called John.

"Have you got five minutes John?" I asked.

"Yes" he said, "Pop down". John's office was only a few yards along the corridor from mine – he liked to have his lieutenants close by.

"No", I said, "I need you to come to my office, I've got something to show you". It wasn't very often that John was summonsed to anyone else's office, he didn't do 'taking orders' but his curiosity was aroused and he duly appeared a couple of minutes later.

My office door opened inwards and as John entered the door shielded the windscreen from his view. "What have you got to show me?" he queried – the tone being "This better be good, I don't take kindly to being told what to do"

"Ah", I responded, "Shut the door and all will be revealed!" I could almost hear the grinding of his teeth as he registered this second instruction, even so, he complied.

The screen was revealed, enormous, leaning up against the wall and totally opaque, no wall to be seen through it. John stared but said nothing.

"That was Peter's problem", I said, "Can you tell which side of it is the broken pane"?

John remained silent for a second or two longer but he didn't touch either side of the glass. Finally he simply said:-

"I see what you mean now".

And that was the end of that. Honour restored all round.

I'm not sure that Peter ever received an apology for having his actions questioned. I suspect not and I've always rather regretted that I didn't speak to him about the ins and outs behind it all myself – but the next time I was in the office where the pilot's records were kept I did make a point of removing all reference to his alleged 'offence' from his file.

34. Airport Evacuation

One of my jobs for a while as a pilot manager was to run the pilot base at East Midlands Airport [EMA]. This required overseeing all aspects that related to the pilot community there and all the elements that went into achieving a smooth – and safe – operation of the flying programme. By and large this wasn't too much of an onerous task. The base at that time was not particularly big. We had around a dozen aircraft there comprising a few remaining Douglas DC9 jets, half a dozen or so Fokker F70 and F100 jets, and a smattering of ATP turbo prop aircraft. This eclectic collection required some 60 crews – or 120 pilots so everyone pretty much knew everyone else.

The routes we flew were pretty stable, the destination airports were generally familiar to the crews and East Midlands airport itself was not too busy so the flying was not over complicated either. I also had a few other management responsibilities, a fair amount of liaison work to be done between ourselves and other agencies – Air Traffic Control, National Air Traffic Services, the EMA airport authorities, Security, etc, etc, but mostly the base ran reasonably smoothly. As far as the pilots were concerned it was rather like being a paid member of a big and glorified flying club.

My modus operandi was to not try and fix things if they weren't broken and to not give the pilots a hard time if I could reasonably avoid it. If I could improve anything I'd try and achieve that improvement – but if an improvement was going to cost money it could seldom be achieved unless I could demonstrate a cost benefit to the company as well – however much the pilots might moan and groan about whatever the problem was.

On the basis that it's not possible to hunt with the horses and run with the hounds at the same time the pilots and I had an unwritten contract – if they turned up when they were supposed to, did their jobs properly, kept their heads below the parapet and didn't give me a hard time, then I'd leave them alone to get on with it and I'd scratch their backs for them when I could. This seemed to work well and we all rubbed along together quite well with few issues and little friction between workforce and management.

'Few issues', of course, didn't mean any issues. There was the odd occasion when I had to get out of bed and do some work in that context. I particularly remember one or two of those occasions, this one involving airport security.

The problem arose because the Airport Authority moved the normal entry/exit point through which aircrew accessed the terminal building from the aircraft parking apron. They had informed everyone except those in the respective airlines using the Airport who dealt with aircrew matters. As a direct consequence of this neither I, nor our pilots, knew about these new arrangements.

Come the day of the changeover, as our crews returned to base from their days work, there was lots of head scratching when they found that the door they normally used to gain entry to the Terminal was firmly locked against them. All used their initiative and worked round the problem by asking the first ground staff member they met [who were all aware of the change] how they could get out. All that is, except for a certain Captain Chaz and his co-pilot, Paul.

Chaz was a bit of a character. I'm not sure exactly what his actual background was but he liked to give the impression that he was a distinctly ex-military man. He walked with a ramrod straight back and was always immaculately turned out. His uniform shoes were only black in the darkest of rooms, the rest of the time they reflected so much of any light that was available that one was almost blinded by their brilliance. His trouser creases were sharp enough to cut a wedding cake and he wore his uniform hat like the archetypal Regimental

Sergeant Major. Chaz was also possessed of a somewhat short and volatile temperament. It wasn't too difficult to wind him up and set him off – at which point his complexion would burn bright red and he exuded so much explosive energy that you could have boiled a kettle on him if he'd stood still. For all that, he was a good pilot, his foibles were tolerated and he was popular with his peer group. His co-pilot, Paul, was an affable character of Scandinavian origin, was extremely laid back and another well liked and good pilot.

Anyway, having finished a short day's work, these two disembarked their aircraft to go home at around 10 a.m. This was one the busiest times of the day at the airport with waves of aircraft landing back from their first sorties before then departing again on their next rotations.

Chaz, with Paul at his shoulder, found himself thwarted in his ability to exit by the usual door, now locked. Not being one to be defeated, Chaz pulled and pushed in an effort to free the obstruction. The door wouldn't yield. Rather than then seek assistance, as had all others who'd gone before, Chaz kept attacking. He shoved and pushed with more determination and with growing strength as his anger grew. The door eventually gave up the unequal struggle and yielded to his insistence.

Three things then happened simultaneously. The door opened, the Airport Security alarm system went off and our two brave pilots walked through door, then through the terminal and then on out to the car park and from there onward and upward to their respective homes.

The consequence of the door being forced open was that the Terminal Building was evacuated due to the alarm sounding. Inevitably, that of course led to the whole of the Airport operation grinding to a halt. It wasn't long before it was established that the trigger for the alarm was the forced door but it took a good while before it was evident that no terrorist activity had taken place. It was at least an hour before order was finally restored and the terminal was again re-opened.

The first I heard of this was when I received a phone call from a very irate Airport Director. He gave me the background and demanded that this crew's heads be served on a silver platter. I told him that I hadn't been advised myself that the system had been changed so hadn't told our crews and he then became even more angry. When I asked him which aircraft the offending crew had disembarked from he couldn't tell me. I pointed out that we'd had roughly half a dozen aircraft landing at about that time of day and it wouldn't be easy to track the culprits down but I'd see what I could do. [Bear in mind that at this stage I had no idea who the culprits were].

I was actually quite amused by the whole episode. It was inexcusable for the Airport management people not to advise the operational side of their customer airlines that they were making this change so it sort of served them right that it went horribly wrong for them. The downside was that it disrupted a lot of flights and a lot of people, including our own passengers. Further, Chaz was clearly not enjoying his finest hour when he decided to attack the door like an SAS commando on manoeuvres in enemy territory.

How was I going to track down this miscreant crew? It was pretty obvious that asking for the offenders to step forward was unlikely to produce a positive result, no self respecting person would volunteer to put their neck in a noose. A more subtle approach was called for. I pondered for a good while about this and eventually came up with a strategy that might just work.

I wrote a memo to all the pilots [these went out by e-mail so receipt by all was pretty instantaneous]. I briefed the crews of the new arrangements for access to the terminal and briefly described the incident that had occurred that morning. I then went on to say that I wanted to see the offenders in my office at 0900hrs tomorrow [or receive a phone call from them if they were flying early] on pain of severe sanction. I further advised that I had clear CCTV footage that showed the entire incident unfolding at the door. I therefore knew who they were and they knew who they were. Non attendance was not an option [needless to say, no CCTV actually existed but my audience didn't know this!].

At 0900hrs tomorrow morning two po-faced and embarrassed pilots appeared in my office. Bingo, sometimes a plan comes together! I briefed them to tell anyone who asked that they'd both had a monumental rollicking and I then sent them on their way rejoicing. I phoned the Airport Director and briefed him likewise. And that was the end of that.

35. The Reluctant Car Park Barrier.

I had a similar clash with the same Airport Director on another occasion, again a security issue was at the heart of it all. This time the problem was centred around Staff Car Parking.

Years ago airport staff were treated quite well in this respect. Before airports became as busy as they now are and before space for parking became constrained, we were looked after quite well and afforded a level of priority and respect which delivered dedicated parking close to the terminal buildings from which we operated. As the industry expanded however, we found ourselves slipping further and further down the V.I.P. list until we aircrew types eventually fell off it and joined the ranks of the also rans. We were forever being shunted further and further away from our places of work and into to ever more remote areas, requiring longer and longer walks in wind and rain alike, to start our days toils. We also ended up having to have stickers on our car windscreens and swipe passes to get into and out of the staff car parks.

We were given notice by the Airport [who ran and administered car parking] of yet another parking change. The car park was to inevitably move to an even more distant part of the airfield as from Monday next week. We were assured however that there would be no change to the entry/exit system, the same passes as currently issued to aircrew would continue to operate the new barriers. All fine and dandy – one would have thought.

And so it was. None of our aircrew had any trouble accessing the car park on the day of the switch over. All that is, until Murray, one of our pilots on an early shift, turned up to report for work at circa 0630 in the morning. Murray swiped his pass through the reader at the barrier controlled entry and waited for the barrier to rise. It didn't move [of course] so he tried again, and then a third time and then several more times, still nothing. Eventually he got out of his car, thumped the barrier mechanism to try and wake it up, then he tried swiping again. Nothing. He tried the same trick again but this time, in order to try and spark the barrier into life, he also attempted to push it up at the same time. He got a positive result at last but not quite the one he'd intended. This time, as Murray tried to force up the barrier it snapped off altogether at its base and he was left holding a long red and white striped pole, looking somewhat perplexed, surprised and rather like an old fashioned barber outside his shop.

Undaunted, Murray proceeded to park his car and then make the ten minute walk up to the company offices in the terminal building. He told me later that by the time he arrived at the terminal he was running somewhat late for his report time and so didn't have time to advise Airport Security of his little argument with their equipment. His intention therefore, was to do so when he got back from his flying detail at lunchtime. This seemed quite reasonable to me.

Almost as soon as I'd arrived in my office that morning the phone rang, with I'm sure more urgency than normal. I lifted the receiver to be greeted by a veritable tirade of anger from my friend the Airport Director. He was apoplectic with rage as he recounted the story – which had all really been captured on CCTV this time. He therefore had all the evidence available, including the car registration and the pilots name. He accused Murray of out and out wanton vandalism, said he was going to have him prosecuted as well as sue him for the damage caused to the barrier. He also said that he was going to confiscate Murray's 'Airside Pass'. This last bit was a serious threat. Airports issued these passes to customer company employees who required access to the aircraft parking apron. Without a pass Murray would not have been able to fly as he'd not be allowed 'airside' to reach his aircraft.

I tried everything I could over the phone to calm down the overwrought Airport Director but he would not be moved. He remained resolute that he was intent on carrying through with his threats and the more I tried to reason with him the more irrational he became. I was achieving nothing that was constructive by continuing this conversation, it was time to get off the phone. I told him that I'd speak to the offending pilot when he returned to East Midlands later that day, as this was the first I'd heard about the incident. I'd then get back to him as soon as I'd done so.

I left a message for Murray to come and see me as soon as he'd landed, which he did. Murray was a perfectly decent chap and made of all the right ingredients. He was pleasant, personable, had a good sense of humour, was a good pilot who got on well with his peer group and he'd previously never found himself in any kind of trouble with the airline. Murray was a bit of a social animal too but was far from being the kind of individual who would lose his temper with a malfunctioning barrier and then deliberately smash it up in a fit of pique.

Murray gave me his side of the story – which was perfectly rational, reasonable and believable – the bottom line being that he'd most certainly not deliberately broken the barrier, he'd merely been trying to coax it into life when it broke. He further said that he'd already reported the incident to the Security Office on his way over to see me and had offered to make good the cost of any damage caused.

I was actually quite amused by the story. Knowing Murray as I did, I knew that it was an unfortunate accident and that he would have been horrified to have caused any damage. I could just picture the look of dismay on his face when he found himself suddenly holding on to nothing more than a red and white striped pole at six thirty in the morning. It was Faulty Towers clumsy humour stuff – or would have been if Mr. Airport Director had had any sense of proportion. Satisfied with Murray's explanation, and the fact that he'd offered to pay for the damage without any prompting from anyone, I sent him on his way. Confident that I now had enough information to calm down my protagonist and get him to call off his lynching. I phoned him to explain.

The Airport Director however, was not to be moved and he stuck ferociously to the same line that he'd spouted when he'd first spoken to me. He finished off by telling me that he'd now spoken to the police who were on their way to interview Murray as we spoke. They were taking this breach of Airport Security very seriously, he said. Goodness knows what yarn he'd spun to Mr. Plod but I was dismayed. Just where was his sense of judgement and perspective!?

We were at this time in the throes of starting up a new 'low cost' airline [BMI Baby] that was going to be based at East Midlands airport. It was to be quite a significant operation and so had a lot of buying power and influence at the Airport and it was in the midst of negotiating various important contracts with the airport for the start up of its new operation. I decided that as I couldn't achieve anything constructive on getting Murray off the hook I'd have to resort to higher authority. I contacted the newly appointed Managing Director of BMI Baby, a Tony Davis, and asked him to intercede. Tony said leave it with him and he'd see what he could do.

I telephoned Murray and told him that I'd not yet managed to call off the attack dogs and that Mr. Plod would be visiting him at home shortly. I suggested that he might like to 'go shopping' for a bit before he returned home whilst we tried to resolve the issue. Tony called me back an hour or so later. I don't know what he'd said to our mutual friend the Airport Director but he'd succeeded where I'd failed and all was now well. Murray was to pay for the damage caused and I was to send round a memo telling everyone that there was now a contact number on the barrier to call in the event of malfunction. Happy days!

I sent out the requested memo without delay. Murray's surname was Orr, so I titled my note 'Staff Car Park BarrieOrr'. I think everyone got the joke – except perhaps our Airport Director friend.

29. Mission Impossible.

One of several sidelines I found myself involved with at one point was running a series of courses on 'The Fear of Flying' at East Midlands Airport. As the name implies, these were courses designed to try and help people who found flying an uncomfortable and stressful business – there are a surprisingly large number of people out there who seem to be in this category.

Before 911 it was perfectly OK for passengers to visit the flight deck to see how it all worked. That changed [very rapidly] after the event which, although as necessary as it was, I thought was a great shame. I've always resented the fact that aviation became the victim of political failure and has been hung out to dry by government in having to meet pretty much the entire cost of maintaining security at airports and on aeroplanes.

Beyond that, I always enjoyed people visiting the flight deck. Not all captains were comfortable for passengers to come up but I was one of those who was quite happy to indulge them. It was surprising how many people paid a visit to our 'office' because they were nervous and were seeking reassurance and it was satisfying to be able to [maybe] give that reassurance and, on occasion, get a real sense that people were significantly more relaxed after their visit.

As an aside [and nothing to do with nervous passengers] I was flying on one particular evening when one of the cabin crew came in and told me that we had Michael Parkinson on board and could he pay us a visit in the flight deck? I was an admirer, enjoyed his programmes and his interviewing excellence and was, of course, quite happy to welcome him into our little boudoir, so up he came. This night was one of those very clear, crisp winter evenings with superb visibility all round. Pretty much the whole of the United Kingdom was laid out below us in full view. As Michael looked out on this vista through the cockpit windows I pointed out the lights of the various towns and cities in sight:-

'That's Belfast over there on our left', I said, 'And down there in the distance is Dublin. That's the Isle of Man and you can see Glasgow and Edinburgh in the distance up ahead. On the right over there are Grimsby and Hull. And down there underneath us is Manchester, and that's Leeds'. Michael interrupted my erudite commentary: –

'Where's Barnsley?', he asked.

Those of us of a 'certain age' will know that Michael Parkinson was/is a peerless television journalist and is also fiercely proud of his native Yorkshire and even more so of his beloved Barnsley. Obviously, when he asks where Barnsley is, he's being serious. So I said: –

'I don't know, where is Barnsley?'.

I thought that this was rather funny but I don't think that he did for he retired back to his seat in the cabin very shortly afterwards. Clearly I was no Billy Connolly in his eyes! Sorry Michael!

Back to the 'Fear of Flying' courses. These were a series of talks and exercises that I ran, in conjunction with a local phobic charity. Each talk was designed to ramp up the candidates' acceptance of flying as a rational activity and to reduce their fear factor. The whole thing culminated in a quick 15 minute flight – for those for whom the course worked – to test and confirm their new found resilience [and courage!].

Each course comprised of around twenty or so people. They were always a very varied bunch, male and female, young, old and in between and they were all members of this phobia charity. There was not much in common between this disparate bunch of people, except that they all had a fear of flying. My job was to just give the lectures on flying and do all the aeroplane interface bits in the hope that this would succeed in achieving the desired outcome for them.

One particular course stands out clearly in my memory, only

because of a chap called Tommy. Tommy was middle aged and there was nothing that I noticed, to start with, that especially made him a stand out individual or one who I would still remember all these years later.

The first couple of sessions of the course, one session a week over a five week period, went fine. These were simple 'chalk and talk' sessions held in a conference room in the Airport terminal where I would explain how aeroplanes worked, what attendees should expect when they went flying, etc, etc. The talks were accompanied with photos, video, Q and A sessions and the usual classroom type stuff. Session three was a practical tour around the Terminal building looking at the passenger check in desks, security checks, visiting the departure lounges, etc, etc.

Session four was when we first ventured out of the Terminal and onto the aircraft itself. This was a big day for these students of course but it was also important to me that the session went smoothly too. Aircraft are expensive bits of kit and they don't make money when they're sat on the ground doing nothing. The opportunities therefore, to find a slot where one was sitting around long enough to be able to show a bunch of people around it was limited. We had a window of about an hour and a quarter available to get the task completed. Then the aircraft needed to be cleaned, catered, checked and fully prepared for its next flight. Time was of the essence if the course was not to get in the way of the airline's operation. A delay to the departure of the next flight would not go down well with anyone, not least the passengers on the flight.

I met up with my charges, briefed them about the musts and must nots of walking out onto the apron – with all that that implied in terms of safety, vigilance, etc. I also expressed the need for us to be fairly slick with it all as there was only limited time available to us.

We assembled at the departure gate through which we were to exit the terminal to reach our subject aircraft, every one sporting a yellow high visibility jacket. The charity co-ordinator and I herded our charges out through the door. Once assembled outside we had to cross the service road that ran between the terminal and the aircraft parking stands. Our aircraft was conveniently parked in front of us on the other side of this road, steps in place and fully prepared for us to board. And this was where I was to first become aware of Tommy.

When the road was clear we chaperoned everyone across it to then gather at the foot of the aircraft steps. I was about to lead us all up and into the aircraft when I glanced back across the road. Standing there, alone and forlorn, was one of our party.

"Who's that, and what's he doing still there?" I asked the co-ordinator.

"Ah", she said, "That's Tommy, he's got a bit of a thing about crossing roads. I'll go and get him". She did.

With the group now fully assembled, I led everyone up and into the aircraft cabin. All that is, except Tommy. He remained at the bottom of the steps.

"Come on Tommy!" I called down. The co-ordinator intervened.

"Ah", she said again, "he doesn't like steps either, I'll go down and bring him up". She did.

I was beginning to think that Tommy was on the wrong course, he'd got more problems than just a fear of flying! Undaunted I showed everyone around the cabin and gave them a few minutes to gather their thoughts, wander about, try the seats, look out of windows, etc, etc. Everyone was fine and quite excited but I noticed that Tommy hadn't moved very far from the front door by the steps but I didn't give this too much thought as I was busy fielding questions and explaining things to the group.

The dénouement of this, the penultimate session of the course, was to finish by closing the aircraft doors and then starting up one of the engines. Those who were not unnerved by this next step would be going for a flight next week. I asked if everyone was now ready to have the doors shut. No one demurred but the co-ordinator quietly advised me that Tommy might find this difficult as he suffered from claustrophobia. I could hardly believe what I was hearing at this point.

What on earth was poor Tommy doing here, there was no way he'd ever go flying?! He'd already eaten up a precious ten minutes or more with his issues and I didn't need any more interruptions. I held my council but asked him directly if he was happy. He nodded his head in agreement so I finally got the doors shut and, having given a further briefing, I was at last able to run an engine which all went well with no one [including the unfortunate Tommy] being upset or panicking. Excellent!

Lesson over [still with some time to spare, despite Tommy's difficulties] all I had to do now was disembark everyone and get them safely back inside the building. Not difficult, merely a reversal of the boarding process. Doors open, I led everyone down the steps. You've already guessed! Every one that is, except Tommy. He was still stood at the top looking as lost and lonely as one of Bo Peeps sheep.

"I'm afraid Tommy suffers from acrophobia". Says my co-ordinator.

I was left speechless [again!] but given all that had gone before with poor Tommy I shouldn't have been surprised and should perhaps have even anticipated this eventuality. Up the steps the lady went to entice Tommy down. No amount of coaxing, cajoling persuasion or reason would get Tommy to budge and the time ticked away seemingly faster and faster. If we didn't get him off the plane soon we'd be eating into its pre-flight preparation time. That eventuality came to pass.

Soon enough we had engineers, crew, caters, cleaners, re-fuelers, Uncle Tom Cobly and all gathered round waiting to do their stuff. And still little Tommy stood his ground. It was like Custer's Last Stand at the battle of Little Bighorn. Eventually we had to call for an ambilift – a specialised kind of truck that was designed with a rear cabin that was a lift, specially made, to allow disabled people access onto and off aeroplanes. It took about half an hour for this device to appear but eventually it backed up to the aircraft door, the lift was raised and Tommy stepped aboard. He was safely transported off the apron and released back into the wild. The next flight on the aircraft departed about forty five minutes late. Not my finest hour!

I never saw Tommy again, I don't suppose he got out of his house much. I have no idea what either the charity or Tommy was thinking when he enrolled on the course in the first place, he was clearly not a suitable candidate from the outset.

Sadly, this was to be the last of the 'Fear of Flying' courses that we undertook. Constructive as these course were designed to be, we couldn't really justify the risk of a repeat of another delay like that, too many fare paying passengers had paid too high a price.

37. A Self Inflicted Wound.

One of the more satisfying conclusions to an argument I had with one of our Captains was settled in the Staff Car Park at East Midlands Airport.

The Captain involved had joined the company as a First Officer on leaving the R.A.F. Gordon was a perfectly good pilot and in due course was duly promoted to command, flying our turbo-prop Fokker F27 aircraft. The F27 was a fairly small twin engined airliner which carried up to forty nine passengers. We had several of this type which operated mainly from East Midlands on short domestic and European scheduled service routes such as Amsterdam, Paris, and the like, as well as then flying our service between Liverpool and Heathrow. All the pilots were based at East Midlands and went to and from Liverpool by company supplied taxi when required to fly from there.

By way of background, as well as rostering pilots to fly, we also had a duty called 'Standby'. This was designed to have pilots available at short notice if, or when, things went wrong. It was a duty where pilots had no specific flights to undertake on the day so they were free to do what they wanted, except that they had to be on the end of a phone and able to report for work within one hour if called out. Mostly things went well and the Standby duty effectively became a day off for the individual concerned, except that he [or she] couldn't go to the pub or stray too far away from a telephone. If called out to fly the pilot had no idea where they might end up going to and/or when they might get back home so it was all a bit of a lottery – but understood and accepted by all. Sometimes the dice roll your way and sometimes they don't.

On this day Gordon had some kind of domestic commitment to keep [I never found out what it was!] but he was also rostered for a 'Standby' duty. He'd obviously gambled that he wouldn't be called out to work and hadn't bothered to protect his commitment by requesting the day off in advance. Unfortunately his gamble failed and he was called out to taxi up to Liverpool and do three return trips, six flights in all [the maximum number of flights our pilots were required to fly on any one day]. He would then return to East Midlands in another taxi, arriving back at about eleven thirty p.m. – far too late to meet his own domestic priority.

Needless to say, Gordon was not a happy camper and he protested mightily to the crewing officer who contacted him to advise him of his new fate. However, there was no one else available to fill the slot and so he had no option other than to comply and set sail – presumably making peace with his wife as best he could before leaving home.

I knew nothing about any of this until, at around six p.m. that evening I had a call from our Operations people. Gordon was on the last leg of his day's work [also his sixth flight] and flying up to Liverpool from London. He had a full load of forty nine passengers on board and he was diverting to East Midlands. Diversions were not usual. They happened of course but even in bad weather most flights ended up at their intended destinations. Today was not a bad weather day, merely a mild winters evening. Gordon must be diverting for some good technical reason. I was immediately alert as it could well be that something was seriously wrong and he might need some assistance with his problem.

I was flabbergasted when the Operations Controller told me that the reason for the diversion was that the port navigation light on the wingtip of the aircraft was not working – and that was it [i.e. one of his sidelights] – how trivial can you get?! I was about to ask what the heck Gordon thought he was doing when the controller filled me in with the background story about him being upset at having been called out. Then I understood.

Landing at East Midlands, en route to Liverpool, would get him back to his home base still in time to make his domestic assignation. Further, he wouldn't have to continue the next flight on up to Liverpool as he'd now already have completed the maximum six flights. We'd have to call out a replacement Captain to do the last leg whilst he went home to domestic bliss. Meanwhile forty nine passengers were now to be hugely delayed and inconvenienced.

I was suddenly very angry but there was nothing I could do. Apparently, as Gordon had taxied out to the runway at Heathrow another pilot in another aeroplane had noticed that his navigation light [the red one] wasn't working and had told him. It's a legal requirement for these lights to be on at night and as it would be dark by the time he got to Liverpool he decided to stay legal and land at East Midlands.

Gordon was fireproof with his decision, the law was on his side. Any disciplinary sanction from me would not be allowed to stand. Never mind common sense, Gordon had the legal high ground. Notwithstanding all that, I determined to go up to the airport from my office to meet up with Gordon when he landed and to tell him just exactly what I thought of him. My biggest single gripe was with his cavalier attitude towards his passengers. How any self respecting pilot could treat his customers with such distain was beyond me. Whilst there was nothing I could do to remedy the situation I could at least derive some satisfaction from giving him a piece of my mind [how petty is that – maybe I'm no better than was he!]. Anyway, up to the airport I went and once I'd met up with Gordon my spleen was duly vented. He listened in silence, and I'm sure with a slight smirk. He knew that I knew that he was untouchable and no doubt he was deriving some perverse pleasure from my obvious agitation.

Rant over, we both departed from the Airport Crew Room to the staff car park. I felt a little better having given him a piece of my mind and I expect, by contrast, Gordon felt quite smug. I was thirty seconds or so behind him on our walk out and I saw him getting into his car to go home. It was now dark and as he turned on his lights to reverse out of his parking space I witnessed a miracle!

Lo and behold, one of Gordon's rear side lights wasn't working! This was truly manna from heaven and an opportunity not to be missed. Revenge really is a dish best served cold and my mood had left me feeling very cold. I stopped him before he'd moved very far, gestured that I wanted to speak to him. He wound his window down: –

"Gordon", I said, "I'm sorry to tell you but one of your rear lights isn't working".

"Oh", he replied, "Thanks, I'll get it seen to tomorrow".

And with that he made to move off but I persisted: –

"No, no..", I said, "It doesn't work like that, I don't think you understand. It's now official night. It's a legal requirement to have serviceable lights on your car, it's no different from your aeroplane. If you leave this car park without a rear light, I'll have no option other than to report you to the Police. Do I make myself clear? Either you replace the bulb or you find another means of getting home".

Gordon looked back at me, at first a little taken aback at my apparently aggressive outburst but then I could see the look of comprehension on his face as he realised that he'd been hoisted on his own petard.

There was a garage at the Airport that probably sold light bulbs but it was a good ten minute walk away. I stood watching, on guard, as Gordon first returned his car to its parking slot and then set off on foot to try and buy a light bulb. I waited until he was out of sight before I jumped into my own car to go home. I didn't check my own rear lights but I probably didn't need to any anyway – I was positively glowing inside the car. I was now happy as I drove home and I do remember hoping that Gordon, by contrast, now felt livid!

38. Gross Insubordination

There's a time and a place for everything – but there's never a single characteristic or person suitable for every time, every place and every occasion. When the constituent parts collide there are always bound to be fireworks and when more than two of the components clash it can often generate an unwanted, but a predictable, firestorm.

One such collision started at Jersey Airport on a busy summer Sunday. Jersey on summer Sundays was always manic. It was a popular holiday destination and Sundays seemed to be the day on which everyone wanted to arrive or to leave. Aircraft were coming and going all day long without let up or hindrance. There was no time for holdups or the finer things in life. It was all go and it needed everything to run smoothly to get the job done cleanly and efficiently. By and large the operation ran pretty smoothly, everyone knew what to do and when to do it and it was generally impressive to see as it mostly ran like the prevarbial well oiled sewing machine.

We were then primarily using the Douglas DC 9 as the mainstay of our short haul jet fleet. The DC9 was a real pilots aeroplane. It was a veritable rocket machine, hugely overpowered, very light on the controls and a delight to fly. We had two versions of this aircraft, a smaller model which we configured for eighty five passengers and a larger model with one hundred and ten seats. Both went well but the small aeroplane went like a scalded cat and had been christened the 'Pocket Rocket' by those who flew it. It leapt down a runway like a cheetah on a mission and it climbed like a guided missile too [for those who like numbers, if the aircraft was light and without passengers on board you could get a rate of climb of sixteen thousand feet a minute out of it at lower levels].

Flying his DC9 on this day, the 'Pocket Rocket' version, was a Captain John Salmon – protagonist number one in this tale. John was a real character. An excellent pilot but a complex personality and one not always easy to handle. He'd started out as an aircraft engineer, serving on HMS Ark Royal and had then made the transition across to piloting in his civilian life. John was no one's fool and neither did he suffer fools gladly. He was quite happy to deliver his thoughts and feelings, without fear or prejudice, at any time of day or night, to anyone who was listening or who had offended him – whatever their status or rank within the company. He was also very loyal to his friends and to the company. In short, John was one of those salt of the earth type of people but he could be a bit prickly when aroused – which was not infrequently!

Protagonist number two was a ground engineer based at Jersey, the inimitable Jim Peacock. Jim was physically a giant of a man, literally. He was tall, he was broad, he was big all round, strong as an ox, heavy but not at all fat. Jim was also a very good engineer. I'd known Jim myself from my days in Channel Airways – where he and Bill Bailey, a fellow engineering colleague, ran the ramp at Southend with military discipline. Jim had migrated to Jersey when British Midland took over the routes that had been vacated with the demise of Channel Airways. Jim was also a strong character and he wouldn't stand on ceremony either if he felt that a mere Captain was being difficult and giving him a hard time.

The particular aircraft that John was flying that day had been having a fair amount of persistent trouble with one of its engines. Nothing dramatic, but pilots kept reporting that the engine parameters were getting close to, and sometimes nudging up to, permitted maximum values – to the point that they were having to take action to keep things within the allowable tolerances. It was an older engine but one still with a reasonable bit of life supposedly in it before needing to be changed and sent away for overhaul. Premature engine changes were a costly exercise and the Engineering Department were anxious to keep this engine 'on the wing' for as long as possible, for obvious reasons. By way of explanation, the phrase 'on the wing' is a term that engineers use to mean that they want to keep using the engine. Most engines are attached to the aeroplane wings but the DC9 had them bolted on to the tail end of the fuselage.

Yet again, that morning the offending motor had been reported by a crew flying an earlier detail, as playing up. Accordingly, our Engineering Director, who had decided to take a close personal interest in this engine, had sent a telex down to Jersey to get the engineers there to request that when the aircraft landed the Captain be instructed to record all the engine parameters on the next take off. That's six different readings, these reading to be taken at the start of the take off run, then again at 80 knots, again at 100 knots, once more at 120 knots and finally at 140 knots – a total of 30 different readings! All to be recorded whilst hurtling down a short runway, conducting a take off and accelerating almost too fast to read even the speedometer accurately, never mind write down a further six different instrument readings every two seconds or so.

Clearly our Engineering Director had never flown an aeroplane, far less a DC9, and he also obviously had no idea what he was asking the crew to do. Jim Peacock went into the flight deck armed with his telex and fully expecting a mouthful from the Captain. He knew that the request would be greeted with derision. He handed the piece of paper to John who duly read the document. Then he turned to Jim and he said: –

"You can tell him to go away".

Actually, he didn't say that at all, that's my polite translation, John's words were somewhat more succinct – but no less clear [bear in mind that John had graduated from 'below decks' in the Fleet Air Arm, hardly the most refined of environments!]. Not to be rebuffed, Jim's response was equally erudite:-

"I'm not [jolly] telling him that, [jolly] tell him yourself!"

As I implied at the beginning of this story, this was an example of the mountain meeting the immovable object – but something had to give, there wasn't time to stand on ceremony.

John reached for his biro and wrote, as requested, his expletive message – in large capital letters right across the telex – which he then handed back to Jim whilst instructing him to fax it back to head office. Jim did [but not before he'd been threatened from further up the Engineering food chain if he didn't].

The first I knew about this was on the Monday morning when I arrived in my office. My secretary told me that John Wolfe wanted to see me [John was the 'big boss' and one of the co-owners of the company]. I called John and was invited along to his office. In his office with him was our Engineering Director. John unveiled the story of yesterday's happenings and handed me the evidence to examine. The message was very clear, loud and stark. Just two words scrawled over the offending telex message and on the subject of sex and travel. Neither John. nor the Engineering Director were amused and John demanded that the Captain's severed head be delivered to him on a silver platter!

This put me in a difficult position. My sentiments were entirely with the Captain of the flight and the author of the message. It was a stupid request to make in the first place and, in any event, it wasn't the Engineering Director's place to tell a pilot what to do. If he'd wanted this information it should have been fed through the operational management side of the company [where the request would have been halted anyway – so the problem would never have arisen]. However, we were now where we were. Equally, I could see John Wolfe's perspective. There's no way you can accept a pilot [or anyone else] telling a Company Director, in highly expletive terms, to go for a walk.

I actually felt like having a go at my Engineering colleague myself, was he not man enough to deal with this in his own right? Why escalate a storm in a teacup, a flash of intemperate language, triggered by his own stupidity, to Board level with a company owner? There was no real issue here that an apology would not have cured. I was not impressed but given the mood in the room, had I expressed my sentiment I would have undoubtedly found myself on the same set of pillories as the unfortunate Captain.

There wasn't much I could do. I explained as tactfully as I could that the request was misplaced and not deliverable but I could not think of a way to mitigate or excuse John Salmon's reaction. How do you defend the indefensible? I said that I'd haul the miscreant in, listen to his side of the story and then deal with him.

I pondered about this problem for a while. Clearly John needed his collar felt. The matter, having reached John Wolfe, could not now be resolved without some kind of severe sanction. John Wolfe would want his pound of flesh delivered and if it wasn't then [quite rightly] my own head would be on the block. The more I thought about it, the more I kept coming back to the same conclusion – as much as I sympathised with John Salmon he was out of order and would have to take the pain. In the end, and very much against my better judgement, I demoted him to First Officer status for a few months.

Sometimes you just have to accept that you can't win 'em all! John got his command back 'ere long and I kept my head too so it all ended up fine – eventually.

39. How to Become Popular

British Midland Airways had always been based, as its name implied, in the Midlands. Originally at Burniston airfield, now the site of the UK Toyota factory, and then at East Midlands Airport as from around 1965 when the airport first opened as a civil airfield having been semi derelict since the Second World War.

With the 1980s came Margaret Thatcher, the deregulation of aviation and the opening up of competition on what were previously State protected routes operated by the duopoly of BOAC and BEA – who had merged to form British Airways in 1974. This deregulation meant that British Midland could now go head to head with British Airways on routes out of London Heathrow. Little by little, and not without the tenacity of our company Chairman, Sir Michael Bishop, we were able to chip away at the near monopoly that B.A. had at Heathrow. Our foothold at London's main airport grew substantially as the airline expanded – by offering better service and cheaper prices than the competition. Before long by far the greater majority [and more profitable] of our services were run from out of Heathrow.

All our pilots were however, still based up at East Midlands Airport. We used to shuttle them in taxis down to London to fly. We then paid for them to stay in hotels adjacent to the airport for three or four nights at a time before then taxiing them back home again for their days off. This suited the pilot community quite well despite them having to spend a lot of time away from home. The taxi time to and from London counted as 'duty' which was regulated by law. This meant that pilots ended up having a greater number of days off as they would otherwise break the rules by working too many hours over a given number of days. Additionally, pilots were paid an allowance, [classed as 'expenses'] over and above their salaries, for every hour they were away from their base. They were therefore racking up fairly substantial sums of money, 24 hours a day, when away, including the time that they spent sleeping! Not a bad little number!

By now I held a reasonably senior management position within the company and it dawned on me one morning that we, on the operational side of the business, were wasting an awful lot of money. The fundamental dynamics of the company had shifted very dramatically, and quite quickly too, over recent years. We were so busy trying to keep up with our expansion processes that we'd missed one or two of the basic housekeeping rules. It made no sense at all to maintain our workforce 120 miles away from where the bulk of the work was done. The pilots needed to be moved south.

I knew full well that rocking the boat would go down very badly with the brave boys and that forcing them to move to the South East would seriously disrupt many families, not least those with children settled in schools and/or with wives who worked. However I looked at it though, the logic of my thinking seemed a no brainer to me, sooner or later I would have to bow to the inevitable. I did some quick sums. Needless to say, these confirmed my first thoughts so I then built a business case to properly demonstrate, and verify, the savings to be made. These savings were of course, very substantial indeed. The downsides were twofold. Firstly, a reasonably significant capital sum would be needed up front to pay for the pilots relocation costs but the payback would be swift and very large. Secondly, the impact on pilots and their morale would not be good.

I knew that my proposal would be accepted by the company owners but I also knew that it would greatly adversely affect a lot of people, so it was with a bit of a heavy heart that I presented my case for the move to our Board. Not surprisingly, the proposal was accepted with alacrity and I was instructed to get on with it without delay.

There was a lot of work that needed to be done to accomplish the task. We still had a reasonable route network out of East Midlands Airport so we'd obviously have to keep some of the pilots there to fly those routes. I'd also have to update the pilot's 'Relocation' package. This hadn't been looked at for a long time and was woefully out of date. The package would require a lot heavy negotiation with the pilot's union [BALPA] to bring it up to a level that reflected the current costs associated with moving house. As soon as the union was approached the cat would be out of the bag and my name would very quickly become mud with the pilots.

And so it was. The self same pilots who before I moved into the management side of the business, as well as working alongside, I used to socialise with, swap small talk with, meet up with in hotels around Europe, etc, etc. and generally rub along with, without fear or favour, these people suddenly now saw me in a very different light. Life is very much changed when on the other side of the fence! This new hiatus was however a whole different ballgame and I became a much vilified personality amongst many of those affected – for all the obvious reasons!

One of the biggest gripes the pilots had was that surrounding the cost differential between house prices in the East Midlands and those in the South East. The price of a reasonable detached four bedroom home in the Midlands would hardly buy you a three bedroom semi in the London area. To mitigate this cost differential we included a reasonable mortgage subsidy within the new Relocation agreement to offset the additional costs of more expensive properties. Even so, most of the pilots ended up with substantially bigger mortgages than they'd had before and/or with smaller properties – or both. They had wanted the company to provide a package that would give them 'like for like' housing – at no cost whatsoever to themselves. They couldn't grasp the fact that in the real world it doesn't work quite like that! As I say, my name was mud.

But it gets worse! Everything in flying is governed by 'pilot seniority' – it's Nature's way of adhering to the hierarchy of Darwin's 'Natural

Selection' when it comes to pilots. It's the old 'first in, last out' principle – as enforced by most pilot unions worldwide. As a result of this it was [volunteers aside], the more junior pilots who were sent kicking and screaming down south. Their more senior colleagues remained smugly undisturbed at East Midlands.

Smug that is, until my friend John Wolfe, one of the company owners, flush with the success of saving so much money by moving crews to London, decided that we should now also move them north. We had aircraft based at Glasgow and Edinburgh and John decided that we should have pilots living at these two bases, as well as at London, to save yet more money. I'd already looked at this scenario but the maths didn't work very convincingly. Savings would be marginal at best and there would be disadvantages that negated any minor potential benefit. I explained the pros and cons but John would not be moved.

I was now left with no option other than to tell a bunch of senior pilots, many of whom had been working for the company for longer than me – and who had thought that they were 'safe', – that they'd now have to up sticks and decamp to Scotland. Few were impressed and I suspect that many would not have treated me too well if they'd met me in a dark alley at night.

I remember flying one day with a fellow pilot manager, one Ron Hardy, at this difficult time. Ron was then our Chief Pilot and had been a management animal for some considerable time. He had lot of 'history' in that context and so was not much more popular than was I. We were flying together on a DC9 on this particular day. This aircraft had a control column that had a removable centre boss fitted to it.

In an idle moment Ron removed this central boss from the steering wheel on his side to see what was underneath. He pulled out a piece of paper from within on which was written:-

"Ron Hardy is a twit".

Actually the last word much stronger – but I write for polite society so have substituted to save embarrassment to those of a more sensitive disposition. We had a hearty chuckle about this revelation and I then pulled my centre boss off too to see if there was another gem deposited within. Lo and behold [each pilot has a steering wheel]another piece of paper was revealed. I removed it from its hiding place and read it out:-

"So is Jim Snee" it said! Quite a coincidence this when you think about it, each piece of paper 'discovered by its intended victim – and at the same time!

It was at this point that I knew that I'd finally 'arrived' as a proper manager. We had a further, more substantial, chuckle. If you can't take the heat, stay out of the kitchen!

Over the next few years, as we recruited new pilots, they were posted to Scotland to replace those more senior pilots who wanted to return to East Midlands. Some of the old guard, once settled up there, decided that it was a pretty good place to live and they preferred to stay put. That side of the thorny problem therefore sort of resolved itself over time.

On the London side of life, ten or fifteen years later, those reluctant refugees to the world south of Watford were almost lining up to shake my hand in gratitude! Such had been the pace of house inflation in the London area that many were now [on paper anyway] millionaires and those who weren't were not far off!

British Midland saved many hundreds of thousands of pounds, per year, as a direct result of these changes – but I never received a penny piece by way of bonus from my Lords and Masters.

Alas, as I didn't move down to London either, neither did I derive any benefit whatsoever from house price inflation. The North/South divide remains as strong as ever! However, the opprobrium that had been heaped upon me in the heat of battle slowly dissipated over the years and by the time I retired most of my pilot colleagues were once again talking to me in friendly terms. A far more important outcome!

33. The Heathrow Bomb.

The 1960s and '70s was a strange time in some ways. There were many paradoxes in play in society over that period. It was, on one hand, a time of great and growing liberation with new freedoms for all. The dawning of The Age of Aquarius, Flower Power and all that. On the other hand there was also a lot of bigotry about and much of it was still pretty well entrenched – think Alf Garnet in 'Till Death Us Do Part' – a television comedy programme but one with very heavy ironic undertones that reflected all too accurately much of the bigoted attitudes of too many in society at the time. It was very popular in its day but it's safe to say that, unlike Dads Army, no repeats will ever be shown in these more enlightened times.

Not least amongst those to suffer from these same levels of bigotry that today's generation would neither understand, nor tolerate, were those in the 'Gay Community'. Homophobia was as rife then as it is now unacceptable and I have to confess that I was, in those days, no less bigoted than many other so called 'red blooded' males.

There were few stewards working as cabin crew in short haul flying when I first started my airline career but as time went on their numbers increased. Not all were gay of course but some were – they were popular with their female cabin crew colleagues [who probably felt safe from wandering hands and unwanted advances] – but most of us pilots were unimpressed.

I was flying out of Heathrow one early morning – up to Scotland and back, probably a couple of round trips, I think but wherever it was it was a routine day's work and nothing to get excited about. One of our cabin crew was a chap called Peter, a rather effeminate steward.

By now [early to mid 1980s] the industry was beginning to become a bit of a target for disaffected and deranged people and occasional bomb threats were becoming a growing concern. Nearly all turned out to be hoaxes – no doubt motivated by a misplaced sense of humour or someone with a grudge against a particular airline – but all had to be investigated and resolved.

As a consequence of this it had become a routine part of the Cabin Crews pre-flight checks, on every flight, to search the cabin for any suspicious packages, just in case. Needless to say no suspicious packages had ever been found on any of our aircraft but the crews still had to check. They also had to check that there was still a lifejacket stowed under each seat – unscrupulous passengers, presumably amateur sailors, would sometimes 'borrow' them without permission. It was a legal requirement that every passenger must have a lifejacket available, even if we weren't flying over water [no I didn't make it up!] so if one was missing it was very inconvenient.

Anyway, this morning I was outside the aircraft checking that nothing had fallen off, etc, whilst inside, the cabin crew and co-pilot went about their respective businesses. Halfway round my external check I was intercepted by one of our cabin crew. She said that Peter had found a bomb on board and that they had all evacuated the aircraft. I was somewhat taken aback, to say the least!

"And where is Peter and the bomb now?", I asked.

"Oh, he's still in the cabin holding on to the bomb!" she replied.

"Why on earth is he doing that?".

"Well, we're taught never to move a bomb in case it explodes and he found it under a seat tucked in next to the lifejacket so he's still holding it – in case it moves if he lets go".

I acknowledged her explanation and told her to go and advise the ground staff, get them to call the Police and Airport Security and to move everyone away from the aircraft.

The cynic in me said that this couldn't be real, it was another hoax. The aircraft had spent the previous day flying to and from Scotland

and hadn't been anywhere else and it would have been searched on every turn round. My guess was that some miss-guided wag on the last flight southbound the previous evening had planted his 'joke' under the seat and the cleaners had then missed it. The non-cynical bit of me said that sooner or later there had to be a first time, why not now? Whatever the truth, I couldn't leave the poor effete Peter alone, holding the bomb and waiting, terrified, to die. I was the Captain, I'd have to lead from the front. I went back into the cabin and there, about halfway down the cabin on the port side, was the unfortunate steward leaning forward with his hand stretched out under one of the seats. He was immobile, or as immobile as he could be.

He couldn't see what he was holding of course, he'd simply been feeling under each seat, routinely as usual, to make sure that the lifejacket was there and that there were no foreign objects secreted within. There never were – until this time! Now poor Peter was both terrified and stuck.

"Are you OK?", I asked – a rather useless question really!

"Yes", he said in a voice that told me that he was anything but.

"Good, I'll take a look", says I, trying to sound helpful.

I knelt down in front of him to take a look under the seat. Pretty much immediately all was revealed. He was holding a bomb all right but it was transparently obvious to me, with no more than a first glance – and with no knowledge at all – that this was nothing more than a toilet roll with a couple of wires sticking out of it. It was a real as a unicorn dancing on ice. Not only that, Peter's hand was shaking so much that had it been a real bomb with any kind of interference device attached, it would have gone off long ago! I gave it a few seconds of proper scrutiny just to make sure and then I told him to drop it.

"Are you sure?", he asked – his voice trembling in time with his hand.

"Yes", I said, "You'll be fine".

He hesitated for a second or two whilst he processed this suggestion and then he decided to act. In one single movement he dropped his bomb, leapt over my crouched figure and was gone – up the cabin, out of the front door and up the jetty into the terminal building, moving way faster than Tom chasing Jerry in any of their cartoons.

I felt very sorry for the hapless Peter who found himself the unwitting victim of this hoax. I didn't know him at all but I don't suppose that he had a malicious bone in his body. As far as he was concerned, right from the very start of this incident, he had been the custodian of a real bomb. For something like five minutes – of what must have been sheer hell for him. He, in his mind's eye, had been literally holding on to the difference between life and death – for him and for anyone else in the vicinity. I took the 'bomb' up to the front of the aircraft and put it on a front seat before leaving myself to deal with the aftermath of this farce.

This aftermath was hardly any less comical than what had gone before. I rendezvoused with our crew and our ground staff. They had alerted the Security people and the Police, as briefed, but there was no sign of either. We waited at least twenty minutes for these people to arrive – at which point I'd had enough. My crew were by now all fine and Peter too had recovered and was happy to continue with his day's work so we re-boarded the aircraft, finished our checks and called for our, now much delayed, passengers to be boarded. I left our 'bomb' evidence with our ground-staff to hand on to the Police, etc, and said that I'd be writing a report about the incident on my return.

Up to Scotland and back we went. On arrival back at Heathrow I was met by a rather angry Security official who proceeded to lecture me about every piece of advice that I'd ignored – I should not have moved the 'bomb', I should not have gone back on board to 'rescue' Peter, I had no right to decide the bomb was a hoax, etc, etc. His attitude made me no less angry than was he. I responded in kind and we ended up agreeing to disagree.

This was the only security threat I ever encountered. The benefit was that I finished that day's work with a degree of admiration for my gay steward. He had been brave, stalwart under threat and uncomplaining afterwards. It wasn't a big thing [for me] but it was the beginning of a thaw in my attitude towards those of his ilk.

Not many months later I did a charter flight for the Ford Motor Company. They were launching a new car and we were commissioned to fly a plane load of motoring journalists on a three day jaunt around Europe where these chaps and chapesses would shoot off and test drive these new model cars in different locations. The crew with me on this trip were all based up at East Midlands Airport but the flight was to depart from Heathrow. We assembled at the appointed time at East Midlands Airport and set off for London by taxi, myself, co-pilot, two stewardesses and one steward – as camp as they come.

I was not hugely excited about having to spend a full three days with this chap but c'est la vie, I'd just have to put up with it. For the life of me I cannot now remember his name so I'll call him Gordon [it definitely wasn't Gordon but what's in a name?]. Anyway, Gordon was to have a lasting effect on me.

As we taxied south, me in the front passenger seat next to the driver, the cabin crew in the second row of seats, Gordon sandwiched between the two girls and the co-pilot bringing up the rear in splendid isolation on the back row, we chatted about this and that and what lay in store for us over the next three days. At one point I turned round to more closely engage with one or other of the crew. To my horror – and amazement – there was Gordon, guarded by his two female sentries, busy doing his knitting!

This couldn't be happening surely? Never had I previously ever seen anything like this. Grown men do not get out their knitting, in public and in a taxi and knit away, seemingly without a care in the world and in front of their Captain to boot! This was a bridge too far for my [narrow] 1980s perspective: – "If you don't put that knitting away now", I said, "I'll turn this taxi round at the next junction and we'll go back to East Midlands Airport where I'll get a replacement cabin crew member!". Somewhat nonplussed, Gordon complied and that was the last I saw of his knitting.

We collected our passengers at Heathrow and flew off to Geneva – goodness knows what Gordon did to the coffees he served me during the flight. Hopefully nothing but I'll never know! We were to spend the rest of the day and that night in Geneva whilst our illustrious passengers went test driving somewhere on the slopes of the Alps. We crew arranged to all meet up at circa 6pm to go out for a drink and a meal. I wasn't much looking forward to spending an evening in Gordon's company, especially as I thought that he might be a bit grumpy after my ultimatum in the taxi but that was the way that things usually worked so that's the way it was.

How wrong I was. Gordon turned out to be the life and soul of the party, we all laughed and joked and got on famously. The more the evening wore on, the more I began to warm to the man. I retired that night having thoroughly enjoyed the evening, and his company, just as much as that of the other three. The same was true of our next evening, this one spent in Milan. Again, Gordon kept us all hugely entertained.

I can't now remember the detail of what it was that made Gordon so entertaining but it was certainly his wit and repartee that came to the fore. By the time we'd had yet another night of entertainment from him, this one with the backdrop of Cologne, all my previous prejudices about gay people had been permanently banished. I was [and remain] far from joining their persuasion but from that day to this I am a changed man in my attitudes – and I'm sure all the better for it! So thank you Gordon and Peter – or whatever your real names are!

34. The Tedasaurus

There are many portraits I could draw of colourful characters who have peopled my flying career. Most have been pilots but there have been others too. Not least amongst these is a ground engineer by the name of Ted. Ted was/is another larger than life character and equally loud. The portrait of him below is pretty much self explanatory. I have merely edited much of it to make it less offensive to sensitive souls. It should also be noted that pilots and engineers, whilst each having great respect for the others professions, would never admit to this. Each is sworn to decry the other at every opportunity. It's Natures way of differentiating the species.

Tedasaurus.

Foreword

This Tedasaurus records the well known pearls of wisdom and oft uttered sayings of one Ted 'Dukes' Hawley, a line engineer of some repute [and considerable noise, notoriety and knowledge]. Ted worked for BMA out of East Midlands Airport [EMA] on one of four shifts operating on the ramp, A, B, C and D. Ted inhabited D Shift – for more years than anyone can remember – before finally calling it a day and retiring to play with his myriad collection of boy's toys. The Tedasaurus was written some 25 years ago [we're now at a time two decades into the 21st Century since the first edition was released – how time flies] for the private consumption of only those engineers inhabiting the EMA locker room.

The Tedasaurus was compiled by Paul Stevens, a fellow spanner man to Ted – but one with a difference. Unlike many of his colleagues, Paul is an engineer well versed in the art of both reading and writing. As the reader will observe, Paul also possesses a veritably good sense of humour and has enviably strong powers of observation – hence the tone as well as the content – which served to amuse all engineers who worked with Ted and knew him well.

As is the way with all engineers Paul was kept so busy repairing aeroplanes that he was able to find the time to pen this document in company time, on company stationery and using a company computer. This would now be neither possible nor acceptable, far less even tolerated. Such is the march of time.

The Tedasaurus was written during a period of history that will not be well understood by the millennial snowflakes who now inhabit the World. Ours was a time that enjoyed real free speech, direct talking and one where no precious 'false offence' was taken, nor indeed was any offence intended or envisioned. Friendly banter was well understood, was given and exchanged in equal measure. With no malice intended, none was taken. All this was long before 'political correctness' and 'woke' [whatever that is] had been invented and were still a curse for the future.

The time has now come to release this Tedasaurus to a wider audience – before it is lost to history. This second edition has therefore been edited, at the invitation of the original author, to allow a greater circulation. Minor adjustments only have been made in order to merely protect the innocent and to ensure some small sanitation of language. The commissioned editor was one of the engineers clients – – i.e. a pilot.

In the world of the engineers pilots were a breed of jumped up pr*ts who took the engineers carefully repaired and maintained aircraft away so that they could do their best to break them and then bring them back for further repair. This all to make sure that the same engineers did the same work all over again. This was good because it kept the World turning and it made sure that everyone had a job. Even so, the cycle was often not appreciated by the engineers but the pilots really were altruistic and were never full of their own bullsh*t and self importance. They also understood irony.

Author's Comment

There were a lot of memories for a lot of people forged on that line at EMA and in today's world of regulation, safety, targets, security and general tosh it's good to think back to how it was once actually possible to do a job, make some money and have a bloody good time and all at once!

So, now to the Tedasaurus itself: –

Tedasaurus

As Revised. 2019

A

Amanco. — A make of stationary engine favoured by Ted and other batty collectors with garages full of junk.

Amoco Cadiz. — Description of an oil leak somewhat greater than a seep. [Amoco Cadiz was an oil super tanker that ran aground off the Brittany coast in 1978 spilling 220 thousand tonnes of oil into the sea].

B

Barny! — To be shouted out any time something is crashed, broken or dismantled and/or there is a sh*t job to do.

Berlin Airlift. — More than three aircraft landing at East Midlands Airport within an hour.

Bob Hope. — Chances of a new job being started after 02.00hrs. [see also ZZZ].

C

Clinking. — Good, satisfactory, bloody marvellous. [Origin unknown].

Check 4'd — To be taken to pieces, sprayed with 3961 [i.e. WD40] and then reassembled [often incorrectly].

Chicken and mushroom curry. — Saturday lunchtime favourite – demoting lunchbox 'rabbit food' to the bin.

Collar. — Hard work. [Origin unknown].

Couldn't spit a tanner. — To have a dry mouth and require a hot beverage. [Used approximately 347 times per shift].

Chogie. — Anyone of non Causican origin.

Curly. — Attractive female to be letched over.

Cracked it. — To clear a long running C.F.D. [only for it to recur
on the next sector – exactly as before]. [CFD= Carried
Forward Defect].

D

Delay. — Something often attributed to, but never accepted by, D
Shift.

Doing all the Collar. — What Ted says he's been doing whilst
actually out chatting up curly, taking bits to Mash [the
welder] and wandering around looking for his glasses.

Dogtosser. — Someone who fails to meet Teds' high standards in
some way. Directed at one or two fellow engineers [none on
D Shift] but mainly at pilots

Dukes. — anyone and everyone, from himself to the Queen.

E

Eat at Joe's. — To carelessly receive an electric shock and light
up like a neon sign [as often seen over American roadside
restaurants].

Epic. — Any job that takes longer than expected due to unforeseen
problems, lack of spares or complete mechanical ineptitude.

'Ere we go'! — The cry from Ted as he departs at the end of his
nightshift – leaving chaos behind him.

F

F**k a Priest. — Exclamation of amazement

F**k a Stoat. — Rather more difficult – and probably less satisfying
– version of F**k a Priest.

G

GO AHEAD! — A radio call response made by Ted – at a volume
only previously required before the advent of electronic
amplification.

H

Honk. — To smell. i.e. like a fisherman's sock or like vomit etc..

Honk. — To vomit. [Thus 'to smell like vomit' in Tedspeak would be 'honks like honk'].

Honking it Down. — Heavy rain, usually applied when tasked with a protracted outdoor job.

I

'I was suppressing Communism'. An oft repeated claim of how Ted saved all people living in the Free World – by drinking beer in a hanger 87 miles away from the front line of a war conducted before any of us were born. [Malaya – doing his National Service].

J

JUDITH! — A gentle call to his spouse when a cup of tea, advice or help to lift a gearbox was required.

K

Kitbag. — Teds tool roll full of VONO bed spanners, loose washers, gramophone needles and turn screws. [i.e. useless rubbish].

L

Like Heathrow. — More than three aircraft on the apron at EMA at any one time.

Left you one in the hanger. — Ritual statement from D Shift on handover to the next shift. [an aircraft assigned to D Shift for repair but not yet fixed].

M

'May as well have one today'. — Ted's answer any time he's asked if a cup of tea is required.

M.G. — A never to be completed project. e.g. Ted's MG TC or his application for an electrical licence, etc.

N

Not on this planet. — An unfounded comment on the collective
state of D Shift.

O

Oil can. — Amongst the most desirable and highly prized antiques
available [to a small group of strange shed dwelling loners].

P

Podded. — To make pregnant, to be pregnant or to give birth. In
fact anything to do with babies and the production thereof.

Pies. — Nickname of Notts County football team – from their style
of play, in which they all appear to have been wrapped in a
heavy coat of pastry.

Q

Queen of The Skies. Any fondly remembered aircraft of yesteryear
i.e. DC 3, Viscount, ATP, etc.

R

Richard the Third. — Human excrement commonly found all over
the apron following a toilet servicing miscalculation.

Ramjam Sam. — Playful nickname for Baz Bansil, Ted's favourite
avionics professional.

S

Shave off. — Exclamation of dismay.

Shave a rats arse. — More specific exclamation of dismay.

Sh*t Shift. — A, B or C Shifts – as seen by D Shift. [To all other
shifts, company management and the entire aerospace
industry, this describes D Shift].

T

That is so! — Ted's agreement with a statement. i.e ; – 'Bunks is
looking a bit miserable today'.

The Stationary Engine. — A magazine that provides lavatorial reading to shed dwelling oddballs.

U

Unsung hero. — Failure by management to realise that Ted has kept the company going for the last last fifty years.

V

Van. — Escort van reserved for Ted as per memo dated 3rd. April 1806.

W

Where's Biggsy? — Query uttered many times per night by Ted when some real 'collar' needs doing.

X

Ex Engineer. — What Ted is now that retirement has arrived.

Y

Youth. — Wasted on the young so continued by Ted never quite growing up.

Yonks. — A long period of time. [i.e. 'I haven't had a sniff of overtime in yonks' or 'Where the f**k's the Chinese, they've been gone yonks?' [they've obviously stopped off at the pub].

Z

ZZZ. — D Shift Crew Room soundtrack.

Footnote to Tedasaurus

For the record, Ted – now aged about 130 – remains alive, well and continues to walk amongst us. He has even managed to complete the restoration of his MG and his vintage Rudge motorcycle. This is not good as the roads of N.W. Leicestershire [and beyond] are significantly less safe when he's out and about. In the world of vintage motorcycling he's become known as 'Scroggins' [no, I don't know either].

More worrying still, Ted is now also the proud owner of an ancient French Citroen HY van hailing from the 1950s [or maybe early 60s]. Ted calls this latest addition to his toy cupboard his 'Sapeur Pompier' van as it spent its' working life in the hands of the French Emergency Service in Paris, plying it's trade as an ambulance.

Like Ted, his van is now retired from active service and the pair of them are another scourge on the roads and lanes around Loughborough. They are frequently to be seen roaring around with the same wanton abandon as Toad of Toad Hall, usually taking his Amanco stationary engine to a steam fair or some other display.

42. The Lodgers.

The rules on alcohol and flying are now very stringent and are also, quite rightly, enforced far more rigorously than in my earlier days of aviation. Now there is a defined blood count, as in the limit for car driving. I'm not sure what the number is for flying, I don't now fly, but effectively it's zero. For pretty much all of my career the rule was '8 hours, bottle to throttle' and there was no defined alcohol blood level count involved or defined. It's pretty obvious that this rule didn't hold much logic or bear too much scrutiny and it was not uncommon for some folk to drink like fish right up until the 8 hour time limit curtailed activities – in the hope that by some miracle they'd be sober enough in the morning to work at full efficiency.

Despite the very obvious flaw in their thought processes these same people could delude themselves that they remained beyond the reach of censure, secure in the knowledge that no regulation had been broken! Somehow and one way or another, the system appeared to work OK and no one seemed too bothered. I never ever heard of any pilot being challenged about their sobriety either. Maybe this did happen from time to time but if so, it was pretty rare.

There were then some pretty accomplished drinkers in the flying community and great volumes of alcohol were not infrequently consumed at post flight gatherings, particularly in hotel bars, not least because there often wasn't much else to do and there was almost always a companionable colleague or two around only too willing to pass the time over a pint or three [or more]. As often as not conversation would focus on how unfair life was for pilots and how the management could possibly be so useless – irrespective of which airline it was that employed them.

In my early days working for British Midland up at Teesside we rented a three bedroom detached house on a housing estate in the town of Eaglescliffe, near Stockton. To offset the cost of the rent we let out one of the spare rooms to one of my fellow pilot colleagues. Initially to one of our captains, Joe and then later on to a fellow co-pilot by the name of John.

Joe was another of those larger than life characters and also an accomplished pilot who enjoyed flying small aircraft as well as airliners. He had a real zest for life and was just as happy in a bar, with a pint in hand, as he was anywhere else. As a result of his pursuance of these two interests in life Joe spent much of his time at the local flying club, both instructing and socialising. He would habitually call in at the club after a day of airline flying and unwind with a beer or three before returning to his digs, more often than not, in the small hours of the morning.

Joe had recently bought himself a brand new, bright red and very shiny Saab motorcar. This was the little V4 Saab 96 version that was currently excelling on the rally scene in the hands of Scandinavian drivers such as Eric Carlson, Stig Blomquist and the like. Joe was very proud of his new car and fussed over it on a daily basis.

On one particular occasion Joe had returned home after a day's work via the flying club – as was his habit. He had also had more than a few beers – as was his habit. Drink driving was, in those days, not considered to be the heinous and unacceptable activity that it is now known to be. Joe had weaved his way home – as was his habit, parked his car outside the house and had then retired to bed feeling no pain – as was his habit.

My wife and I slept in a bedroom at the front of the house that faced the street and at around 2am in the morning we were awoken by an almighty great crashing sound. I peered through the curtains, only half awake, to see what was going on.

What had happened was that our neighbour from the house

opposite us had reversed his car out of his drive and continued straight backwards across the road, broadside into Joe's pride and joy. With his Ford Cortina now embedded in the side of Joe's no longer pristine Saab, he was standing there in the middle of the road, in the middle of the night, scratching his head and clearly wondering how on earth this could have happened. He also didn't seem to be too steady on his feet as he was swaying about in an alarming manner. My first thought was that perhaps he'd somehow hurt himself so I rushed downstairs and outside to help him. It soon became clear that he was not hurt in any way. His problem was that he was so pickled he could hardly either speak or stand up. Relieved that he was OK, but not impressed with the state of Joe's car, I returned inside to wake Joe and break the bad news to him.

It is seldom easy to rouse a man who has had too much to drink and, not surprisingly, I had some difficulty in waking Joe but eventually he staggered, bleary eyed, to his bedroom door. I explained to him what had happened. I'm not sure he really understood but he re-appeared a short time later in his dressing gown and slippers and went downstairs to investigate. Our neighbour was still outside cogitating and the two of them engaged in conversation. My wife and I observed proceedings from our bedroom window.

It is simply not possible to accurately convey in writing just how funny a spectacle the two of these grown men made. I have no idea which of the two of them was the more drunk but the simple fact was that neither of them could either stand still or speak properly. They stood in front of each other, well lit by a nearby street light, swaying backwards and forwards, almost in unison, one in a dressing gown and the other with his shirt hanging out, with both indulging in an occasional stagger to steady themselves. If they'd been on Strictly Come Dancing they'd probably have scored four tens.

To this day I have no idea what they said to each other and I have no idea how they understood each other either. All that issued forth from the pair of them was a continual babble of slurred drivel and an occasional expletive. There was also some pointing and gesticulating but it didn't seem to help much. Eventually they both gave up the unequal struggle and staggered off to their respective beds – no doubt agreeing, somehow, to resume hostilities in the morning. The story did have a happy ending. Once sober the next day, Joe and our neighbour made peace and Joe's car was restored to its former glory after a spell in the car hospital.

Following on from Joe as a lodger, he moved on to fly in the Middle East, came John. John was a fellow co-pilot and a really pleasant individual. He was a little older than was I and he lodged with us because his family were well established in their present home. With his children happy in schools in Oxfordshire John didn't want to move them up north to make them start again at new establishments. He therefore commuted between home and work, staying with us when up at Teesside.

John, like Joe, enjoyed a tipple or two and he also liked his fish and chips. A combination of these two ingredients had endowed John with a somewhat fuller than average physic over the years and it also rendered him with less energy than he otherwise would have possessed. The consequence of all this was that John slept very deeply and it was not infrequent that he would sleep through his alarm when on an early morning flight. Many was the time that there was a mad scramble and panic as he desperately endeavoured to get up and get out of the house before he was late for his flight. Reporting late for duty was always considered a heinous crime and if a flight was late because of a 'no show' there was hell to pay!

A year or so later we moved house and I was by then a captain. John then had no lodging to fall back on and so had taken to living in his VW camper van – parked in the airport car park – when he was working.

On one particular morning when I was flying with John he didn't turn up on time. This was not especially unusual [for him] and we had a pretty well tried and trusted system to cope with this particular foible; one of the ground staff was simply dispatched to his camper van in the car park to arouse him. In the meantime I carried out all the necessary pre-flight duties myself and we proceeded to board our passengers to be ready to depart when John finally deigned to arrive. He was always there in time for us to leave before we'd encountered a delay and this morning was no different.

What was different this time however, was John and the state of his dress. He came running across the airport apron, properly kitted out in his full uniform, trousers, jacket, hat, etc, the full kit and caboodle [as one would expect] except that from out of the bottom of each of his trouser legs were protruding the two ends of the legs of a white and blue striped pair of pyjama bottoms. A more comical sight you've never seen in your life. Goodness knows what our passengers thought as he puffed and panted up the aircraft stairs and into the flight deck full of profuse apologies. Still, as usual we departed on time so no real damage was done.

Eventually John's habit of oversleeping resulted in too many early morning flights departing late and he landed himself in deep trouble. Summonsed down to head office to face the music, John again managed to turn up late, even for that important interview! This was considered to be a bridge too far and there was a parting of the ways. I always thought that this was a sad way for John to finish his time with the company. He was worth a lot more than that but que sera, sera.

43. The Pilot Myth Broken

I had always thought that pilots were both sensible and intelligent. It wasn't until long after I'd become one myself and had moved into a management position that I began to question that assumption and to think, on occasion, that I was mistaken in granting such accolades to the breed.

Before anyone gets the wrong impression let me say that most aviators fit the description pretty well. Even those whose actions have surprised me and given rise to my scepticism are quite bright too and generally speaking, perfectly safe and competent aeroplane drivers. It's just that sometimes common sense, propriety and/or a sense of proportion seems to desert their powers of reason and they become devoid of rational thought.

One such was Harry. Harry was a captain who found himself posted to Glasgow from the East Midlands, much against his will. He hadn't wanted to move so kept on his house in the Midlands as well as having a place up in Scotland. He used to commute between his two abodes by air on the company's schedule service flights, as did a few of his fellow colleagues who found themselves in the same boat. All fine and dandy so far.

The problem was that Harry had a chainsaw. Unfortunately it would seem that this one chainsaw was not enough to service the demands of his two estates and he needed to use it at each end of his two house property empire from time to time. Rather than invest in a chainsaw for each end of his commute, Harry decided to take it with him to whichever end of his portfolio it was needed at the time. Again, not a problem in itself. All Harry had to do was pop it in the aircraft hold when he boarded his flight and then take it out again at the other end. Simple – or so one would have thought.

Unfortunately this airline captain, this shining example of gravitas and responsibility, this icon of safety management, fully trained to deal with dangerous goods and volatile substances on his aircraft, on this occasion, either forgot to empty the fuel tank of his chainsaw or decided that it didn't need draining in the first place. Either way Harry loaded his saw into the aircraft hold with fuel still sloshing about in the petrol tank.

As luck would have it the flight – from Edinburgh to East Midlands was uneventful. That is, until it parked up and the baggage handlers opened the hold door. At this point they were assailed by an overpowering aroma of petrol fumes. Investigation soon revealed the source – none other than Harry's chainsaw of course. Luckily for Harry this piece of sheer stupidity didn't cost him his job – but it very nearly did.

On another occasion our Harry had been on holiday to some sunny Mediterranean hotspot. He flew with Britannia Airways, then one of the larger UK holiday airlines. During the flight the cabin crew came round with a survey form that they asked passengers to complete. This survey was designed to give the airline feedback on what people thought about their service, etc. Thinking that he was being helpful, good old Harry duly completed this survey with a very long list of aspects that he felt were wanting in Britannia's service – poor food, slow cabin service, late flight, etc, etc. Harry's list went on and on, all negatives and no positives.

This would have been all well and good – except that we had an arrangement with Britannia for staff travel concessions and Harry was actually flying on a ticket that was absolutely free – his flights, there and back, weren't costing him a penny piece! As he'd attributed his name and details to his survey return this was picked up by Britannia when the form got back to them a day or two later. Needless to say they were not impressed and they lodged a complaint with us with a threat to withdraw concessions to all BMI staff. Again Harry found himself in the doghouse and his collar being felt – quelle surprise!

Sometimes pilots showed what [to me] seemed to be a surprising lack of initiative. Either that or they just wanted to pass the buck. Taking responsibility was for someone else to do, they weren't paid enough to make decisions [I hope you detect the irony!]. I had a phone call from our Operations people one evening whilst I was at home. Apparently we'd had an aeroplane land at Heathrow having come in from some far flung destination, Addis Ababa or Freetown or somewhere similar. Anyway, it was now flying on to Glasgow and the fresh crew had found insects on board. The captain was worried about this and he wanted to know what he should do about it – would the aircraft need fumigating before it flew again?

From the information given to me I assumed that the aircraft was alive with bugs and this seemed like a fair question. The trouble was I hadn't got a clue, probably it should but I was neither the Minister of Health nor the Chief Medical Advisor to the Government. I was but a pilot, what did I know about these things? I asked what kind of insects they were and how many. Our Ops. people called the pilot back and asked the question. Back came the relayed answer,

"Only one insect, it looks like a locust but they weren't sure".

"And where is this locust now?". I asked. Again a relayed answer:-

"Oh, they've got it in a plastic bag in the flight deck". I have to say that at this point I ran out of patience. What had started out as a plague had now been reduced to one solitary item.

"OK", I said to our Ops. chap, "Tell the captain to put the bag with the locust in it on the captain's seat, sit on it and fly the bloody thing to Glasgow!".

I didn't hear any more from them but the plane departed on time [and nobody became ill or got bitten].

Another example of these displays of lack of initiative and stupidity came one winters evening. Again I was at home and I had a call. One of our aircraft was stuck in some airport or other in one of the 'Stans,

I forget which now but they'd been flying our schedule service to Baku [Azerbaijan] the day before and had had to divert to an airport elsewhere in the region due to snow. They'd had to spend the night there and had apparently endured a horrendous, and long, taxi ride to their hotel [all hotels close to this airport were already full due to earlier and multiple diversions]. Likewise, the return taxi ride to the airport the next morning was no better and they'd all thought that they were going to die. They were now back on their aircraft waiting to depart – and had been for some four or five hours.

The problem was that the airport they were at was now itself closed with snow and wouldn't re-open for at least another hour or two. The captain said that they were running out of duty hours. If they couldn't take off soon then they would have to spend another night there. What was I going to do about this? And, by the way, they point blank refused to go back to last night's hotel [far too dangerous], we'd have to find another one for them.

I listened with mounting incredulity to this sorry tale. Just what did this captain think we could do to clear the runway or even find them another hotel when every bed in the area was already taken? Not only that we were something like 2,500 miles away from their locality and possessed with about as much local knowledge as the captain had of the Moon. It was clear that the Operations Controller who had called me felt the same and had been beating his head against a brick wall with this pilot. I suggested that the captain might like to call me direct so that we could try and sort out the mess. The captain duly called me.

Our conversation was rather brief. I pointed out the distance between us and the improbability of our ability to clear the snow any quicker than those on the scene. I also spelled out the various options that I saw as being available: – 1. He could find an alternative, more local, hotel himself in the event that it became necessary. It was simply not possible from England, we'd already exhausted our repertoire, as had our handling agents on the spot, working on his behalf. 2. If he couldn't find another hotel then he'd have to return to last night's hotel as there were no other choices. 3. If he wouldn't go back to that hotel and there were no alternatives, then he and his crew would have to spend the night on the aeroplane. 4. Failing all of the above, then he was best advised to await the re-opening of the runway and to then fly the aircraft back to the UK using his 'Captain's Discretion' [a legal concession allowing the Captain to extend the duty hours when in extremis].

I also asked what he thought the words 'initiative' and 'leadership' meant and why he thought we paid pilots the salaries they commanded. He was not impressed but as soon as the runway re-opened he flew his Airbus back to the UK.

Why did any of us back at base need to get involved in the first place?

44. The Fiery Izzie.

I described in an earlier story the incident at Leeds Bradford airport when one of our Viscount aircraft skidded off the runway and broke its undercarriage.

The sequel that first story was that not only was it necessary to investigate the detail of the two pilot's actions, the same was true of what had transpired in the cabin during the incident.

We carried two cabin crew on the Viscount, it wasn't a massively large aircraft and we had it configured for a maximum of seventy three passengers so two cabin crew were considered to be sufficient to cover all eventualities. On this particular flight both the cabin crew members were based at East Midlands and were staying in the same hotel as were we, the management team investigating the cause of the incident. Both these cabin crew members were seasoned professionals who'd been in the job for quite a while and they both really knew their stuff.

One was a steward by the name of Stuart [he and his wife, Heather, were to become lifelong friends of ours in later years]. Stuart was a very competent operator, quiet, knowledgeable and very good with people, especially those who were nervous about flying. His colleague, Izzie, was no less competent and professional but was a different character altogether. Izzie was Irish and full of beans, lively, brash, loud, always a smile and always a quip just round the corner, if not already delivered. Izzie was also a bit of a disciplinarian and she wouldn't stand for any nonsense from her passengers – or us pilots either! Anyone who transgressed the rules, or her instructions, would soon know about it – she was definitely no shrinking violet and not one for taking prisoners alive.

It hadn't been too difficult to establish that the actions taken in the cabin by these two following this sudden – and totally unexpected – emergency had been exemplary. As luck would have it, there was also a third cabin crew member on board who was travelling up to Leeds as a passenger, Trish. Trish was also a seasoned and very professional team player. They had all reacted exactly as they had been drilled and trained to do and everything had been handled like clockwork within their domain.

Both Stuart and Izzie had rapidly assessed the situation and as soon as the aircraft had come to a grinding halt in an 'unusual attitude' [i.e. tipped to one side because the undercarriage had collapsed], without further prompting from anyone, had used their discretion and ordered the passengers to evacuate the aircraft. Their clear instruction was for everyone to get out from the left hand side only.

This was because the right wing of the aircraft had been damaged and there were jagged bits of metal sticking out of the top of it. Anyone going out of the emergency exits over the right wing risked been severely damaged by these jagged shards. Not only that, the inner fuel tank in the right wing would almost certainly have been punctured and so presented a significant fire risk. Best to keep that risk outside the aircraft by leaving the exits on that side closed. How these two reached such logical conclusions so quickly [and which were both totally correct and aligned] and in the dark and on a very stormy night and during what must have been a very frightening experience, was very impressive – but that's what they had done, ably assisted by the redoubtable Trish. Everyone therefore got off that aeroplane in short order and without harm or injury.

Everyone that is, bar one. There's always one! On this occasion it was but one chap who ignored Izzie's instruction not to use the emergency exits over the right hand wing. Izzie had seen him making his move but in the heat of the battle and before she could do anything about it he had opened one of the exits over the offending wing and disappeared into the dark of the night. As it transpired no damage was done, the passenger didn't hurt himself on any torn metal and the ruptured fuel tank didn't catch fire either, so all was well.

The following evening, after the accident itself, Stuart and Izzie were still up at Leeds in the hotel – it had taken all day to de-brief them and they were by now pretty drained and in need of nothing more than a bit of relaxation. Roger, our company accident investigator, Dave – our Operations Director and myself had now been joined by John Wolfe, one of the company's co-owners.

It was decided that we should take our very well performing cabin crew out for a slap up meal in one of Leeds finest dining establishments by way of some small token of recognition of their performance in the hour of need. Research was conducted, a suitable establishment identified, reservations were made and we all turned up at the appointed hour – each of us looking forward to a pleasant and relaxing evening with some good food and a good bottle – or two – of decent wine. Best of all John Wolfe would be picking up the tab! It would be a fine contrast to the events of twenty four hours previously, especially for Izzie and Stuart.

And so it was. The wine was flowing, along with the conversation – which was light, cheerful and a long way from the events of the previous twenty four hours. We were all just beginning to come down from what had been a very difficult, traumatic and highly charged experience when – without warning or explanation – Izzie suddenly vacated her seat and made a bee line track across a very full dining room. Izzie's target was a distant table occupied by a couple. On arrival at said table Izzie engaged in animated conversation. We couldn't, of course, hear what was going on but there was much pointing and gesticulation from our excited Irish colleague and looks of incredulity and incomprehension from the seated pair.

It rather looked to me as if this was a bit of a one way conversation that wasn't going too well. A bit of diplomacy seemed to be required I thought, so I arose to intervene. It turned out that the chap seated at the table with his wife/girlfriend/fiancé/companion was the very man who had defied Izzie's orders the previous evening and had escaped from the aeroplane via the wrong exit over the wrong wing! Izzie, somehow or another, had recognised him – across a crowded room – and was intent on pointing out to him the error of his ways, as was Izzie's wont. He, by contrast, thankful to still be alive, had decided to celebrate this fact by taking his partner out for a good meal in a good restaurant and in an intimate setting. He had been sitting there, minding his own business with his lady love, when all of a sudden – and out of nowhere – had appeared this Irish apparition intent on accusing him of crimes more heinous than those carried out by Attila the Hun.

Having eventually caught and understood the nature of Izzie's complaint I was able to extricate her from the engagement and persuade her to rejoin our little party. Honour was restored, I hoped, by my application of a few words of diplomacy to the couple – so unexpectedly interrupted – and a bottle of good wine [or maybe it was champagne – I can't now remember] delivered to the hapless and unsuspecting pair at their table and underwritten by John Wolfe – who probably picked up their whole dinner bill as well!

As for Izzie, what could be done? The answer was 'not a lot'. She would have argued that she had been right to issue the instruction that she did at the time of the incident [as she was] and so it was right that she should pursue any violation. Who can say that she was wrong? In any event she'd done a good job – as had Stuart – and none of us management types present had either the heart – and certainly not the courage – to take her on!!

45. Customs Surprise

Back in the '70s we used to run a schedule service on the Viscount from East Midlands to Frankfurt. For various reasons this service went via Birmingham and Brussels before then hopping across the Belgian border to finish in Frankfurt. Once in Frankfurt we had a stopover of about five hours. We then retraced our steps back to East Midlands via the same two cities, Brussels and Birmingham.

This all made for a bit of a boring, and long, day. Not so much the flying but the time spent on the ground whilst at Frankfurt. Not only that, but at the end of this long and tedious day's work we still had to go through the formalities of customs clearance when we finally landed back at base. This was, more often than not, a bit of a pain. Aircrew were not entitled to the same 'duty free' allowances as the rest of the travelling public and the Customs people seemed to take a perverse delight in making us jump through hoops with form filling and bag searches when all we wanted to do was to go home.

Five hours at an airport is a difficult time period to fill – it's too long to do nothing and not long enough to do anything. Even back then, Frankfurt was a large airport with a lot of cafes, restaurants and shops, etc, but there's only so much coffee you can drink, or food that you can eat and once you've been over there a few times there are no more shops through which to interestingly browse either. The company provided us with a 'rest room' in which to while away the time but even a book or a magazine or two can become somewhat boring after a couple of hours or more.

On one particular day I was over in Frankfurt doing this round the houses flying day and we, the crew, had as usual been cruising the terminal. We'd done the leisurely coffee and the longish lunch bit and were now, rather aimlessly, wandering around the shops, not looking for anything in particular but rather just passing the time, running down the clock and feeling rather tediously bored.

One of the cabin crew with us was a lively young lady called Lyne. Lyne was not at all an unattractive lady. She was also rather predatory and had a roving eye for the pilot community. In her time she'd kept a lot of like minded aeroplane drivers very happy and fully occupied whilst on trips away from home and she was quite open about her hobby and her preferences. As well as being very friendly, Lyne was also blessed with a good sense of humour, even if often of a rather lavatorial nature.

There was one particular shop at Frankfurt Airport in which Lyne took a more than casual interest. It was called 'Dr. Muller's' and it concentrated on the sale of those specialist items for adventurous couples who required only their own company, vivid imaginations, agility and much privacy. Lyne spent a long time in this emporium and we followed suit. I suppose we lived in less enlightened times in those days. Certainly the Germans, or Dr. Muller at least, seemed to be more liberated [and imaginative] than were we Brits. There was 'stuff' in this shop that I had no idea even existed and certainly had not the first idea of what to do with, even if I'd possessed any of it. I'm sure that If I'd asked Lyne she'd have been only too happy to explain all – demonstrate even – but I hasten to add that neither of these eventualities ever occurred!

What did occur however, was that I had a bit of an idea. Lyne was somewhere in the shop doing her own thing and I was with the rest of the crew. I outlined my plan to them; we'd buy one of the battery operated items in the shop [the large 'face massage' model] and one of the cabin crew would hide it away in Lyne's crew bag on the flight back home. When we arrived back at East Midlands and the Customs Officer came into the flight deck to collect the necessary paperwork I would tell him what we'd done, he'd search Lyne's bag, find the offending item and we'd all have a jolly good laugh – such fun! Everyone thought that this was a good wheeze so we then proceeded to execute our plan.

I suppose that this all goes to show that people get pretty silly and are easily pleased when they're bored out of their minds. Anyway, that aside, we then flew back to East Midlands in some anticipation and, for a change, looking forward to a baggage search from Mr. Customs man. The only gamble was that we had to hope that we were met by one of the Customs people who had a sense of humour and who would then play along with our little joke. There weren't too many of that type but on this occasion it turned out that Lady Luck was on our side.

Back at base our passengers disembarked and we were duly met by the Customs Officer. I explained what had been going on and he readily agreed to play along. With greater than usual gravitas he then advised us all that we would have to accompany him to the Customs Office for a 'routine' inspection. We were to bring our bags with us and they should not now be opened unless in front of a Customs official. We all trooped off to the Customs office, everyone knowing what was in store. That is, everyone except for poor Lyne of course, who had no idea of what was to come.

Suddenly it struck me that maybe this hadn't been such a good idea after all – what if Lyne had unwittingly sneaked an illicit carton of cigarettes or a bottle or two of gin into her bag, what then? I should have thought of that before, now it was too late and we were going to be stuck with a problem and some explaining to do if that eventuality arose.

As it was all was well. Once in the office Mr. Customs picked out Lyne and asked her to open her bag. Lyne happily complied, knowing that she had nothing to hide. Mr. Customs then dutifully and studiously rummaged around within and amongst the content of her valise. We, of course, all waited expectantly for the offending item to be produced – except for Lyne who had no idea what was going on. Mr. Customs rummaged on and I began to think that the plan had failed, the rest of the cabin crew had thought better of it and hadn't placed the item in Lyn's bag after all!

Then, without warning and at last and with a flourish of triumph, Mr. Customs extracted not one item but two! One still in its shop box wrapping and another, naked and unwrapped and which had, clearly, long since already been introduced to the delights of the big bad world and Lyne's desires. Lyne was the one who laughed loudest and longest!

46. Business and Pleasure

It's expensive to fly any aeroplane. The bigger the aircraft and the faster it flies the more expensive it becomes. At the point where the aircraft becomes as big and as fast as a passenger jet it becomes virtually essential to use aircraft simulators for training. Flying the real thing – when no revenue is returned – is eye wateringly expensive. Not only that, a simulator makes for a much better standard of training as all manner of failures and problems can be replicated in these machines, which obviously can't happen in a real aeroplane.

There is a problem with simulators though which is that the simulators themselves are also pretty expensive, nothing like as expensive as an aeroplane but they're still expensive to buy and to operate. Most large airlines will buy their own simulators as they have the economy of scale to be able to justify the necessary investment. Smaller airlines then buy time on these simulators – a win, win for both sides. When British Midland first bought it's jet DC9 aircraft we used the Finnair simulator based at their offices up in Helsinki. Later we switched to using KLMs machine in Amsterdam – much closer and more convenient – and much warmer too [although Holland can get pretty cold in winter as well!].

All good things come to an end however and over time, as KLM replaced its DC9 fleet with other aircraft, they no longer needed to retain their own simulator. The upshot was that they decided to sell it. This gave us a problem. There were no other DC9 simulators within striking distance that we could move to. Unless we bought the KLM machine we'd have to start sending our crews over to the USA for their regular six monthly training and testing sessions – this would be both expensive and time consuming.

I put a business case to our main Board to justify buying the KLM simulator and received clearance to do a deal with them to purchase it outright. My partner in crime for this project was to be Ron Hardy, our Chief Pilot. Ron was a very experienced and longstanding senior manager as well as being a seasoned and very experienced pilot. Ron was also an Olympic standard beer drinker and he had led me [and countless others] astray many a time and oft over the years. Not only could Ron see me under the table without blinking [as he could most people], he never even seemed to suffer from any kind of hangover whatsoever, however much he'd imbibed. An added bonus, for him, given his proclivity for a pint or two.

Our problem with the simulator deal was that we had a very limited budget and KLM were asking a very high price – for what was, in truth, a pretty old and long since depreciated asset. They also knew that we were between a rock and a hard place – if we didn't buy this simulator from them then we'd be in trouble with our future pilot training programme. Hence the disparity in the relative prices put on the simulator by each side. All this put KLM very much in the driving seat as they could afford to play hardball and so, not unreasonably, they did.

KLM was also a very large outfit and had their own internal legal department. This, and the difference in our two contrasting end price targets, made for a very protracted period of negotiation. It was to be several months of hard meetings before we were finally able to settle on a price that was acceptable to both sides and only then were we able, at last, to sign a contract. On the way to concluding the deal with KLM Ron and I had many journeys to and from Amsterdam. This generated many a small adventure and more than a few enjoyable days out together in the Dutch capital.

Negotiations took on a regular pattern. We had two flights a day between East Midlands and Amsterdam. When a meeting was required we'd catch the early morning flight out, arriving in Amsterdam at about 10 a.m. local time. We'd then pick up a hire car and drive over to KLMs offices for our meeting. Although we went through a protracted negotiation process our individual meetings would rarely last beyond lunchtime. Ron and I would then have nothing to do until catching our evening service back to East Midlands. This was manna from heaven to Ron – all afternoon and nothing to do except drink beer, what could be better! Ron seemed to know every pub and cafe in Amsterdam and all their opening hours as well. As one bar shut mid afternoon he'd deftly move us on to another with seemingly no interruption to the flow of fizzy continental lager.

There was one infamous occasion when we moved on from one pub to another, happily parking our hire car close by our destination in a convenient gap along a line of similarly parked cars. When we returned an hour or two later, not only had our car disappeared, so too had all the other cars. We were mystified and wondered if we'd got the wrong street but were pretty sure we hadn't. I asked in an adjacent shop why the street was now devoid of parked cars. It turned out that parking was prohibited after 4 p.m. All the locals had decamped and our car had been towed off to the pound.

Ron threw the keys down the street in disgust and we had to order a taxi to get back to the airport. Christian, the chap from whom we regularly hired our car [at a good rate] was not impressed when we told him that it had been stolen – by the police. He was even less pleased when Ron announced that he'd lost the car keys into the bargain.

When on these negotiating missions, we used to buy our 'duty free' allowances on our outbound flight from East Midlands as, not infrequently, the cabin crew had sometimes run out of stock on the return evening trip, having sold everything on the outbound leg.

On one particular occasion we went over on one of our expeditions and it happened to be my birthday. As usual we bought our duty frees on the way out to Amsterdam. Stupidly, during the course of the day I let slip that I was now another year older. On our flight home that evening – already replete with many beers from the afternoon and having availed himself of yet further alcohol in the form of gin and tonics from the aircraft bar, Ron tried to buy a bottle of brandy when the cabin staff came round with the duty free trolley:

"Bottle of Courvoisier pleeesh", said Ron.

"Ron", says I, "You can't have any more alcohol, you bought your full allowance this morning and you don't even drink Brandy either!"

"I can buy what I want, don't interfeeere – bottle of Courvoisier pleesh".

"Ron, you don't even drink brandy!"

"Who careshs!'", said Ron and he bought his bottle.

No sooner did he have the bottle in his sticky hand than he turned to me and, with a big grin across his face, held it out to give to me. I grabbed it before he dropped it. His smile broadened even more and he said: –

"Happy Birshday, get out of that!".

I was in a pickle now. I couldn't spurn his generosity, nor could I lose face by refusing to accept the bottle. Customs would not be impressed if they caught me with a bottle over my allowance and if I declared the bottle and paid the duty I would be failing to rise to Ron's challenge.

What to do? I pondered my problem as the flight progressed and was still pondering when the Captain came over the P.A. and announced that we'd be diverting to Birmingham due to snow closing East Midlands airport. This was not good news, I wanted to get home. Ron however simply said:-

"Ah good, time for another G. and T." and promptly ordered us one each.

We landed at Birmingham in a snowstorm and taxied to the terminal. The handling agents hadn't been expecting us and so when we parked and the flight crew shut down the engines we were all plunged into darkness because no external electrical power had been plugged in.

Ron and I were sitting at the back of the aircraft, immediately adjacent to the rear passenger door. As soon as the door opened a howling gale carrying freezing air and snow flakes invaded our space and everything immediately turned to chaos! Ron stood up and, clutching his duty free bag, moved to disembark.

Unfortunately, his glasses fell off and when he picked them up to put them back on he discovered that one of the lenses had fallen out. He stooped to search, in the dark, for his missing lens. I seized the opportunity that was suddenly and unexpectedly presented – as deftly as the Artful Dodger picking a pocket I reversed the process of our carrier bag contents. I took out my bottle of surplus cognac from my bag and slipped it neatly into Ron's, temporarily unguarded, bag!

Now reunited with his lens Ron marched off the aircraft clutching his, now overloaded duty free bag, fully believing that he was immune from interference from Customs and that I was the one 'at risk'. Little did he know! We both walked through the 'Nothing to Declare' channel, me following behind Ron. No sooner was he in this Customs baggage inspection area than he stopped and put his bag on the counter – directly under the nose of the only Customs official in sight – and he then bent down to re-tie his shoe lace! I was mortified: – "Come on Ron, you'll miss the coach – do that outside", I said. Ron ignored me and, oblivious to his parlous position, happily continued to fiddle with his shoes. I walked on, abandoning my friend to his fate. Eventually he re-appeared without a care in the world and as happy as Larry – and still with both bottles in his bag.

"Thanks Ron," I said "I'll have my bottle of brandy back now, if that's OK with you?" and with that, I calmly reached into his bag and retrieved my bottle of birthday Courvoisier. "You crafty bar steward, when did you manage that?!" said Ron in wondrous tones.

Not too many people ever got one over on Ron so I was secretly quite pleased to have scored a point. There's a whole book to be written about him, he was a man very much of his time and a character whom many knew and few forgot – mostly for all the right reasons!

47. A Difference of Opinion

One of the people I came to much admire in my world of flying was John Wolfe, one of the three partners who owned British Midland Airways. As I've said elsewhere, there was much about John that was less easy to understand [or even to forgive] but on balance he was a very smart individual who did a difficult job with limited resources and who took a lot of flack that was not always justified, even if he did sometimes make judgements that were either plain wrong or had unintended consequences.

One of John's less impressive decisions [I would say this wouldn't I!] involved a mistake that I had made – yes, even I was capable of making a mistake – occasionally!!

We had fourteen DC9 aircraft, eleven of which had fuel gauges calibrated in kilos and three which had their gauges calibrated in [imperial] pounds. As a pound of fuel represents approximately half the amount in a kilo of fuel this was not a very smart way of leaving things. One day, because Sod's Law can come into force at any time, some unsuspecting pilot was going to get airborne with about half the amount of fuel on board that he thought he had.

Both myself and other management pilots had argued that this was not a satisfactory state of affairs and that the three aircraft with the 'oddball' gauges should have them changed to kilos so as to fall in line with their brothers. John, who held the purse strings on such matters, would have none of it. Too expensive, he argued, if we trained our drivers properly no one would make such a stupid mistake. Try as we might, none of us could convince him to change his mind. And so we lived with it. Why our regulators, the CAA tolerated this obvious

231

trap, I don't know – but they did.

On one inevitable day the mistake that so many pilots had forecast, was made. You're ahead of me already for, as you've guessed, I was the pilot who fell down the hole. It was a fine summers evening and I was flying to Glasgow and back from East Midlands. I ordered four tons of fuel to be loaded – 4,000 kilos – for the trip. More than enough for the flight itself and enough to allow a good contingency surplus for any unforeseen circumstances. This was duly loaded and off we blasted.

We'd not been flying long, no more than five minutes or so, when I began to feel uncomfortable about our fuel state. To this day I still don't know what it was that triggered the unease that made me query our fuel situation. Maybe it was the position of the fuel gauge needles, maybe it was that they were moving too fast, I don't know but whatever it was, something intuitively alerted me and made me feel uneasy. I mentioned my concern to the co-pilot. He checked the fuel state for himself and couldn't find fault. We continued but I persisted. Suddenly the penny dropped, we were in one of the three 'pounds' aeroplanes and so had only half the fuel we'd thought we had! Frantic calculations from my co-pilot then commenced but I'd already made my decision.

"We've still got enough to get there", he said.

"No", I countered, "Tell Air Traffic that we're diverting to Teesside – for operational reasons"

"We don't need to divert, we can still make Glasgow." he insisted.

He was right of course, we could have flown on to Glasgow – and on a good day with nothing going wrong, anywhere, we would have had no trouble. But the slightest hitch, the smallest delay and we would have been in desperate straits. As it was, we still had enough fuel to comfortably get to Teesside in safety, with enough to spare to cover any problems of delay, etc. and without any hassle or compromise to safety or regulation. Needless to say, we diverted to Teesside for a quick 'splash and dash' before carrying on to up to Glasgow.

One of the interesting things about this faux pax was the difference in reactions from us two pilots. Whilst I was highly embarrassed by falling into such a stupid trap I was intent only on finding a solution that was based on safety and not reputation. My co-pilot, younger, less experienced and no doubt worried for his job, was more concerned with avoiding retribution than anything else. This was how things worked in those days, there was a lot of 'blame culture' and not enough emphasis on the priority of safety. Too many incidents became major problems, or even accidents, because too many pilots made bad decisions merely to cover up their mistakes. Happily things are very different now in aviation. A lot of hard lessons have been learned along the way and a very different Safety culture now exists.

Not surprisingly I was summonsed to see a very serious and sober looking John Wolfe the next morning. He had Dave Court, our Operations Director with him [whose position I was due to take over in a month or two when Dave retired]. I didn't have much to say other than what had happened had happened and, as the captain of the aircraft, it was my fault. It was embarrassing, yes, but there was never any exposure to danger for either the passengers or the aircraft and neither were any safety regulations compromised. We'd never gone below the legal limits for minimum fuel.

John however had a different perspective. He'd recently had bit of an argument with the CAA over another issue and felt that the company didn't need any more hassle from them. As I was the designated heir to the position of Operations Director, John felt that he needed to make an example of me to keep the Authority on side. I was therefore to be sent on gardening leave for three months and not only that, this suspension would be on half pay! And I was to be banned from entering any company building!!

I was a bit nonplussed to put it mildly, I hadn't seen that coming at all. I knew I'd face harsh words – and quite rightly too – but I hadn't thought that any sanction would be quite so severe. Then again, I'd not been aware of John's concerns about the CAA breathing down his neck either. Also, a reduction in salary by fifty percent was a bit of an unexpected blow [and I thought rather unfair – as well as being illegal, but that's another story]. We had four children at school by then and money was in short supply. We needed to keep feeding the bottomless pit of education.

Still, at least the upside of the story was that I'd be out of purgatory after a while. Also, it was a good thing, in a way, that it was me who had made the mistake. I had further to fall than the rest of the pilot community, had it been one of them they'd have probably lost their job altogether! The final piece of silver lining was that within 48 hours of this incident occurring, our three 'oddball' aircraft had shiny new fuel gauges – all now calibrated in kilos! I wonder why John changed his mind!?

There's always a positive but this particular episode was to turn out to have further consequences for me.

48. The Day of The Long Knife

I was, not to put too fine a point on it, somewhat miffed at being sent to Coventry following my misadventure with fuel quantities. I reasoned however, that this wasn't really the end of the world, worse things happen at sea and at least I'd have some time at home with the family.

It did present a new problem though, I'd already booked our summer family holiday – a fortnight in South West France – and this was due to start on the self same week that I was now scheduled to return to work. It didn't need much imagination to work out that it would go down like a lead balloon with the grown ups in the Airline if, following my return from enforced absence, I was to then disappear for a further couple of weeks by announcing that I was now off on holiday. My friend John Wolfe would have wanted to see me hanged, drawn, quartered, my head skewered to a pike and then put on display above the ramparts of the Tower of London. Something needed to be done.

Not without some difficulty, the internet was not yet a tool for everyman, I re-arranged our ferry bookings, accommodation, etc, etc, and moved our holiday into the last two weeks of my enforced time off – problem solved and everyone now happy.

All was well and my grounding was being put to good domestic use when, out of nowhere, a second dose of Sods Law then intervened. About a month in to my sentence the phone rang. It was John's secretary, Rosemary. John wanted to see me at nine o'clock sharp, in his office, tomorrow morning.

I turned up at the appointed hour and was ushered into the inner sanctum with a high level of curiosity as to what this meeting was to be about. John was again with our Flight Operations Director, Dave Court. Courtesies over, John cut to the chase. Enough was enough, he said, he'd made his point and there was no real mileage in letting my suspension drag on any longer. I was to pick up where I'd left off a month ago and all was now forgiven!

This was entirely unexpected and came as a bit of a bombshell! I'd just re-arranged for our family holiday to fall within my sentence of suspension and now the carpet had been whipped clean out from under me. I was back to where I'd started from, with a holiday booked on the wrong side of the time line.

John had offered me an olive branch and were I to throw it back at him by telling him that I couldn't start back at work again for two weeks because I was going on holiday I would be toast within five seconds flat and nothing more than a distant memory. There was no choice other than for me to cancel our summer break. This would be a great disappointment to my wife and the children but to do otherwise would be foolhardy in the extreme – assuming that I was minded to continue working at British Midland and to retain an uninterrupted ability to continue paying our mortgage.

I left John's office with Dave Court and in rather subdued mood. "You're a bit quiet", he said, "I rather thought you'd be pleased!". I told him about my holiday problem and that, whilst I was pleased to be back in the fold at work, I was not looking forward to having to tell my wife and children that they'd now not be going on holiday.

"You can't do that!" said Dave.

"Well, I'll have to", I said "If I go off now John will have a fit and that'll be the end of me".

"Well can't your wife go without you?" Dave suggested.

"No way", I said, "For a start she won't drive in France. Also, having to keep control of four young and lively boys, on her own, for a fortnight, would be a bridge too far. Plus, we're 'self catering' so it wouldn't be much of a holiday for her anyway". Dave pondered all this and then he said: –

"OK. I'll tell you what – you take your leave, as planned – and then you can start work again when you get back. Leave it with me and I'll square it all with John."

I could see that Dave was trying to be helpful but I was very doubtful that John would be happy with this plan so I said that I'd think about it overnight before making a decision. In fact I knew damn fine that John would explode if this happened!

Back at home that evening my wife and I kicked the issue around and we came up with a plan that I thought might just work to keep everyone happy. I would drive the family down to SW France over the weekend, as planned, and then catch a flight back on the Sunday evening so as to be in the office for Monday. At the end of the fortnight I would then fly out on the Friday night, drive us all back over that weekend and be in the office again on the Monday morning. As we'd be anyway having friends [with children] to stay whilst we were in France my wife wouldn't be left with everything to do entirely on her own so this seemed to be a reasonable compromise.

There was a slight issue in that the only flight I could find to get me back on the Monday morning was into Gatwick, landing at about seven a.m. This would mean a hire car drive back up to the Midlands and so I'd not be in the office until around eleven in the morning. All in all this didn't seem to be too bad a plan to me. I outlined my scheme to Dave the next morning and told him that I'd be back in the office next Monday at about lunchtime due to the flight timings, etc. All sorted and settled, I was once more a happy bunny.

At this point in the evolution of the airline we were in head to head competition with British Airways on the Heathrow – Glasgow and Heathrow – Edinburgh scheduled service routes. They'd been flying these two routes with what they called their 'Shuttle Service'. This was a no frills service but with a monopoly and so had high fare levels and not much by way of good cabin service. Following deregulation of the industry by Margaret Thatcher, we'd come onto the routes with a full service offering – good food, free drinks, newspapers, etc, with what we called our 'Diamond Service'.

This had hit B.A. hard and we'd taken a good deal of the market share from them, not least because we also offered our fares at a significantly cheaper rate. B.A. had now re-launched their own offerings in an attempt to win back their customers. Our reaction to this was to convene a cabal of the great and the good from our airline to develop an ongoing strategy designed to maintain and grow our market share and to keep B.A. at bay. John Wolfe headed up this think tank and I was also a part of it.

John called a meeting of this illustrious brain storming panel for the Friday afternoon of the day I was due to take the family down to France. Not a problem but I needed to get away sharpish at 5pm to drive down to the south coast to catch our overnight ferry. The meeting dragged on well past close of play and I was becoming anxious to get away. At last John wrapped it up and announced that he was off to the pub and that we'd resume at nine o'clock sharp on Monday. My heart sank!

I wouldn't be back until two hours after nine a.m and I just knew that this would not go down well with the big man. However, there was nothing much that I could do about it, except to let him know, which I did as we all left the room to go our separate ways. He acknowledged the information but didn't make any particular response, either good or bad. I scuttled off, keen to get on my way.

My plan went like clockwork over the weekend and with the family safely delivered to their holiday destination I was back in the office by eleven o'clock on the Monday, tired but intact. The place was like the Marie Celeste, none of my fellow 'management' colleagues were around. I'd not long been sat at my desk when the phone rang – John Wolfe wanted to see me in his office.

I entered. John had a face like thunder and Dave sat meekly next to him, nervously shuffling bits of paper. This wasn't a meeting, it was a firing squad. I was told, in no uncertain terms, that I was not fit for purpose, that I was not management material and that I was now history, never again to be invited back into the human race. With immediate effect I was to be stripped from all management responsibilities, associated salary increments and from all management privileges. I was no longer to be a Training Captain either and furthermore, I was never to darken his step again.

Well that put me in my place! I had no response of course – and neither was I invited to give one. I was shown where the door was and invited to walk through it. The irony was that some ten minutes later as I was clearing my desk the phone rang again. This time it was John himself. He wanted another meeting, this one in the Bull, a local hostelry – where he bought me several beers. He was nothing if not full of paradox.

I was to learn later, from others at that meeting on the Monday morning, that the first question that John had asked was: –

'Where's Jim?'.

Dave had apparently said: –

"I don't know, I'll go and find out". He'd then left the room and returned some few minutes later and announced: –

"He's down in France!".

John hit the ceiling and that was we me cooked, there and then! I never quite understood why Dave reacted how he did and although I rubbed along with him quite well and he remained a friend over the future years of his retirement, I never had quite the same respect for him that I had held before that day.

There was eventually a happy ending to this saga. A year or so later John once again admitted me into his inner sanctum of management and there I remained, in one form or another, until eventually walking off into the sunset of retirement!

49. A Close Call

One of many more or less parallel questions that are often asked of airline pilots is "Have you ever had any scary moments?" – or "Did you ever have any emergencies?" – or something similar along those lines. I suspect that, like most other pilots, I've long since lost count of how many times this genre of query has come my way!

By way of response, I can say, with total honesty, that in all my years as an airline pilot the answer to that question is "No – not even once!" [It was a bit different for me in small aeroplanes but that's not the subject of this particular tale!]. Of course things went wrong from time to time but I have no recollection of anything really seriously threatening ever coming my way. I never even had a single engine failure or had to shut an engine down – other pilots did but I always seemed to be on the right aeroplane at the right time. I shut engines down many times whilst flying but these were always only when either training other pilots or conducting air tests, never did it happen in anger because something had gone wrong with one.

As an aside, – for those of a more mechanical bent, I flew nearly ten thousand hours in the Viscount aircraft, which had four engines – that's forty thousand engine hours. And in all that time I never shut one down in anger. If you do the sums that adds up to four and a half years in the air! Quite a testament to the Rolls Royce Dart engines that were fitted to the beast.

A question that would yield a different answer from me would be "Did anything life threatening ever happen to you?". The answer to that one is "Yes, but only once" – and the thing that might surprise people is that I wasn't even in the aeroplane involved at the time!

This event happened at Teesside Airport circa 1975. I had arrived at the airport to fly the afternoon and evening service down to Heathrow but the incoming flight, the aircraft I was due to take over, was running late and had not yet landed so I wandered down to the airport coffee shop with my crew, to while away some time over a coffee whilst we waited. We bought our coffees and settled into a set of comfortable chairs around a table in the coffee shop, which overlooked the aircraft parking area and beyond that, the runway which ran left to right in front of the windows and was fairly close at probably no more than three hundred yards or so away.

Teesside was not a busy airport at all. Normally there was very little activity to be seen through the full height windows of the lounge there, which also stretched the full width of the wall overlooking the apron and framed, not just the apron and the runway but also offered a panoramic and splendid view of the Cleveland Hills in the distant background.

Because the airfield was little used it was an ideal place to carry out flight training for pilots and it was therefore frequently visited by various different airlines undertaking their aircrew training exercises. On this day there was a solitary British Airways 'Merchantman' aircraft pounding round and round practicing take-offs and landings – to bring new pilots qualifying on the type up to speed [the Merchantman was a large four engined turboprop aircraft used for carrying cargo and was a derivative of the 139 seat Vickers Vanguard passenger aircraft].

I sat there, sipping my coffee and idly watching this seemingly endless and repetitive series of manoeuvres unfold. The aircraft would land, roll along the runway for a bit, full power would be applied and it would then take off and climb away again, only to once more turn left and then fly back down to the beginning of the runway to repeat the exercise again and again. It all looked typically smooth and routine but I knew, from my own experience, that the trainee pilot would be working like a one armed paper hanger and that the Captain training his student would be paying close attention. It could all go horribly wrong, very quickly, if the student pilot made a bad move and didn't quickly recognise and correct any basic mistake.

I watched as the aeroplane came in for another one of its landings, rolling along the runway and as before, applying full power to once again accelerate down the runway before lifting off into the wild blue yonder. No change from any of the previous departures. Or at least that was what I thought until just after the nose of the thing had been rotated to the take off position. They'd just got the aircraft into the air, literally no more than a few feet off the runway, when it did indeed go all horribly wrong, exceedingly quickly.

Suddenly the aircraft did two things. It banked over to an angle of very nearly ninety degrees and it also turned right by about the same amount. I sat there open mouthed and mesmerised, too transfixed to move. This massive, four engined beast was now heading straight for the end of the terminal building, directly in front of where we were sat, at probably over one hundred and thirty m.p.h. plus and also at an impossibly steep angle of bank. So much so, in fact, that its right wingtip was ploughing a furrow along the grass as it headed straight for us, fully filling the picture windows of the building – and growing ever larger as it approached.

As soon as that wingtip hit the edge of the apron concrete the whole aeroplane would cartwheel into the terminal and we'd all evaporate in a ball of flame and from there into instant and permanent oblivion. I remember thinking that I now had no more than five seconds to live. Not only was I anyway transfixed to the spot, even if I'd had the presence of mind to run, there was nowhere to go. As athletic as I was back then, even I couldn't outrun an airliner ploughing at two miles a minute, or more, and heading straight for me!

Miraculously, the outcome was not instant death in a fireball. Nothing at all happened to us in the terminal and the aircraft didn't end up turning itself into a crisp packet either. Somehow or other the Training Captain managed to gather it all up and regain control of his errant aeroplane. He must have had full opposite aileron and full left rudder applied, no doubt ably assisted by his trainee and a good deal of willpower to boot but, even now, I have no idea how the pair of them did it, so extreme was the situation. Even so, somehow, the wingtip undug itself from the turf before it hit the concrete and the aircraft slewed a bit to its left as it began to right its wings and turn away. It missed the end of the terminal building, still at a very steep angle of bank and disappeared almost as suddenly as it had presented itself. We all listened, still transfixed, for the inevitable crash and explosion as it ploughed into the car park or the hotel behind the terminal. But there was no sound, save a growingly distant drone of aircraft engines. The aircraft and captain went on to make a successful landing a few minutes later and then taxi over to the hanger – where the aircraft was quickly hidden away inside one.

At the end of my days flying that evening I went down to the hanger to have a look at the aircraft. About three feet of the right hand wingtip was either missing or was otherwise torn and bent. The jagged metal now forming the end of the wing was full of mud, grass, and even a lone dandelion had joined this party to add some colour!

It turned out that what had happened was that on takeoff, the training Captain had 'simulated' an engine failure by closing the throttle on the outboard engine on the right wing. As the power reduced on that engine the propeller control, by sheer coincidence, malfunctioned and the propeller 'ran away'. Put simply, this meant that the propeller, instead of being four blades cutting smoothly through the air, went out of control and span so fast that it took on the aerodynamic properties of a fifteen foot diameter dustbin lid pointed flat side on into wind. This resistance was enough to tip any aircraft over and was one of the worst power related malfunctions that could happen on any propeller driven aeroplane. For it to happen at the precise time that it did on that day defies all odds!

Even more remarkable was that a piece of the outboard aileron had been damaged beyond recognition but still the Captain and his trainee had managed to salvage the flight and bring the old girl home.

A truly remarkable piece of flying. I never met the chaps flying that day but if they read this account and get in touch I'll happily buy them a pint – and a fresh pair of underpants each!

For me those two pilots are up there in the same league as 'Sully' Sullenberger and Jeff Skiles of landing on the river Hudson fame. The only difference being that the story of this propeller failure flight never even made the local news, far less world wide acclaim! Unsung heroes, both.

And that was as close as I ever came to a true emergency involving an airliner!

50. The fickle Finger of Fate.

By and large I led a charmed life in my flying career – and outside it too, but that is not a part of this collection of stories! One of my early pieces of nearly amazingly good fortune happened when I was flying [as a passenger] from Miami to London. In the end it turned out to not actually be as amazing as it could have been but it kind of shows that Lady Luck was often not far away from me.

The year was 1967 and I'd not long started my flying training at the London School of Flying. At that time my parents were living in British Honduras [now Belize] and I'd been out there to visit them and was on my way back to the UK, flying as a passenger with BOAC. There were no direct flights from the UK to Belize or vice verca. You had to travel via Miami and switch airlines there to get from A to C.

Once on board the BOAC flight at Miami and now bound for London, I found myself sitting next to a middle aged lady. It could just as easily have been anyone else but it was this particular lady and it was she who was going to make the difference. After a while we started exchanging pleasantries, as one does when rubbing shoulders with an enforced neighbour sitting at rather close quarters and destined to remain immediate 'friends' for several hours. I suppose that our idle chat meandered around whilst we both searched for common ground, shared interests, etc. She asked me what I'd been doing in Miami and so I filled her in on the background. Amongst the information I imparted was that I told her that I'd taken a short break from learning to fly.

On hearing this piece of information I was suddenly deluged with a whole string of questions about my flying activities. This lady seemed to be genuinely interested in what I was doing and where I thought it would take me in terms of my future career. Soon she revealed what lay behind this interest and curiosity. Her husband, she said, was a chap called Harold Bamberg and he, she added, "Owned an airline". Quite a good throw away line when you think about it! I'd never heard of Harold Bamberg but the airline she told me he owned was called British Eagle International, of which I had most certainly heard!

British Eagle was a pretty big UK airline back then – one of the biggest independent UK airlines of the day, if not the biggest. Suddenly my whole approach to this lady was changed. One minute I'd been having a casual and polite conversation with my random neighbour about nothing in particular and the next I found myself sitting next to someone who was suddenly revealed as being very important in the world of aviation [in my eyes anyway]. This was demanding of even more respect and courtesy than I had employed up until this point – but I did wonder what she was doing sitting back with me in the economy section – rather than relaxing 'up front' in the cosseted First Class cabin!

Anyway, I determined to ensure that I would leave a good impression on my new found companion, not that I would have done otherwise even if she hadn't had an aviation connection but somehow this now seemed to be important. I don't suppose that I thought that anything would come of my rubbing shoulders [almost literally] with the wife of an airline owner and engaging with her in polite conversation but if I did then I was proved to have been almost right!

When we landed back at Heathrow and before we disembarked Mrs. Bamberg told me that she'd enjoyed my company and she gave me a piece of paper on which she said she'd written her husband's office telephone phone number. If I cared to a call this number, in a couple of days time – after she'd had time to talk to him, she was sure he'd give me some good advice as to how to get on once I'd qualified as a professional pilot.

A few days later I summonsed up the courage to take up her offer and call the number she had passed on to me. I had no idea as to how the conversation would unfold and my call was made with more than a little trepidation. However, I reasoned that the worst that would happen was that I'd get a big brush off. On the other hand I might well get some good advice on the best way forward so it was worth doing. What was there to lose?

I needn't have worried. Harold Bamberg was very friendly and personable. He told me that his wife had enjoyed her flight back from Miami. She hadn't been looking forward to it beforehand because she wasn't in First Class 'as usual'. This, he told me was his fault because he'd forgotten to get his secretary to arrange her ticket for her until it was too late. The flight was full and he'd only been able to secure a seat for her in steerage. However, she'd enjoyed my company he said and all was well! Would I like him to arrange for me to meet his Chief Pilot for a chat? How could I not take up such an offer?

A week or two later I met up with British Eagle's Chief pilot at Heathrow. He gave me a lot of his time and fielded a whole series of questions [that must have seemed rather inane] from this young man who didn't really know the difference between his elbow and the dark side of the moon.

At this stage I was still in the very early stages of my flying training and really didn't know very much about the business side of the airline world at all. However, I had learned that it was a tough game in which to secure a job once you'd got your licences. Airlines liked pilots with experience so 'new' pilots were already disadvantaged. Not only that, there weren't many flying jobs to be had. We were still living in the shadow of the aftermath of the 6 day war in the Middle East, resulting in many airlines struggling and more than a few even going out of business. This meant that there were lots of experienced aviators chasing very few openings. Back at my flying school, few trainees had any secure future [apart from our Middle Eastern colleagues] mapped out and I was no different.

At the end of our chat the Chief Pilot gave me his business card and told me to give him a call once I'd got my qualifications [scheduled to be in about ten months time]. Then, he said, he'd 'see what he could do' to find me a flying position with British Eagle! This was an amazing development and made me the envy of my trainee colleagues. Apart from a contingent of Middle East aspirants, sponsored by their own emerging state airlines, I became about the only student with his future potentially mapped out. What a lucky boy was I!

This happy and random meeting with the wife of the owner of a prominent U.K. airline, which had ended up with so much promise, was not to culminate with the implied fairy tale scenario which should have been the result. Instead, the fickle finger of fate was to intervene! Such were the vagaries of the aviation industry back then [and still are!] that British Eagle went to the wall before I finished my training – and with their demise went any chance I'd had of making a smooth transition from trainee pilot to employed pilot.

Although I was to fly to and from Miami a few times more as a passenger I never did see Mrs. Bamberg again but I was grateful for her and her husband's efforts, even if fate and politics conspired to thwart them.

51. Freddie Burkett

The first time I saw a British Midland Airways Boeing 707 was when I was working for Channel Airways. I was at Stansted Airport and driving to [or from] the airport whilst doing some Viscount flying from there. This would have been around 1970 or '71. Back then the road to the terminal buildings at Stansted took you through a cutting not far off the end of the runway and across its extended centreline. There was a set of traffic lights set in this dip, operated by the Air Traffic Controllers, which were strategically designed to stop the traffic using this road from crossing past the end of the runway when an aircraft was taking off or landing. Stansted was a far from busy airport in those days and was actually very little used at all so this sort of arrangement was perfectly practical.

On this particular day the traffic lights were set on red as I approached so I dutifully stopped my little Triumph Herald [actually it was my wife's car not mine] to await for the airborne crossing of an aircraft and for the green light to then indicate safe continued passage. You couldn't see the runway from the road as you sat waiting in the dip but you could see the wooden perimeter rail fence at the top of the banking, there to stop people and/or animals straying too near the runway.

As I sat waiting, l heard only the quiet tick over of my car engine as it idled away. Suddenly and out of nowhere, there was the most enormous roar and almost simultaneously a huge four engined jet aeroplane burst into view, it's undercarriage wheels filling my windscreen a mere few yards in front of me and hardly any higher than the top of the banking on each side of the road. No sooner was it there, darkening the sky ahead of me, than it was gone, leaving behind only the veritable howl of its four engines, all set on full power and screaming in unison.

This aeroplane was so low however, that it also left a huge gap in the wooden fence at the top of the banking as its wheels ripped through the wooden rails, scattering them like an exploding box of matches! Bits of this fence flew past me tangled up in the aircraft undercarriage whilst the rest of it rained down on the road and onto the bonnet of the car! The aircraft was in sight in front of me just long enough for me to make out that it was a British Midland Boeing 707. Wherever it was going it had barely clawed its way off the ground and into the sky to get there. No doubt there were some very relieved people in the flight deck when they realised that they were actually flying rather than ploughing through the field beyond the runway end!

Normally a departing aircraft from Stansted would be a few hundred feet up in the air by the time it got to the end of the runway, even if it was heavy. Stansted had a very long runway, even for a large aircraft. Clearly as it had only just managed to scrape itself into the sky at the eleventh hour, this aircraft and its occupants, had had a lucky escape on this particular departure. It was pretty obvious to me that something, somewhere had gone a bit awry with this take off. It should never have been as marginal as it had turned out to be.

It wasn't until I joined British Midland myself a year or more later that I discovered what had actually happened to cause my overly close encounter with this particular Boeing.

Apparently, the aircraft had been chartered to transport a load of pedigree cows to some far flung destination. Not only was it full of live cows, it also had a full load of fuel on board and so it was at, or close to, it's maximum allowable take-off weight.

I don't know how many cows there were on board but it was a lot. In calculating the total weight of these beasts the 'average' weight of an individual cow had been used and this had simply then been multiplied by the number of animals on board – I have no idea what an 'average' cow weighs [or even that an 'average' cow weight even existed then or does now] but the logic at least sounded plausible to me. Presumably this logic seemed equally as logical to the Load Controller who had then used these weights for the necessary 'weight and balance' calculations for the flight. These calculations, as is normal, had then been passed on to the Captain, one Freddie Burkett. He was also happy to accept these numbers. Why wouldn't he, what did he know about cows? And so these weights were also then used as the basis for the take-off performance and fuel load calculations for the flight.

What neither of these good folk had been told though, was that all of these precious cows, now happily ruminating in their stalls in Freddie's stripped out aircraft cabin, were heavily pregnant and so weighed significantly more than the 'average' Mrs. Cow! The aeroplane was therefore unwittingly, but even so, dangerously overweight – shades of a similar experience that I had had with lobsters in my little Beech 18 a year or two earlier!

When Freddie trundled down the runway to take-off, by the time he realised that he was running out of tarmac, it was far too late to stop and he just managed to scrape himself, the aircraft and his pregnant cows into the air in close formation. Despite it being a 'close call', in the end the only casualty had been the perimeter fence at Stansted. And the bonnet of my wife's Triumph Herald!

Whilst on the subject of Captain Freddie Burkett, he was an interesting character. He had few airs and graces, called a spade a spade and liked his money so much that he never wanted to part with more of it than he had to. He'd also been round the block a few times, survived a torrid time as an RAF pilot in the war and he knew which way up was.

Freddie, like many of his generation, didn't talk much about his wartime service but he flew mosquitoes and saw a lot of action. There was one occasion when he made reference to his wartime service though, which was relayed to me by one of his crew on a particular flight. They were at some far away foreign airport, I can't remember where now but it was somewhere where there'd been a lot of wartime activity. Anyway, they were being driven out to their parked aircraft and as they passed a rather large mound, or small hillock, not a million miles from the end of the runway, Freddie, addressing no one in particular said:-

"We lost half the squadron on that mound in 1942…and before any of you lot say anything, I know what you're thinking… it was the wrong half". Very self depreciating was Freddie!

In April 1975 when the USA finally pulled out of Vietnam at the end of hostilities there, one of the last civilian flights into, and out of, Saigon was a British Midland Boeing 707. This aircraft had been chartered by the Daily Mail newspaper, [then edited David English] on an humanitarian basis, to rescue children orphaned as a consequence of the conflict. It was a far from easy flight as the Viet Cong were, by then, in close proximity to the city and were merely awaiting orders to march into Saigon itself. It would not be without some risk to undertake flying into and then out of the airport with that kind of backdrop. 96 orphans were flown to safety from Saigon and then back to the UK on that flight. The crew were all volunteers of course. And the Captain? – none other than Freddie Burkett.

Another Freddie story happened at Sana'a in the Yemen. Goodness knows what they were doing there but Freddie had flown some charter or other into the airport there and now he was stuck. The Boeing 707 needed compressed air to start the engines. The company had been told that this facility existed at the airport but when Freddie got there, either the machine was broken or there wasn't one there at all. So relatively remote was Sana'a from anywhere else that It was going to take three days to get an air start machine to him. Aeroplanes can't hang around for three days doing nothing. They're expensive bits of hardware that need to keep earning their corn and this aircraft was no different. There were other flights to do after this trip and a three day delay was untenable.

It looked like there was nothing that could be done. No air start meant no aeroplane, full stop. But then Freddie had an idea. There might well be no air start machine at Sana'a but there were some military aircraft there in the form of the Jet Provest, a military trainer. These aircraft produced compressed air and lots of it too, out of the back of their single jet engine. To Freddie it looked like the exhaust of the Provest was about the same height as the engine intake on his 707. If he could persuade the military to back one of these little jets up to his engine intake and run up the engine, he might be able to use their exhaust air pressure to spin up his own engine! Once he'd got one of the Boeing engines running he could then use his own compressed air to start the other three.

This was worth a try. His own engine might get a bit hot on start up but he might just about get away with it into the bargain. The military boss was happy enough to play along and a Jet Provest was soon in position and ready for the experiment. Fortunately the heights of the two orifices, exhaust and intake, were more or less compatible and so they gave it a go. Lo and behold, it worked! Freddie managed to get his own engine running. Goodness knows what engine temperatures were reached during this start, Freddie always said he 'forgot to look' [with a big grin]. This bit of lateral thinking and ingenuity cut things down from a three day hiatus to one of a few hours only. Quite a win. In today's world this sort of antic would just simply not happen!

Freddie retired many years ago now. I heard that at one point that he'd taken up a 'retirement ' job as a Trade Union official – which sounds very plausible, he would have relished the argy bargy that went with that kind of territory! Freddie had a pretty good innings but alas, he moved on fairly recently. In 2018 if I remember correctly.

52. Ron and The Boeing 707

No record of the British Midland Boeing 707 story would be complete without mention of Captain Ron Hardy. I've written one or two tales elsewhere in this tome mentioning, or even featuring, Ron but such was the character of the man that he's worthy of a full chapter in his own right, if only devoted to drawing a more detailed picture of both himself and of his antics. Beyond any limited portrait that I might paint of him, Ron is another pilot who should have written an autobiography. Not only did he lead an interesting and colourful life, his voyage through aviation would also have made an interesting read.

Ron had many, many stories about his past and his flying experiences, a good number of which which could not possibly be repeated in print but I will recount one here that is acceptable – and which I think gives a good indication of the calibre of the man and his distain for petty regulation.

Ron was not one who much took to kowtowing to authority. Respect in his book had to be earned. It was never there by right or by rank alone. Ron had learned to fly in the RAF and had been a 'Sergeant Pilot' rather than an 'officer. Despite the fact that you needed to be a cut above the average to be afforded the chance to train as a pilot from within the ranks, apparently sergeant pilots were not really considered to be 'one of us' by their officer peer group. This didn't bother Ron at all and he was quite happy with his status, just as long as he got to fly his aeroplanes.

At some point in his RAF service Ron was posted to fly the Bristol Brigande, a twin engine fighter/bomber. On one occasion, following a routine flying sortie, Ron had completed his written post flight report by advising the ground engineers that there was a problem with the cockpit undercarriage indication lights – the lights that confirmed whether or not the wheels were properly extended and locked down for landing. In an effort to be helpful to the engineers in diagnosing the fault, his report said that he 'suspected a faulty micro-switch' was the problem [rather than the locking mechanism itself].

Apparently, the officer in charge of engineering had taken offence at this comment and had complained to Ron's boss. As a result Ron was hauled in front of his commanding officer and told in no uncertain terms that his job was to fly aeroplanes and most definitely was not to diagnose the cause of any technical problems that arose. This was the engineers domain and Ron was to desist, forthwith and with immediate effect. The next time that Ron flew an aeroplane that then developed a fault he followed his orders to the letter. He simply submitted a report that said 'Aircraft unserviceable' and left the engineers to work out what on earth was wrong with it!

Ron was, for many years, the Fleet Manager [the boss] of the piloting side of the 707. After many years of working for British Midland Ron had had to hang up his uniform [when he reached the age of his sell by date for flying aeroplanes]. He had then taken to running our Boeing 737 simulator programme but eventually and inevitably he had to walk away from that too and into the sunset of retirement – which he enjoyed for a good number of years.

Sadly Ron said his final goodbyes a few years ago now, in 2011.

I wrote a piece about Ron for his funeral but it never saw the light of day. I plagiarise and reproduce it here because I wouldn't be writing anything different now were I to start again:-

"Ron was not just a pilot, and an extraordinarily good one, Ron was the complete aviator – known to many in the industry, world wide, and respected wherever he went. He might have been 'only' a Sergeant pilot in the RAF – he took a perverse pride in not having been an 'Officer' – but he proved himself to be an exceptional General when it came to leading his men on the Boeing 707.

The challenges in those early days of the introduction of this fleet came thick and fast. They were constant and unremitting – Never enough crews, never enough time, always too much training, never enough training captains, never enough budget to get the job done, constant moaning from the pilots union, never a stable operating programme, never enough aircraft to fly the schedule. And so it went on.

Whatever the challenge, Ron rose to, and overcame, every problem thrown at him and every riddle set for him to solve. All was taken in his stride and always he enjoyed his flying. And always he carried the crews with him. Not for nothing did his catchphrase 'keep attacking' become a part of the British Midland culture.

It was no surprise when Ron was appointed British Midland's Chief Pilot. Ron led from the front, he set high professional standards and he always followed them. He didn't however, suffer fools gladly.

To be in attendance when Ron occasionally had to deal with a miscreant pilot was a thing of beauty to behold, it was a master class in the art of the soliloquy.

The poor recipient was barely allowed to speak, was subjected to the highest levels of a blatantly politically incorrect perspective, a complete disregard for the niceties of polite conversation and/or employment law, a veritable lesson in the best use of profanities and a clear understanding of why he was in the dog house. Ron made the fiercest of Regimental Sergeant Majors look like mere pussy cats. There were never any repeat offenders to one of Ron's interviews. Afterwards, Ron would happily buy a beer [usually several] for his erstwhile victim.

The Boeing 707 was undoubtedly the aircraft that was closest to Ron's heart. He knew it inside out, he flew it with the consummate skill and professionalism that few could hope to emulate and he never tired of flying it.

His exploits in a 707 [painted in Kenya Airways colours] at the 1976 Tees-side Air Display have become the stuff of legend – 40 years later and those who witnessed it still want to talk about it.

I happened to be at that particular event and witnessed this display first hand. It really was a superb piece of flying. Ron flew the aircraft fast, he flew it slow, he flew it clean and he flew it with everything hanging out. He made plenty of noise and so steep were his turns that I don't think he ever strayed very far outside the airfield boundary. Wonderful stuff!

Ron used to refer to above average pilots as having 'a good pair of hands'. Well, he certainly had an exceptional pair himself. He truly was made of 'the right stuff'.

53. The Viscount Simulator

In 1972 South African Airways put their entire Viscount Fleet up for sale. The story goes that British Midland, which had been in the market for a single additional aircraft to add to their fleet for the coming season, had a look at the South African offering – with a view to picking off a single aeroplane. However, such was the bargain basement price being asked that Midland ended up purchasing all thirteen aircraft, plus spares and also plus a Viscount simulator. Seven of these aircraft were flown back to the UK to join the British Midland fleet whilst the rest were broken up for spares.

The simulator came back by sea – apparently travelling as deck cargo. This didn't do the poor old machine much good, salt, water and electrics never make happy bed fellows. However, back at base on the airport at East Midlands someone had had the foresight to recruit a simulator engineer to rebuild, and then to maintain, this tired old and now much abused, machine. That individual was a chap called Dave Whitfield.

Dave was a redoubtable genius when it came to valves and relays and wires and wiggly amps and all things electric and he rose to the challenge of bringing this, already piece of history, back to life. This new life was to last all the way through until we finally moved on from flying the last of our Viscounts [they were replaced with the jet Fokker [100 and 70] and the British Aerospace ATP aircraft] in the mid 1990s – some 20 years of pretty much uninterrupted service from this venerable old simulator. All this down to the ingenuity of Dave, who kept the thing going despite a lack of spares availability and/or any support from the original manufacturers.

The Viscount simulator was a very different animal from those that are in service today. It had no visual screens so there was never anything for the pilots to look at through the cockpit windows – they always flew in cloud – even for take off and landings! Also, it was on a fixed base and so there was no sensation of movement for pilots flying it either. In fact, it didn't really simulate a Viscount flying at all but for all that it was still a very useful training tool and a combination of training in this 'simulator' and of flying the 'real' aeroplane, in parallel, gave a much better understanding to the pilots of the aircraft and of how to deal with its foibles and problems and it was to save the company a great deal of money over the years.

The simulator was housed in a corner of one of the hangers on the airfield. The actual flight deck bit where the pilots sat wasn't very big at all but the machinery behind it and driving all the instruments, lights, bells and whistles, was huge. There were rows of racks crammed full of relays and wires and glowing valves and widgets and all sorts of things that went bump in the night – and some that didn't. It looked like a more complicated version of Alan Touring's Enigma breaking computer at Bletchley Park but one that had been fed and then run on steroids. That Dave knew how it all worked and kept on top of it was a mystery to all but himself. It was his baby, he cared for it, caressed it, he kept it warm, he understood its moods and he tended to it its every need just as avidly, and with the same enthusiasm, as Monty Don looks after his garden.

But what to do with the simulator, Dave's baby, when the last of our Viscounts was retired and we no longer required its services? None of us on the management side of the company had given this any real thought at all – there were always more important opportunities and challenges to resolve. In any event, the simulator had served us well, we'd had good use from it for twenty odd years and any residual value it had ever had had long since been written off the books. In short, It owed us nothing. There were now very few Viscounts still flying, world wide and there would be no real market for it, save perhaps for some beer money to be made in exchange for the very few 'proper' aircraft parts that were used on it.

One day Dave came to see me in my office. Could I spare him a few minutes he asked? Of course I could. Dave outlined his plan. He would like to keep the simulator going when we finally decided to dispose of it. He would like to buy it from the company and would dismantle and remove it himself and at his own cost. He had already found himself a new location for it [I think he said at Tollerton Airfield, Nottingham but I can't really remember now] and he named a price. This seemed like a lot of money to me and it was clear that he was seriously keen on keeping this machine going.

Dave had done a fantastic job over the years looking after the simulator and it seemed to me to be pretty mean to make him pay for it after all that, especially the amount he was offering. If he took it away himself this action alone would save a lot of hassle and labour for the company, which would be more than payment enough in my opinion. However, it wasn't my machine and I wasn't empowered to give it away. I therefore said that I'd think about it and get back to him in a day or two.

I then spoke to John Wolfe, the company co-owner who looked after the operational side of the company. I outlined Dave's offer and argued that Dave had been a loyal company servant, etc, etc, and that we should let him have the thing as long as he dismantled and removed it. John must have been in a good mood because he readily agreed with my sentiments and confirmed that Dave could indeed have the simulator. I was mildly surprised because I thought he'd be less easy to convince, he didn't very often do 'sentimental'! Still, Dave had the green light to waft his beloved simulator off to paradise and yet another new life, this next chapter as a part of aviation history.

Sadly this story was not to have the fairy tale ending that it deserved. It was not yet quite time for Dave to put his removal plans into action, there were still a few more chunks of pilot training that needed to be carried through before the final curtain call was made. As the clock ticked down Dave was approached by a start up Viscount airline which wanted to buy time [on the soon to be] Dave's simulator once it was installed in its new home. Seemingly Dave had not turned down this expression of interest outright.

Somehow or another John Wolfe got to hear of this potential use of the simulator and he took an immediate and hostile attitude. He interpreted this as giving succour to the opposition – a competitor – this could not be allowed to happen.

John ordered that as soon as the last training detail on the simulator had been completed the engineers were to move in, sledge hammers in hand and that the whole thing was to be broken up and sent to the scrap yard. The simulator was to vanish without trace. And so it came to pass. Nothing remains. It should, by now, be housed in a museum somewhere – Brooklands or similar. Instead, it remains as no more than as a memory. Even this will only fade over time as we 'old farts' also move on.

As for Dave, he remained in the company and became a ground instructor on our Boeing 737s, teaching pilots converting onto type, what they needed to know to fly this aircraft. He never expressed any regret [to me anyway] that the viscount simulator had been lost to posterity but I suspect that it must have all but broken his heart.

As for the airline, or 'The opposition' as John labelled it, that had wanted to use the simulator, it came and went in one season and then disappeared, probably with all its investors cash, never to be seen again.

54. Petty Regulation – Customs.

Everyone can probably think of a good example of some petty regulation or another, probably several, they're everywhere. However, I doubt that there is any other aspect of governance in the whole of the United Kingdom that had more pettiness running through it, nor more officials better suited to that kind of mindset, than that of H.M. Customs and Excise when they policed our borders. These people really used to get under the skin of us aircrew and none more so than under my skin. We rubbed shoulders with these people pretty much every day of our working lives and far too many of them went out of their way to make our landings back on British soil as difficult and unpleasant as they possibly could.

In short, Customs officials were, more often than not, a set of cloned caricatures of the archetypal 'Jobsworth' type, shrouded in the protection of myriad petty regulations – gifted to them in turn by another bunch of self serving Jobsworths – our politicians. They knew it and they exploited this petty regulation regime – and their powers – to the full.

Aircrew were not entitled to the same 'duty free' allowances as the rest of the travelling public. Oh no! We were singled out for some reason and restricted to a mere two packets of cigarettes, rather than the two hundred that the rest of the population enjoyed – including our politicians. [I did once write to our illustrious Chancellor of the Exchequer to point out that this was a discriminatory law, and therefore unfair, but I was not even given the courtesy of a reply, never mind a change in legislation].

This 'two packet' rule was actually based on a specific weight of tobacco that equated to two packets. However, it was later reduced to thirty nine cigarettes when a, presumably bored, customs officer [at Teesside Airport] decided to pick apart a packet of fags and actually weigh the tobacco. He then discovered that two packets was over the weight limit and that the real allowance was 39 cigarettes – any more than that and you were over the top! Thus our allowance was further reduced, starting at Teesside but then subsequently permeating every UK airport.

Not long after this new limit had kicked off I was rostered to operate a series of flights to/from Jersey which were to end up at Teesside. From there I was then scheduled to passenger back to Jersey and on to my home base at East Midlands. Being a somewhat cantankerous individual when the mood took me, I decided to pick a fight with Customs over this cigarette issue when we landed at Teesside.

We aircrew had to complete a 'Crew Declaration' form every time we landed in the UK from abroad [Jersey was classed as being 'abroad' for customs purposes] on which we had to declare any, and every, item we'd purchased whilst away and were now importing into the UK. I, very deliberately, 'declared' on this form that I was in possession of forty cigarettes. We landed and Mr. Customs duly came into the flight deck to collect and peruse our declarations. I waited to see what would happen – would he rise to the bait or would he let it go? Of course he rose to it! In fact he started off very much on the wrong foot as far as I was concerned. "Which one of you is the Captain?", was his opening gambit when he entered the flight deck. This was an insult in its own right. Captains wore four stripes and sat in the left hand seat in the cockpit, facts that he well knew. I looked at him witheringly over my shoulder and, acknowledging my signalled response, he continued:-

"I see you've declared forty cigarettes Captain, you're only allowed thirty nine you know."

"Yes", I said, "Correct on both counts".

"Well," he said, "As I say, you're now not allowed forty, only thirty nine".

"No", says I, "I don't think that's correct, I think that I can bring in as many cigarettes as I wish, as long as I declare them – which I have".

"O.K., yes, that's right, but then you have to pay the duty".

"That's fine", I said, "I'll pay the duty".

This was going to be interesting, I had no more idea than did Mr. Customs as to what the duty on one cigarette would be but it would certainly require him to complete a lot of paperwork! Mr. Customs asked me to report to his office once I'd finished my flying paperwork and handed the aircraft over to the engineers/next captain, etc.

Now in the Customs office we continued our conversation. I asked to check our Crew Declaration form to ensure that it was correct and Mr. Customs passed it across the counter. I took out my biro, crossed out the forty, substituted it with thirty nine, countersigned the change and handed the form back. Mr. Customs looked at me with shock and incredulity: –

"You can't do that!" he said, "You've altered your declaration, that's illegal!".

"I can", I said, "I still haven't cleared Customs yet as I'm in your office and I've now smoked another cigarette so I've only got thirty nine left".

"No, no. It doesn't work like that, you'll have to pay the duty!".

"Well I don't want to pay the duty – I bet you don't even know what the duty is on one cigarette!".

"If you're not prepared to pay the duty then I'll have to confiscate the cigarette!".

I couldn't believe what I was hearing and I looked at him with incredulity, waiting for some sign of humour but it didn't come. The man was serious, I really had got him going! "Fine", I said and with that I took a single cigarette, placed it between the palms of my two hands and vigorously rubbed them together, deliberately shredding the cigarette and letting the strands of tobacco , paper and filter scatter all over his counter. I was really enjoying this silly game! "What did you do that for?", Mr. Customs said, "I'll have to complete a Damage

Declaration form now!". "That's fine by me." I said, "Not my problem. I just didn't want you smoking my cigarette later on. By the way," I added. "I'd like to put the bits in the Bond so that I can export them when I next leave the country!". Even more paperwork for him!

Mr. Customs was now furious but there wasn't much that he could do and there then followed a ten minute interval whilst he brushed my destroyed cigarette into a plastic bag and completed the various forms that had been generated by this jousting session.

Barely ten minutes after I'd departed from the Customs office I was back there again and in front of Mr. Customs:-

"Hello again", I said, "I thought you'd like to know what I'm doing now. I'm going back out to Jersey – as a passenger – and then on up to East Midlands, also as a passenger. En route, I will be purchasing two hundred cigarettes and a bottle of gin which I will import at East Midlands Airport, without paying a penny in duty… and by the way, I'd like to export my damaged cigarette too, can you complete the requisite paperwork please and have it delivered to the aircraft?!".

Aircrew: One. Customs: Nil.

Another run in I had with Customs was at East Midlands Airport where there was one particularly draconian officer. I was based at East Midlands and we knew each other quite well insofar as we rubbed shoulders quite often in the line of duty. I had been called out, with a fellow Captain, to take a taxi to Birmingham and to then fly a Viscount, with passengers on board, across to East Midlands Airport – a ten minute trip. The aircraft had come up from Jersey to Birmingham and was scheduled to then continue on to East Midlands but the flight had been badly delayed and the inbound crew had run out of duty hours, hence the requirement for us to do this final leg.

As far as my fellow Captain [a chap called George] and myself were concerned this was a purely domestic flight with no customs implications at all. However, the flight had come from Jersey to Birmingham, where some passengers disembarked, with the duty free bar and goods sales trolley having been locked and sealed before landing at Birmingham [as required by Customs regulations]. The remaining passengers then flew the last hop on to East Midlands with no bar and no service.

When we parked up at East Midlands and our work was complete George and I wandered back across the apron to go home. There was a tap on our shoulders and we turned round to be greeted by our obnoxious Customs Officer friend: –

"You haven't cleared Customs", he said. We explained that we didn't need to as we'd only flown from Birmingham to East Midlands, so hadn't left the country, had no access to any Duty Free goods and so didn't need to trouble Customs. Our obnoxious friend pointed out [quite rightly] that it didn't matter that we'd only flown the one domestic sector, technically this was what was classed as a 'Split Clearance' flight and we'd therefore need to complete a Crew Declaration form so we had to accompany him to the Customs Office to complete this formality. The Customs Officer was quite right of course, in this case both myself and my fellow captain were out of order and had miscued.

Back then I smoked quite heavily and I used to jot down the details of my flying day on my cigarette packet. When the packet was empty I'd put it in my Flight briefcase for safekeeping and then, every so often, I'd transfer the flying details from these, now empty, packets to my log book before discarding them. At the time of this discussion with Mr. Obnoxious my Flight bag was stuffed full of empty cigarette packets awaiting this processing procedure.

Having completed the declaration form, both of us having positively declared that we had no Duty Free goods, Mr. Obnoxious then asked to search our briefcases. George happily complied. Our days work was done and I now had all the time in the world to argue with, and wind up, this Customs man. I knew that my bag was chocker block full of empty cigarette packets and that he would eventually get to open it but I refused to co-operate: –

"You're obliged to let me search your bags, as you well know". He said.

"Yes, but what if I had passengered back from Amsterdam yesterday and bought two hundred cigarettes and a bottle with me and haven't yet emptied my bag? – You'd confiscate them or charge me duty – or both".

"Well, have you got those items in there?".

"No, but I could have!".

I continued this bear baiting for as long as I could make it last and then I cut to my punch line. I knew what I knew and you know what I knew but Mr. Obnoxious had no idea. At last I yielded and I opened my bag. For the first time in my life I saw eyes literally come out on stalks! Never have I seen a more energised or excited man, he veritably exploded: –

"You told me that you didn't have any cigarettes, what do you call this?", he shouted, positively glowing in the glory of his perceived victory!

"That", I said, in the most even voice that I could muster in my moment of triumph, "Is my log book!".

Obnoxious grabbed a packet and flipped the lid open – no content. He opened another, still empty but much in the way of written hieroglyphics on the packet. And then it dawned, he had been caught, hook, line and sinker!

Customs: Nil. Aircrew: Two!

55. The Best and The Worst.

I have often been asked what was the best thing and what was the worst thing that ever happened to me during my flying career. It's a reasonable enough question and my assumption is always that what the questioner is really fishing for are a couple of dramatic stories about some high drama or other that unfolded in the cockpit at some point and which we the crew, fought manfully to control and to overcome.

The problem with that though, is that – as I've already said earlier – I never had any high drama escapades, not even a single engine failure, in my entire career of airline flying. Yes, there were a few bits of daring do involving small aeroplanes in the early days but there was never anything of that ilk in all the years of my airline flying – and I suspect that it's exactly the same for very nearly all airline pilots.

I do have an answer to this question though and it's always the same. Both of these extremes for me – best and worst – are bound up in the same issue, different sides of the same coin. Making people redundant or having to 'let them go', in other words management issues, not flying challenges.

I spent a lot of time flying aeroplanes, yes, but I also spent a sizeable part of my time flying an office in one pilot management role or another. This inevitably meant a lot of dealings with people, mainly pilots, either directly making decisions that affected them, or being party to decisions that affected them. Pilots and people [not always the same thing!!] are not like aeroplanes. Pilots and people have feelings and emotions, they have responsibilities and dependents and they can sometimes be dramatically affected by decisions that are made for the wellbeing of the company rather than for them, particularly if those decisions have an adverse effect on the smooth running of their lives.

Any manager in any business will confirm that it's easy to pass on the good news – you're getting a pay rise, you're being promoted, you've got an extra days holiday, etc. That's the easy stuff, anyone can do that. It takes no real effort, it generates no drama and there are no adverse impacts or emotions that need to be managed.

The hard part comes when the news is not good – when there's an adverse effect on the individual, or individuals, involved. That's when managers earn their corn and is one of the reasons that they [generally] earn a few quid more than the rest of their peer group. Handling the bad news requires planning and thought and emotion and more than just a little care and empathy.

It really isn't very funny when you have to call someone in and tell them that they're being made redundant [or worse, dismissed], that there is no longer a job for them, that they're surplus to requirements, that as from such and such a date there will be no more pay, etc, etc. Admittedly it's even less fun for the recipient of such news but when it has to be done, it has to be done and it is always of course a manager who has to plan how to, and then to actually deliver, the bad news.

I had to face that challenge a few times in my career and on each occasion it was undoubtedly the most difficult thing I ever had to do. Telling a colleague that they're now on their way to the scrapheap, that they won't have the income to cover the mortgage, etc, etc, is a horrible piece of news to impart – however you dress it up. Not nice at all and very definitely the worst thing. It's all very well to think, with a management perspective, that 'it's only [say] 5% of the pilots, it could be a lot worse'. If you're one of those in the bracket, then you will get 100% of the hit.

So what about the best then? Well, the first time I had to 'lay off' a bunch of pilots was as a consequence of yet another flare up in the Middle East. The catalyst was the Iran/Iraq war in the 1980s. The conflict had, as is usual with all these disputes in the oil rich Middle East, played havoc with fuel prices. These had gone through the roof, dramatically affecting the aviation sector. Again, as usual when these flare ups occurred, it had also badly affected consumer confidence and so people were just not flying. This hurt British Midland of course [as well as all other airlines] and we had to do something to cut our cloth to counter the downturn in business – hence my having to make twenty six pilots redundant.

At this time, BAF [British Air Ferries], an airline based at Southend, had recently bought a bunch of ex BA Viscounts and they were looking for pilots to fly them – on an oil contract they'd won out in Libya. I contacted the Chief Pilot at BAF and outlined our predicament and the shortly to be carried out set of redundancies. This, I pointed out, would release twenty six current Viscount pilots to the market and was he interested in taking them on?

Needless to say he was more than interested, he was as pleased as a fortune teller winning the lottery. This would save him a whole heap of work in having to advertise and then organise a long and painful recruitment process and it would save a huge amount of training work too – and cost to his airline. If he could easily land a bunch of good, and current, Viscount drivers without difficulty he'd be in clover. His pilot shortage problem would be largely solved with minimum cost, minimum difficulties, in minimum time and with maximum efficiency – job done. All he had to do was find out if our pilots were as good as I claimed they were – and/or that they were prepared to work in Libya.

In no time flat my new friend from BAF was in his car and up the road from Southend, sitting in my office at East Midlands airport and exploring his opportunity [rather like I had done a good few years earlier when Channel Airways went to the wall]. I went over the details of all our soon to made redundant pilots and I made available their training records too to give him a flavour of their abilities. We then arranged a few dates on which he would make himself available to interview those who were interested in possibly joining BAF. Obviously, he would need to satisfy himself that our pilots would come up to scratch and fit into BAFs requirements.

The upside for me of course, was that although I was going to have to deliver a tough message I was also going to be able to perhaps mitigate the shock a little by offering a further message which said that, in all probability and all being well, the brave boys would be able to walk straight into a new job if they so wished. Libya might not be the best location but it was probably better than being unemployed.

Come the day of the long knives for my fellow flying colleagues, I was able to deliver each of them the dire news but news tempered by a light at the end of their otherwise now very dark tunnels. Every one of these people left my office, probably not feeling too good at all but at least with some hope that something positive could yet be salvaged. And so it was. Every last one of these redundant pilots who wanted a job with BAF was accepted and most of them came back to British Midland too, when the better times returned.

It was not a difficult thing that I'd achieved, it was made possible simply because I was lucky that our downturn in business just happened to coincide with another airline finding themselves short of Viscount pilots at the very time that we had a surplus of them. The fact that I was able to facilitate the transition for these people and in doing so was able cushion the blow of redundancy for them was, in my book anyway, one of the best things that I was able to achieve. I was quietly actually quite proud to have spotted the opening and to have acted as the middle man in a successful transaction.

The same sort of thing happened again years later following another Middle East debacle, the first Gulf war. My brief was to make another tranche of pilots redundant, I think it was sixteen of them this time. Again I was able to engineer a replacement job for these people to go to.

This time it was with Cathy Pacific [based in Hong Kong] who were looking for Second Officers to fly on their Boeing 747s. In all honesty it probably wasn't the best flying job in the world, even if it was on the 'Jumbo', an aircraft that seemed to carry a lot of kudos for some pilots. These 'Second officers' in Cathay were not well paid and didn't get much flying time either but a job was a job and most of them made the transition. Again, I was very pleased to have been able to let these pilots down relatively gently.

As an aside Cathay and I ended up having a big falling out over this transition which ended up not going too well for them. Cathay had had to train our ex pilots onto the 747 – an expensive and time consuming exercise. These chaps had been flying the Douglas DC 9 with us. Unfortunately, and rather carelessly I thought, Cathay hadn't contracted the pilots to stay with their airline until their training costs had been amortised, a normal practice within the industry. As a consequence, when the market picked up again a year or so later and we needed to take on pilots again these boys came back into the fold. Cathay was not impressed by this and I was contacted by their Personnel Manager who read my fortune to me. He told me, in no uncertain terms, that I would be black listed and would never be employed by his airline! I have to say that I didn't lose too much sleep over this dire revelation!

56. A Pilot's Lot Exposed

Another hotel incident involved a captain called Eugene and this particular event occurred at a hotel we used to stay in when night stopping in Southend.

Following the collapse of Channel Airways in the early '70s, British Midland took over their routes from Southend to the Channel islands [this was when I joined the company, arriving from Channel myself]. These were busy and profitable routes in the summer months and on a Saturday night we'd often have four, or more, crews staying in this hotel.

There wasn't much to do whilst at this establishment, it was too remote and far out of town to easily get out from to a pub, restaurant or find other entertainment. However, there was quite a good country club about a ten minute walk away down a nearby country lane and hotel guests were accorded associate membership to this establishment and so could use it without charge. This was a gratefully received little perk for us aircrew as it was a well equipped and appointed set up and not only that, they also had a restaurant down there and on Saturday evenings they held a regular dinner dance.

Thus we all found pretty much instantaneous entertainment on our doorstep – and just a few minutes walk away. Those who wanted gymnastic exercise could get it, those who wanted a meal could have one, those who wanted to dance could do so, those who wanted a drink could get one, those who wanted a swim could indulge and those who were minded to indulge in all five pursuits could do so as well. What could be easier?

On this particular Saturday evening a whole crowd of us [as usual] went down to spend our evening at the club. I now have no recollection of who else I was with, save Eugene. I'd known Eugene for a few years and we got on well. We'd done our flying training together at Elstree a few years before. Eugene had been on a course ahead of me, had joined Midland a good year or two before I did and was already a Captain when I arrived. He's a very modest and unassuming chap, very thoughtful and rather one of life's gentlemen. He also has a lovely twinkle in his eye and a tuneful chuckle for a laugh.

Anyway, the evening passed very pleasantly and eventually our party broke up as various people dropped out to go back to the hotel, myself included.

There was a rather good indoor swimming pool at the club, the entrance to it being just off the main club entrance lobby itself. Unbeknown to me, for some reason at this late stage of the evening, Eugene had decided that he would go for a swim. As I walked through the lobby on my way out I was assailed by the face of a frantic Eugene urgently hailing me over to the pool entrance door, the rest of him remaining hidden behind a pillar.

It turned out that he was stark stone naked behind his hiding place. He had decided to go for a swim but had no trunks. No one was around as it was late so he'd decided to simply strip off next to the pool and dive in for a bit of a skinny dipping session. Unbeknown to him, a bevy of our illustrious air hostesses had seen this action unfolding and, when Eugene was swimming away from his mound of clothes, they'd rushed in, scooped them up and disappeared off the face of the earth with them!

No doubt the girls had thought that this was hilarious, certainly I did, but poor Eugene was not happy and was obviously in a difficult position. He now had a mile or so along a country lane to negotiate before reaching the hotel, then the hotel entrance to traverse [bathed in light], followed by the hotel foyer itself, lit and peopled, before he could reach the stairs or the lift, both situated on the far side of the lobby near the reception desk. And all this without a stitch of cloth to cover his modesty. Not only that, he had no key to his hotel room either. What to do? Could I, he asked, see if I could find a towel or something to help him in his hour of need.

In all honesty, I'm now no longer sure of how hard I did actually try to find him some comfort, I think I was probably too exhausted from laughing at his plight but I said I'd have a look around. In truth, I certainly did look a bit. There were no handy towels lying around, there were no napkins or table clothes in the dining area and there were no handy staff around from whom to seek assistance.

There was a house rule at this club that said that all males must wear a tie at all times. All I could present him with was a spare tie that I found in the reception desk draw. I gave said tie to Eugene. He solemnly fastened this forlorn tie around his waist and it dangled down in front of him. The tie did nothing effective to cover his modesty and he looked absolutely ridiculous! My hysteria mounted as his frustration grew, both of us knowing that the tie was the best that he was going to get and he now faced the ordeal of what lay ahead!

Now he had to negotiate the route march back home to the hotel. We set off along the narrow county lane. It traversed flat and open land and there was no real cover on the road verges available, nothing but brambles and stinging nettles spilling over from neglected ditches on either side. The road surface itself was not kind to bare feet either, no grass verge and no pavement, just all pebbles and dirt at every step. Poor Eugene was not a happy bunny [which of course, made me even more perversely amused]. Worse, although the lane didn't seem to go anywhere it was quite busy with passing cars [probably at this time of night these were carrying clandestine couples seeking each other's company in isolated and discreet surroundings]. Whatever, with each approaching set of headlights, Eugene was forced to throw himself into the undergrowth of the ditch to find sanctuary. I could already see the newspaper headline for tomorrow if the wrong car caught us out: – 'Airline Captain caught flashing on Southend Common'!

Eventually we reached the hotel, Eugene now in a bit of a state, sore feet, his torso and limbs having suffered death by a thousand cuts from the brambles and he looked to be in dire need of a course of antibiotics to counter the stinging nettle rash that covered his body [and all its intricate bits!]. And still we had the key and the lobby problem to negotiate.

I didn't have the heart to deny poor Eugene access to his room and his, by now, well earned bed, so I approached the reception desk whilst Eugene remained outside lurking in the shadows. I presented myself as 'Captain Eugene' and explained that I'd lost my key. In those days we weren't yet embroiled in the security issue debacles that followed years later and I was soon armed with a replacement key and with no questions asked. I returned to Eugene and gave him his precious ticket to salvation. He was grateful and much relieved.

The arrangement then was that I would place myself at the hotel entrance, in sight of the still hidden tie wearer, and give him the signal when it was 'safe' for him to cross the lobby to the stairs. On my command Eugene would make his charge across the room and disappear upstairs having remained unseen and undetected.

Thus it was, except that with one last twist of the knife, horrible sadist that I obviously am, I waited until the lobby/reception area was as busy as it ever gets early on a Sunday morning before giving Eugene the long awaited signal. He charged across the lobby faster than a submariner goes home after six months at sea and disappeared up the stairs, tie flapping in the breeze. Happily, no one bar me, even noticed! Probably those still up and about at that time of the early morning were no less inebriated than were Eugene and myself.

History does not relate whether or not Eugene ever got his clothes back from the girls – I must ask him when next we speak!

57. Curacao.

Sometimes what, on the face of it, seems like a fairly straightforward trip turns out to be not quite as smooth as it might otherwise have been. In fact it becomes anything but. Sometimes the complications that appear on the way are difficult, frustrating and generate an awful lot of work for both the aircrew and other staff. Very occasionally, such a trip throws up a whole host of problems that are entirely within the remit of others and all the pilots can do is sit back and wait for all the ducks to align themselves before being able to launch themselves and their aeroplane into the wide blue yonder. Whatever the problems are, they are so far out of the remit of the crew that they can't contribute anything positive at all to the solutions required.

One such trip I did was to bring a newly purchased aeroplane back to the UK for subsequent addition to our fleet. This was mid 1980s and the aircraft in question was a DC9 – 32 series. The company was acquiring this aircraft from an airline called NLM, a subsidiary of the Dutch airline KLM and based on the Lesser Antilles island of Curacao in the southern Caribbean.

The business of aircraft financing and purchase is a complex process and pretty much a closed book to most pilots, me included. Likewise, so are the legal and insurance niceties involved in the process, all of which remain as obscure as the science of gynaecology is to most of us. One or two bits of this dark art we might grasp but that's about it. In the same way, aircraft financing is best left to the experts. This is the territory of the lawyers and the accountants and us pilots are best kept out of it.

This was a winter trip, to be undertaken during the month of

January and I was quite looking forward to it. A day or two in the warm sun of the Caribbean in mid winter would make for a pleasant break, plus, I'd not been to Curacao before so that would be a new experience too.

Come the appointed day, myself and my fellow pilot, Dave, accompanied by a lawyer and the aircraft broker who were dealing with the sale, departed Heathrow for Miami as passengers on a BA flight. From Miami we flew on down to Curacao with NLM who ran a scheduled service between these two cities.

The company had sent down a couple of our engineers in advance who had spent the previous two or three weeks crawling all over and inspecting this aircraft, to both ensure that it would be safe enough for us to fly back and that the company was actually getting an aircraft that was fit for purpose, rather than one that was a bag of nails and overpriced to boot. Our engineers had just about finished their work and were satisfied with what was on offer. The plan was that the day following our arrival on the island, having had a good night's rest, Dave and I would undertake a fairly exhaustive test flight on the aeroplane. Assuming that we found no major problems with it, the lawyer and the broker would then complete the paperwork, money would change hands and we'd set sail back to the UK the following day with our engineers and these two paperwork men on board with us.

That was the plan. Unfortunately, I don't know what it is about aviation but hindsight in the business invariably teaches us that plans like these, always, always go wrong. The trouble is that hindsight, as wonderful a gift as it is, is invariably ignored. In the same vein as all illustrious politicians act, somehow or another everyone assumes that this time it will be different and everything will happen like clockwork and that history won't repeat itself.

So was it different this time? No, of course not! Dave and I did the test flight as per plan. There were a few snags that needed fixing before we were going to be happy to fly back to the UK, including repairing the H.F. radio which was not working [a required piece of kit needed to fly across the Atlantic at the higher, fuel efficient, levels demanded by jet aircraft] but there were no show stoppers. We arranged with NLM that they'd fix these minor issues over night, we'd do another, quick, test flight bright and early the next morning and then, all being well, we'd be on our way.

We packed our cases the next morning and headed out to the airport for the second test flight. This went well, the defects, including the radio problem, had all been fixed and we were hot to trot. I headed off to file our initial flight plan back to the UK. The DC9 was not a long haul aircraft and we would need to refuel a couple of times on the way across. Our first stop was to be at Bermuda where we would spend the night [which meant flying over the dreaded 'Bermuda Triangle' – if you believe in these things!]. The next day, we'd refuel again, at Goose Bay, Newfoundland, then at Keflavik, Iceland, before flying the last leg of the journey over to East Midlands Airport.

The first problem I had was that when I submitted our flight plan [a detailed notification to Air Traffic Control of where we were going and the route that we planned to take to get there] it was refused. The plan said we were flying direct to Bermuda. The ATC agent advised me that this was not possible – we'd have to go via Miami, direct routings to Bermuda from Curacao were banned under their regulations. Sadly NLM had had a nasty accident some years before when one of their aircraft had got itself lost on a direct routing, had run out of fuel and all, bar one had perished, hence the ban. I could understand the sentiment behind the ruling but this would seriously derail our schedule, as well as add additional fuel costs to the trip. Fortunately, I could see our aircraft in full view through the windows of the ATC building behind the reluctant controller.

"Ah, yes", I said, "But if you look out of the window behind you, you'll see that the aircraft is now on the British register as G-PKBM and so runs under UK regulation Therefore, your [Dutch Antilles] rules don't apply". Happily, he accepted my interpretation and our plan was duly filed.

Problem solved, I went back out to join Dave and our engineers. We were now ready to go but there was no sign of our lawyer and his companion, they were still locked in battle in a nearby office. To cut a long story short, something had gone badly awry somewhere in the huge paper trail that made up the sale/lease of the aeroplane. I know not what the hiatus was but it was to be a full 10 days before we were able to set sail from Curacao back to the UK.

Curacao is an absolute gem of an island, or was back then. Pretty and unspoiled with lots of wild, rich, green jungle type foliage interspersed with thousands of orange groves. Seemingly endless sunshine warming assure seas, white sandy beaches and an amazing coral reef. Our hotel was a fully fledged high end tourist abode and there were plenty of good restaurants in which to eat. All in all we had a very good ten days of rest and recuperation, leading the life of Riley whilst Tweedledum and Tweedledee sorted out their mess of paperwork.

In the meantime, back in the UK everyone was suffering with an amazingly harsh cold snap of weather. Even Goose Bay and Keflavik were warmer whilst we were there, than was the UK.

Our trip back to the UK was uneventful except that the crafty engineers at NLM at some point after our second test flight and whilst we were waiting for the aircraft to be released by the lawyers, etc., had swapped our, now working, HF radio for the original broken one! We didn't discover this until we were actually on board the aeroplane and about to depart for Bermuda. Delaying further would have been a real pain so we decided to fly back without this radio which meant that we couldn't climb up to the altitude that would give us the best fuel economy. This was not too much of a problem but we had to be a bit more careful with how we managed our fuel en route.

One of the more amusing episodes on our flight back was that at one point we were flying along the same routing as a British Airways Boeing 747 going to London from the States. At that time in the evolution of British Midland Airways we had no scheduled service flights across the Atlantic but on this ferry flight we were using a British

G-PKBM Before departure from Curacao – Still in NLM colours

Midland call sign and were calling Air Traffic Control from time to time to give our position reports. The B.A. pilots could hear our calls and eventually curiosity overcame them and they asked us what sort of flight we were doing,

"Scheduled Service", I said, very tongue in cheek. This was rubbish of course but the BA man didn't know this and we were then giving BA a hard time with competition on some of their short haul routes so it was a bit of a leg pull. Curiosity aroused, the B.A. pilot then asked,

"What aircraft type are you?".

"DC9" I replied, quick as a flash. The DC9 was a short haul twin jet and was no more suitable for flying the Atlantic than was a Reliant Robin. I don't know what he made of it but we didn't hear any more from him and I often wondered whether or not our exchange ever reached B.A.'s commercial department!

I actually felt quite guilty when I got home. My wife and our four boys had had a miserable time in the freezing weather, with power cuts and impassable roads and everything else that goes with the usual British inability to deal with bad weather events. On top of that, I'd told them all that I'd only be gone for 5 days or so but in the end it was pretty much a full two weeks. And all of that time away was really beer and skittles for me!

The crowning glory was that no sooner was I back at home that the weather thawed out and we moved into a benign mild spell. Happy days!

58. One of life's Casualties.

I learned an important lesson about one of the more sober aspects of taking over a management position early on in that particular element of my career. As I've mentioned elsewhere in other tales, this lesson concerned the business of imparting bad news to people. The good news stories are easy, it's the other side of that particular coin that is definitely not. With responsibility for the working lives of others, there also comes a requirement and a responsibility to exercise empathy and understanding.

The catalyst to this revelation came in the form of one of our more junior and inexperienced co-pilots. Rob had been taken on to fly the Viscount aircraft as a co-pilot. At the time of his appointment he had little experience of airliner flying having previously operated only in the world of light aircraft. I well remember my own transition across this great divide.

Still, everyone has to start somewhere and Rob, having been presented with his opportunity to break into the world of airline flying, was not going to let it get away from him. He had applied himself with full vigour and diligence throughout the long and hard training process. He had found it difficult but had persevered and those training captains who tutored him encouraged and mentored him to the point of achieving a happy and a successful conclusion.

Rob had finally been released as a fully qualified Co-pilot on the Viscount and he came to work every day just like all the other pilots in the company. After Rob had been 'on line' flying for a month or two, the odd report and story started to filter back through the system about Rob and his landings.

Generally speaking Rob was fine, he was doing all the things a co-pilot should do, even doing them quite well. The one problem that Rob seemed to be having was that his landings were not consistent and more often than not were not too good at all. Sometimes he'd make a nice smooth touchdown but then his next attempt would be very hard, or too far down the runway, or even a bit short, or off to the side rather than down the middle. Questions began to be asked and Rob eventually found himself to be unfortunately under close scrutiny from a series of flights where he was teamed up with training captains, who soon confirmed that there was substance to the background rumours that had been doing the rounds.

Our training team spent some further time and effort trying to turn things around for Rob and to help him find some reliable consistency in getting his landing technique up to par. This was, of course, not entirely altruistic. It takes a lot of time and effort, as well as expense, to train a pilot to fly any particular type of aircraft and having already invested all that time, effort and money in Rob, it would pay both him and us if we could finally complete the deal and get him properly up to speed with this one last piece of required skill.

However, it didn't seem to matter which training captain was detailed or what weather conditions prevailed or even which airport at which Rob landed, the results were always the same; consistent only in the fact that their quality was highly erratic. Clearly the situation was not sustainable and something was going to have to be done to resolve this problem.

Thus, as I was now the Fleet Manager for the Viscount, the problem ended up migrating across from our training department to finding itself placed firmly on my desk. I now discovered that I had been promoted again, this time without appointment! All of a sudden I was now Solomon and I would have to exercise his wisdom. I was poor Rob's last line of defence. Either I would have to help him cure his problem [somehow] or I would have to 'let him go' – with all that that implied.

I called Rob into the office. He was far from stupid and he knew he was in a big hole. He was distinctly, and wholly understandably, very nervous and apprehensive when he appeared. He was fully aware of his problem and of all the effort and activity that had been going on around him and on his behalf to resolve this landing issue. As I say, he was an otherwise good pilot and he was perfectly capable of judging the outcome of a landing, even if not of executing one. He knew only too well that he had been lacking in this particular skill set and that make or break time now approached for him.

I tried to relax Rob as best as I could whilst we chatted and I prodded around trying to ascertain whether or not he had any underlying issues that might be affecting his performance but nothing was forthcoming. Eventually I cut to the chase and gave him the bottom line. I would fly with him tomorrow. We'd do a series of trips [we then had some pretty short flights in our repertoire of services] and would fly six trips around our usual network and he would do all the landings. Based on his performance tomorrow would hinge my decision as to whether or not Rob would retain his position with the airline.

Rob knew it was coming but even so it must still have been a terrible ultimatum for him to receive and I still feel the weight of the lead in my own stomach that was there when I made the statement to him. What kind of sleep did the poor man have that night, knowing that tomorrow would almost certainly end his career with British Midland? What too, did he tell his wife [if anything]. He had a young family and a mortgage too and if his new found airline pilot job and salary were to be snatched away from him, what then?

We flew our six sector day the following day and sad to say poor Rob was way off the mark. Partly I'm sure because of nerves and the importance of everything in his world that hinged on the outcome of this day's work.

From my point of view there was obviously a higher priority. It was pretty clear to me that for all Rob's strengths in the flight deck, and he had several, he simply had no perspective through his eyes.

He was unable to accurately judge distance or height, or both. For whatever reason, when he got close to the runway and needed the skills to co-ordinate the final couple of feet it simply wasn't there – it was all guesswork. He might as well have held his breath and closed his eyes whilst awaiting the thump onto the ground. That kind of scientific approach was never going to cut the mustard, for me, for our fellow crews and/or, even more importantly, for the safety of our passengers.

As we both traipsed silently back to my office for his debrief I felt awful but I was reminded of a line from Rudyard Kipling: –

'If you can meet with triumph and disaster and treat these two imposters just the same..'

and then I lost my guilt trip feeling. Finally sitting Rob down and reading his fortune to him was certainly a disaster for him and hardly a 'triumph' for me but I knew I'd done the right thing.

I never saw, nor heard from, Rob again but I rather think he knew the truth of his limitations also. Whether or not he continued in aviation I don't know either but I rather suspect that he would have ended up in the same position wherever he went in aeroplanes.

Whether true or not I don't know, but I subsequently learned that at some point in his flying career prior to joining British Midland Rob had been involved in a light aircraft accident in which he'd been quite badly banged about. Certainly, Rob had a scarred face – maybe he'd had a knock on the head in this accident sufficient to skew his eye alignment to the point of adversely affecting his judgement of depth and perspective. I guess we'll never know. What I did know was that, even if I didn't like it, I didn't end up feeling guilty about what I'd had to do. Mr. Kipling occasionally wrote exceedingly good poetry!

59. The Sublime.

I'm sure that in any walk of life there are examples of the two extremes of outcomes when something unexpected happens – the best and the worst. This tale explores one example of these two categories. The next, the other – by way of contrast. I was involved in neither event, I merely record them here for posterity [with my own, subjective, view!].

Captain Churchill was one of our pilots. Like ninety five percent of his colleagues he was anonymous. I don't mean that unkindly, he had his own personality and he got on well with his peer group and working colleagues. No, what I mean is that, like most other pilots, he came to work, he did his job and he went home. No drama, no histrionics when things went wrong, no poor decision making and no problems generated that required intervention from outside. Rather Winston [we'll call him that, it goes with my confected surname for him!] just got on with it. He ran his flights on time, he upset no one and he worked to a good standard. In short, his name never came up in lights – just what any pilot manager wanted from all of his captains and co-pilots.

On this particular day Winston was flying his DC9 jet from Heathrow on one of our many scheduled service routes from that airport. All perfectly normal and routine. Those who know about these things will know that the DC9 was a jet airliner with its' engines nestling at the back of the fuselage behind the wings and tucked under the tail. It was also the flying equivalent of a sports car in the take-off department and it roared down the runway like a scalded cat with everything happening very quickly once released for flight at the beginning of the runway.

On this particular day, a day like any other, Winston, once cleared for take off by Air Traffic Control at Heathrow, unleashed his phantom Ferrari and sent it hurtling down the runway – all routine stuff so far. Unfortunately for Winston this was not going to be his lucky day. Just as he passed the point of no return, V1 we pilots call it – it's the point where you've now run out of tarmac on which to stop. This means that if something now does go wrong and you do try to stop you'll have an accident anyway – off the end of the runway. Best therefore to keep going.

A major problem at 'V1' in an aeroplane is amongst the most critical of scenarios that can be visited upon a pilot in terms of decision making and a requirement for heightened flying skills. You'll be pleased to learn therefore that pilots constantly practice, and are constantly trained and tested on dealing with such problems. There are precise and defined drills and protocols to be followed so as to minimise creating any further untoward difficulties in the event of this happening. You'll also be pleased to know that the coincidence of these two events coming together at the same time is vanishingly rare.

In Winston's case, what happened was that at pretty much exactly the same time that he hit his 'V1' speed he heard a loud 'bang' coming from somewhere behind him. A second or so later his left hand engine began coughing and spluttering as it ran out of power and then failed. Winston did exactly as he'd been trained – he concentrated on getting his aircraft safely airborne and then flying away from the ground before assessing the situation and looking at how to best mitigate his problem and the damage.

Winston pretty soon diagnosed that he'd had a tyre burst on the left side of the aircraft and that bits of rubber had been thrown backwards and on their way back had been swallowed by the left hand engine. Engines are designed to swallow air, not big chunks of rubber so the engine had given up the will to live in a fit of pique.

The trouble was that Winston and his co-pilot now faced a whole series of challenging decisions. The drills that the pilots were trained to carry out said that if an engine failed then the wheels should be retracted so as to reduce the drag from the air pressure acting against them. Fine in theory, but on this occasion the aircraft was not heavily loaded and there was still plenty enough power available from the one engine to keep things safe.

Winston deduced that as a tyre had burst and that he had no idea what secondary damage might have been caused to the undercarriage and that the aircraft was performing just fine on the one engine that it was probably just as prudent to maintain the status quo and leave the wheels down. What if he put the gear up and then it wouldn't come down again because of secondary damage? He'd be in a whole set of new problems that didn't bear thinking about. He decided therefore, to leave the wheels dangling.

Then there were the flaps – the bits that hang down along the back of the wings when taking off or landing. Again, there was a decision to be made. As things stood the aeroplane was flying fine, perfectly balanced and trimmed and with no struggle to either climb or maintain the wings level. The formal drill required that the flaps be retracted [again to reduce the drag with only the one engine working]. Winston decided to leave the flaps where they were, reasoning that if flying rubber had killed the engine, what damage might it have done to the flaps, also positioned behind the wheel? If he ended up with an asymmetric flap situation that could really be very serious indeed. So Winston left the flaps alone – if it ain't broke don't fix it.

The upshot of this saga is that Winston and his co-pilot calmly and efficiently flew their way round the circuit – with a bit of help from Air Traffic Control – and they made, without drama, a successful, and safe, landing back at Heathrow.

Except that it wasn't quite as simple as that!

After the event came the 'investigation'. In my world an engine failure at this critical 'V1' speed is a once in a lifetime event. It's the equivalent of the RAF fighter pilot having to bail out of his aircraft – it hardly ever happens. So much so that the RAF even has a club for pilots and observers who've 'banged out', either by parachute or by ejection seat – the 'Caterpillar Club' they call it [I have no idea why either!]. In my opinion we should have an equivalent for civilian pilots who have experienced an engine failure at V1. It hardly ever happens but they too should have a club – or at least a tie! There are precious few who have ever experienced it – but Winston is one.

To me he was to be commended. Winston used his initiative and his acumen and he got the right result. The bottom line is that no matter how many drills and checklists might be written to help deal with problems, it's just not possible to cover every eventuality. Thus Winston found himself using good basic airmanship to best deal with what was thrown at him. He was the man in the hot seat, in the best place to make the correct calls and judgements. We, the armchair critics can be just that, nothing more.

In reality, back in the real world, he was given a hard time because he had failed to fully follow all the rules, protocols and drills to the letter. As it was Winston carried on to complete a full career, without blemish and with head held high. Were the naysayers just being 'politically correct' or were they secretly jealous that Winston had used his initiative when the chips were down?

It can be a funny old world on occasion!

60. The Ridiculous

If Winston's experience had a sublime element to it then the ridiculous contrast came via the hand of my old friend Derek. I wrote about him earlier – not my favourite captain. This incident preceded Winston's by a good few years and occurred in the early 1970's when the Viscount turboprop aircraft was still a carriage of choice for short haul flights. Derek was at the helm on this occasion [anyone else and it would never have happened!].

The Viscount was an aeroplane with four jet engines, each one driving its own propeller so there two props on each wing. Each engine was fitted with its own electric starter motor which was used in the same way as a car starter motor works. This was all fine in theory but the problem was that the aircraft batteries weren't really man enough for the job of driving these starter motors. To overcome this design fault an external 'Ground Power Unit' or GPU was plugged in to the aircraft electrical system to provide the necessary electrical power. This was also fine, again, in theory. All too often however these GPUs were not up to par either and didn't pump out the requisite number of wiggly amps that the starter wanted.

On these occasions the engine wouldn't spin up as quickly as it should have done and [if the captain didn't do anything about it] the result would be a huge great spout of flame shooting out of the back of the engine and from under the wing, caused by neat fuel burning when the engine did finally decide to burst into life. It could be quite spectacular but was not a big deal, as soon as the excess fuel burned off the flame would disappear.

All decent captains knew that this eventuality was possible, indeed even probable, and so they would minimise the effect by metering the fuel being pumped into the engine during the start process. As you may remember from my earlier tale though, Derek did not fit into the category of being a 'decent Captain'. Indeed, he was the very antithesis of this far more usual breed – uncaring, slovenly, clumsy, lazy and arrogant. Derek wouldn't bother with any of this kind of finessing, he'd just let the engine run its course and carry on and to hell with his passengers feelings.

On this particular occasion four ingredients combined to create the dénouement. A still and dark early winters morning, a below par GPU, a newly trained air hostess and, inevitably, Derek as the Captain.

Everything started off fine and running as smoothly as these things should. The passengers boarded, the paperwork was completed, the doors were shut and the co-pilot obtained start clearance from ATC. Derek pressed the starter button for the first engine and it wound into life but, as was pretty common, the GPU was not strong and the engine turned only slowly. Derek ignored the tell tale signs – he would, wouldn't he?! Eventually the engine fired up and a veritable wall of flame shot out from under the back of the wing, highly visible to all the passengers in the back half of the cabin [the Viscount had big windows] as it was still a very dark morning. Soon the flame disappeared but it had frightened our [very green and inexperienced] air hostess and probably some of the passengers too.

Derek started the next engine. Needless to say the result was the same and our girl had now seen two sheets of flame erupting from under the right wing. Derek now repeated his ham fisted starting procedure with the third engine [this time an engine on the left wing] with the same result. Babs [the young new airhostess] was now becoming very agitated, three engines started and each had been on fire. I dare say that a fair number of passengers were also of like mind! Undaunted, [none of this was visible to Derek of course, sat as he was in the flight deck] he now fired up the last of his four engines. Same result – a great sheet of flame emanated from under the back of the wing.

This was just too much for Babs. She'd now witnessed all four engines on fire and it was time to act! Nothing had been said from the flight deck and no order had been given but the cabin crew had been taught in training to use their own initiative in the event of 'unusual circumstances'. Babs reasoned that four engines on fire was an 'unusual circumstance' – and with some justification. No one had told her about the probability [or frequency] of 'hot starts' as this phenomenon was called so she was totally unaware. Plus, Babs also had initiative – and courage – and she used both!

Independently and without reference to her more senior cabin crew member, who was at the other end of the aeroplane, Babs ordered an immediate evacuation. I don't suppose that too many of her passengers needed a second bidding and before you could say 'boo' to the proverbial goose they'd ripped out the emergency exit windows over the wings and were swarming through them!

In the meantime back in that 'other world' of the flight deck, Derek carried serenely on without a care in his head – for either his passengers, his cabin crew or even his co-pilot [who was probably wholly appalled at Derek's clumsy handling of the start procedure]. He ran through all the 'after start' checks and then asked the co-pilot to call for clearance to taxi out to the runway. The conversation went like this:-

Co-pilot: – "Tower, Midland 456, request taxi".

Tower: – "Midland 456, you do realise that you've got passengers crawling all over your wings don't you?".

You couldn't make it up and it couldn't have happened to a better man! The irony is that there wasn't an ounce of reaction from any quarter. Derek had to shut down of course. The passengers were re-grouped, the windows were replaced, the flight re-boarded and Derek then rebooted and set sail to wherever he was going – without fear or favour! It was as if the incident never happened.

Whilst, on the one hand it's quite amusing in the telling, the truth is that it was also pretty horrendous! How no passenger was severely hurt, or even killed by one of the spinning propellers, no one will ever know. Equally, why there was no subsequent investigation, I'll never understand either. Different times and different views I guess!

Definitely this story has to be filed in the 'Ridiculous' section. It simply defies belief 50 years later. Clearly [and happily] the world has moved on – and very much for the better! As for Babs, I'm happy to report that she also escaped any serious recrimination and went on to forge a successful and long career with the airline as a senior member of our Cabin Services Department.

61. Retired and Missing Flying.

I have to be honest about this particular piece. I wrote it some time ago and have a feeling that I plagiarised an original version from an unattributed and incidental article that I picked up on from one of the many thousands of jokes and snippets that are circulated amongst us sad aviation types via email, etc. There are a lot of pilots out there who have more imagination and humour than I possess but this summarises very well – tongue in cheek – the day to day life of the average airline pilot. I have merely added a fair few bells, whistles and other embellishments to the original skeleton to create [I hope] an even better lampoon of the business of flying and the daily lot of the airline pilot!:-

Now that I've retired and I look back over my working life through those ubiquitous rose tinted spectacles I find myself seeing it all as a rather glamorous career. The longer my time in retirement grows the more romantic becomes my perception of how it all was. Sometimes I can't for the life of me understand why I don't seem to miss it more than I do, something must be very wrong with me.

To remind me of what the reality was in the cold, hard world of work and just how happy and enthusiastic I actually felt when my alarm woke me at some ungodly hour of the early morning to tell me it was time for another trip, my wife has very kindly built me a cockpit simulator in the house. Whenever I mention to her that I miss flying she puts me in this home made device – around about bedtime – for eight hours at a stretch.

This simulator is housed within a cupboard in our bedroom. It contains a single chair on which I can sit. It also houses a switched on vacuum cleaner [to replicate ambient cockpit noise] and the complete flight deck ambiance is achieved by means of a dim light in front of me which replicates the cockpit lighting of an aircraft at night. There are also some Christmas Tree lights on a timer that occasionally burst into life and flash red and green lights in front of me and overhead. These are designed to keep my adrenaline flowing and to stop me from falling asleep too easily.

In the middle of the night my wife will come in to the simulator and serve me with a meal of luke warm chicken accompanied by cold and overcooked vegetables – on a tray that's too small. There will also be a plastic knife and fork on the tray, with which to eat this offering, but one or other of these will always snap when put to use. Sometimes she serves salmon instead of the chicken but it's always only one or the other, never anything different.

When I get sleepy and attempt to doze off she will knock loudly on the door to simulate a CAA Inspector entering the cockpit to carry out a snap inspection. Then, after about six hours or so, she turns on a floodlight mounted directly in front of me to simulate the sun coming up as night turns to dawn and I'm inevitably flying east. I then get a cup of coffee that's been in the coffee maker all night and to make the sunrise even more realistic she'll throw sand into my eyes at the same time.

Eventually she lets me out and I have to get into the back seat of her car while she drives to the shops – this is to simulate the bus ride to the hotel after arrival at my destination. When we get back home and I tell her that I'm going to bed she locks the bedroom door [for an hour] before she lets me enter. This is to remind me that, all too often, my hotel room was not yet ready when I'd arrived at the hotel reception desk after my overnight flight.

When I then promise to never again complain about being retired and missing flying I am finally allowed to enjoy my 'layover' and go to bed. Then, just after I've finally fallen asleep, she stands outside the bedroom door and talks loudly to her friends. This is designed to simulate the hotel maids chattering in the hotel corridor, as they do, usually in a language I can't understand, thus ensuring that I have a disturbed rest.

After two hours of sleep and never until I'm really buried deep in happy slumber, she gets out her mobile, calls the phone next to the bed to wake me and says: – 'Crewing here, you have a roster change, we'll call you back when you've had your legal minimum rest period – and by the way, you might as well know that the company called in the Receivers this morning... sleep well'.

Oh, how I miss it all!

WS - #0163 - 091224 - C4 - 197/132/16 - PB - 9781784567613 - Gloss Lamination